D0403028

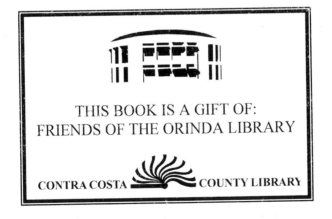

TALES

from a

TIN CAN

TALES
from a
TIN CAN

~ *The USS DALE* ~
from Pearl Harbor *to* Tokyo Bay

Michael Keith Olson

ZENITH
PRESS

To the men and women of the U.S. Navy
Past, Present, and Future

Anchors aweigh, my boys.
Anchors aweigh!

First published in 2007 by Zenith Press, an imprint of MBI Publishing Company LLC, Galtier Plaza, Suite 200, 380 Jackson Street, St Paul, MN, 55101 USA

Zenith Press titles are also available at discounts in bulk quantity for industrial or sales-promotional use. For details write to Special Sales Manager at MBI Publishing Company, Galtier Plaza, Suite 200, 380 Jackson Street, St. Paul, MN 55101 USA.

To find out more about our books, join us online at www.zenithpress.com.

For more information on the USS *Dale* and tin can sailors, visit the author's website at www.tincan.us.

ISBN-13: 978-0-7603-2770-8
ISBN-10: 0-7603-2770-X

Maps: Marlene Olson
Layout: Jennifer Maass
Cover: Tom Heffron

Printed in United States of America

Library of Congress Cataloging-in-Publication Data

Olson, Michael, 1947-
  Tales from a tin can : the USS Dale from Pearl Harbor to Tokyo Bay / by Michael Olson.
    p. cm.
  Includes bibliographical references and index.
  ISBN-13: 978-0-7603-2770-8 (hardcover)
  ISBN-10: 0-7603-2770-X (hardcover)
  1. Dale (Destroyer : DD-353) 2. World War, 1939-1945—Naval operations, American. 3. World War, 1939-1945—Campaigns—Pacific Ocean. 4. World War, 1939-1945—Personal narratives, American. 5. Oral history. I. Title.
  D774.D27O48 2007
  940.54'5973—dc22
                            2006010868

On the front cover: USS *Monaghan* (DD 354) and USS *Dale* (DD 353) emerge from smoke during fleet exercises off San Diego. *U.S. Navy photograph*

On the back cover: Robert Olson aboard the *Dale* somewhere in the Central Pacific circa 1944. Enlisted men were not allowed to have cameras during WWII, but Earl "Jitterbug" Pearson always kept one secreted beneath his dungaree shirt. Whenever he wanted to take a photo, he would simply unbutton his shirt and shoot! *Earl Pearson collection*

CONTENTS

LIST OF MAPS

PREFACE

Perhaps it was the moment our fathers became our sons.

They were lining up for a reunion photograph in a Virginia Beach, Virginia, hotel lobby. We, their middle-aged children, watched as the shorter ones lowered themselves slowly, and with much protest, onto their arthritic knees. But just then, two attractive young women in low-cut dresses and high-heel shoes walked into the lobby and paraded along in front of them. In an instant, the eighty-year-old veteran sailors of the USS *Dale* (DD-353) became twenty-year-olds, and we saw them as James Michener found them nearly six decades earlier on the island of Espiritu Santo, where they provided the inspiration for his *Tales of the South Pacific*, and the subsequent Rogers and Hammerstein musical, *South Pacific*. ("There ain't nothin' like a dame!")

Or maybe it was that moment of epiphany on a bus ride into Washington, D.C.

The veteran *Dale* sailors were on their way to visit the Navy Museum and have a look around the city. I was using the time to record John Cruce's recollection of the attack on Pearl Harbor. The background noise on the bus was making it hard to hear John, and so I was leaning close with the microphone. As John described the absolute surprise of *Dale* sailors that Sunday morning, so many years ago, my attention was drawn past him out the window to where a giant crane was at work repairing damage inflicted on the Pentagon by airliner-armed terrorists.

Somewhere along the line, I came to the realization that the USS *Dale* had a story that needed to be told, and her sailors were finally willing to tell it.

My interest in the story of the USS *Dale* began when my father, Robert "Pat" Olson, came out to California for a visit. "I've got a shipmate that lives up the way a bit," he said. "Mind if I give him a call?"

Harold Reichert did indeed live up the way a bit, and we soon found ourselves sitting down to lunch in a restaurant with a view of the Pacific Ocean. Within a moment or two, Olson and Reichert were back on the deck of the USS *Dale*. When Reichert began telling the story of the Japanese attack on Pearl Harbor, I exclaimed, "Wait! Please wait!" I then ran for the tape recorder in the glove compartment of my car. *Wow,* I thought, *Dad's ship was at Pearl Harbor when the Japanese attacked!*

Despite growing up with a keen interest in sea stories, I knew very little about my father's World War II navy ship, the USS *Dale*. Father simply did not talk about his experiences during the war. In fact, my only source of information was a shoebox containing a few faded black-and-white photographs. Some of the photos were of a navy ship with the number 353 stenciled on its bow. For a child growing up in an era of giant aircraft carriers, the 353 was, well, diminutive! Other photos in the box were of sailors dressed up in strange costumes—a burly, cigar-chomping sailor as a baby, several hairy-legged guys as women in dresses, one particularly gruff fellow as a king with crown and trident. I did not understand the reason for the costumes until I crossed the equator one day in 1968 as a sailor aboard the aircraft carrier USS *Bennington* (CVS-20). Father had his crossing. I had mine.

As the tape rolled and Reichert's story of the *Dale* at Pearl Harbor unfolded, I became captivated by the intensity of his story telling. By the time he finished his story, tears were rolling down his cheeks. It was time for me to dig a little deeper into the story of the USS *Dale*.

The USS *Dale* was one of eight *Farragut*-class destroyers built in the 1930s by Bethlehem Steel Company. As originally outfitted, each was powered by four boilers, which produced forty-two-thousand horsepower and a top speed of thirty-six knots. Armament consisted of five 5-inch guns, eight 21-inch torpedo tubes, and four 50-caliber machine guns. The *Farragut*-class was the cutting edge of the U.S. Navy's Pacific fleet, and, like all destroyers, they were called "tin cans" by sailors. (The destroyers' thin hull plating, along with their small size, led sailors to claim they were made from tin cans.) All eight were moored at Pearl Harbor on the morning of December 7, 1941.

From that day in December 1941, to its decommissioning in October 1945, USS *Dale* steamed back and forth across an eighty-three-million-square-mile battlefield—from the west coast of the United States to the east coast of China; from the Bering Sea in the north to the Coral Sea in the south. During this time, *Dale* steamed through nearly every major naval engagement in the Pacific Theater, collecting twelve battle stars along the way. And, despite the Imperial Japanese Navy's best efforts, *Dale* never lost a crewman to enemy fire. She was, as one of her crew said, "the ship that would not be sunk!"

I began following *Dale*'s sailors with my tape recorder as they gathered for annual reunions in Virginia Beach; Rapid City;

Washington, D.C.; Billings, San Antonio; New Orleans; and Albuquerque. I discovered that, when alone, the World War II vets were quite reserved with respect to their wartime experiences. But when thrown into the melting pot of a reunion, they would let go and tell stories. During these reunions I recorded more than one hundred hours of stories about the World War II experiences of the USS *Dale*, as told by the men who served aboard her.

Even Pat Olson finally talked about his life aboard the *Dale*. We were returning to his home in Billings, Montana, from a *Dale* reunion in Rapid City, South Dakota, and cruising along the interstate near Devil's Tower in northeastern Wyoming, when he finally demonstrated a willingness to talk. And so, with one hand on the wheel and the other on the microphone, I asked him to talk, and talk he did, all the way into Billings.

The stories I collected from *Dale* sailors were six decades old, and thus presented some management issues. First, I had to find the right time and location for each story. This was not as easy as it might seem. Often the sailors had no idea as to the proper time or location for their stories. Some simply forgot, but most did not know in the first place. Only a few *Dale* sailors knew the exact location and mission of the *Dale* on any given day; everyone else had to rely on "scuttlebutt." Second, the stories, like stones worn smooth by a rushing mountain stream, had been well polished by six decades of telling. Some lacked the sharp edges of inconvenient detail and caused one to wonder about their veracity. Finally, some of the story-telling sailors simply talked themselves into situations in which they did not belong. Many, for example, told of how *Dale* had sailed through Typhoon Cobra in December 1944. This storm sank three sister destroyers and drowned nearly eight hundred fellow sailors. Actually, *Dale* was in a floating dry dock at Ulithi at the time.

To anchor *Dale*'s stories in context, place, and time, I traveled to the Library of Congress in Washington, D.C., and obtained a copy of her war diary. It helped. Still, there was the problem of justifying the taciturn nature of the ship's diary with the exclamatory nature of the sailor's story. Consider how a January 1944 storm was portrayed in two ways. First, read from *Dale*'s war diary:

18 January: Steaming as a unit of TU 30.8.2 in formation with TG 38.2 and in general company of TF 38. Because of continuing heavy seas, the fueling exercises scheduled for this day were not held.

Now listen to Bob Johnson, an engineering officer aboard the *Dale*, describe the storm:

I remember looking out over the waves and seeing a tin can do something that scared me out of my socks. That destroyer went completely airborne, like a fish jumping out of the water! I clearly remember seeing both of its propellers spinning in the air. Its sonar dome, which extends down from the bottom of the ship, cleared the surface of the water. I thought, "If this is what's going on, we don't have a chance!"

Were the *Dale*'s diary and *Dale*'s sailors talking about the same storm? Sometimes it was difficult to tell whether the writers of the war diary and the tellers of the stories were aboard the same ship!

I came to rely for direction on those who had sailed the waters before. There was, of course, the *History of the United States Naval Operations in World War II*, by Samuel Eliot Morison; seven volumes of this seminal work focus on the history of the Pacific Theater. There was also *Victory at Sea* by Dunnigan and Nofi, *How They Won the War in the Pacific* by Hoyt, *The Pacific War* by Ienaga, *Blood on the Sea* by Parkin, *Last Stand of the Tin Can Sailor* by Hornfischer, and many others. There was also the collective wisdom of the internet, which was of immense value for tracking details like time and place. And yet, even the experts left me with head-scratching anomalies, like the performance of Rear Admiral Charles "Sock" McMorris at the 1943 Battle of the Komandorski Islands.

Read how Morison described McMorris's performance:

> Although retiring actions never seem as glorious as advancing ones, the odds against which McMorris fought, his bold handling of the task force, and the magnificent manner in which all ships responded to his leadership should make Komandorski a proud name in American naval history.

Now listen to how Mike Callahan, a gunnery officer aboard the *Dale*, described the performance of the admiral:

> The first thing the admiral did in the *Richmond* was turn and run! The real commander of the battle was the skipper of the *Salt Lake City*. Funny thing about this war business is that you can send people to the Naval Academy and teach them to fight, but you can't make them fight when the time comes. Sometimes to save the body you have to lose a foot, and commanders who are afraid of losing troops should not be commanders. There is no substitute for leadership in combat. You can never be certain you are doing the right thing, but you have to make a decision and fight!

Morison and Callahan were looking at the same admiral in the same battle, and yet where one saw bravery, the other saw cowardice. If the first law of writing history is to tell the truth, as Cicero would have us believe, then this writer is in water over his head. But wait! Here comes Voltaire with a life preserver: "History is filled with the sound of silken slippers going downstairs and wooden shoes coming up." There it is! Clearly, navy historian Morison was listening to the sound of Rear Admiral McMorris going down in history, whereas sailor Callahan was listening to the sound of Japan's 8-inch naval guns walking up on the *Dale*.

As I followed the octogenarian veterans of the USS *Dale* around the country with my tape recorder, I came to realize that every one of them possessed a fully developed and unabashed sense of pride in a job well done. As a veteran of the Vietnam War, I had never experienced that sense of pride, but rather always carried the thought, way down deep, that I had somehow made a mess of things! Rubbing shoulders with *Dale's* sailors brought healing to this wound. I will remain forever grateful.

Tales from a Tin Can is the story of the USS *Dale* during World War II, as told by the men who served aboard her. As I write, these sailors are being ordered back, like Virga under a warming tropical sun. I write so their tin can will not be forgotten, and their stories will not go untold.

ACKNOWLEDGMENTS

I am grateful to the sailors of the USS *Dale* for taking me into their family and sharing their stories.

I am also grateful to the following institutions for providing invaluable guidance and material: National Archives, Washington, D.C.; Navy Museum, Washington, D.C.; National D-day Museum, New Orleans, LA; and National Museum of the Pacific War, Fredricksburg, TX.

I want to extend a special thanks to Bill Nolan and Marlene Olson for their countless hours of proofreading; to Marlene Olson for crafting the maps contained herein; and to my father, Robert "Pat" Olson, for the swift-kick-in-the-butt "Are you done yet?" phone calls.

Finally, I am most grateful for the loving support of wife, Marlene, and daughter, Kelsey.

1941

Japan was ten years into its campaign to conquer China when it ran out of oil. The campaign had begun in 1931 with the annexation of Manchuria (although the official start of the Second Sino-Japanese War is generally considered to be the Marco Polo Bridge Incident of 1937). It would end in 1945, when Japan surrendered to Allied Forces at the end of World War II. By 1941, however, many of the world's nations had already become involved by supporting one side or another—including France, Germany, Great Britain, and the Soviet Union. For its part, the United States, fearful Japan might come to dominate the entire continent of Asia, organized an oil and steel embargo that made it impossible for Japan to continue its operations in China without developing a new source of oil. Japan was left with two courses of action. It could cease its effort to conquer China, or it could secure the oil it needed by taking the natural resources of Southeast Asia by force.

The first course of action was rejected by the military, which then dominated Japan's government. After all, the militarists believed, the immensity of China represented hope for their tiny island nation's future. Furthermore, the only obstacle preventing the taking of Southeast Asia's oil was the U.S. Pacific fleet, which had recently been relocated to Pearl Harbor, Hawaii.

To be certain, the Pacific fleet presented a formidable obstacle. In fact, the U.S. Navy sheltered the largest collection of warships in history within the confines of Pearl Harbor. There was, however, opportunity in the consolidation and concentration of the Pacific fleet. If the U.S. Navy could be caught unaware, and put out of action for six to eight months, Japan would be free to establish military strongholds throughout Asia and the western Pacific. To avoid a prolonged war, the peace-loving American public would surely force its government to negotiate a settlement with the all-powerful Japanese.

The task of exploiting this opportunity was assigned to Admiral Isoroku Yamamoto of the Imperial Japanese Navy.

Yamamoto graduated from the Japanese Naval Academy in 1904. Within a few months he was wounded in action while participating in the Russo-Japanese War, a bloody fight over the Chinese town of Port Arthur (Lushun) and the Liaodong Peninsula. Japan had tried to negotiate a division of the area into spheres of influence, but Russia refused. On February 8, 1904, without a declaration of war, Japan attacked Port Arthur and bottled up the Russian fleet. The decisive Battle of Tsushima occurred on May 27 and 28, 1905. The Japanese fleet, under Admiral Heihachiro Togo, met the Russian fleet, commanded by Admiral Zinovi Petrovich Rozhdestvenski, in the Tsushima Strait. Of the forty-five ships in the Russian fleet, only nine survived. The Japanese loss was limited to three small torpedo boats.

Later, Yamamoto attended Harvard University as a student and, after achieving the rank of captain, was appointed to be Japan's Naval Attaché to the United States. During the 1930s, he held a number of important positions involving the development of the Imperial Navy's fleet aviation.

To realize the opportunity presented by a concentrated U.S. fleet, Yamamoto would have to answer the question all predators must ask of themselves: "How can I strike down this prey without causing harm to myself?"

Many veterans of the Russo-Japanese War, now Japan's senior naval officers, argued that Yamamoto should engage the Pacific fleet with the Imperial Navy's massive battleships and simply blow the Yanks out of the water. After all, it had worked for Admiral Togo at Tsushima. But Yamamoto had his eyes on a different battle.

In April 1940, outmoded British Swordfish biplanes carrying jury-rigged torpedoes attacked the Italian fleet in the shallow waters of Taranto, Italy. The British attached fins to their torpedoes, which enabled them to function in shallow water. Because of this simple innovation, the British torpedo attack inflicted significant damage on the Italian ships. Yamamoto had his staff construct models of Taranto Harbor to study how the British carried out their successful attack.

During the past decade, Japan had developed two weapons that could, if employed with skill and cunning, make the British attack at Taranto look like child's play: aircraft carriers and torpedoes.

By 1941, Yamamoto's fleet of aircraft carriers exceeded that of the United States. This superiority in carriers was much greater than raw numbers might indicate, as American carriers were divided between the Atlantic and Pacific fleets. Yamamoto's carriers were well stocked with the finest ship-borne aircraft made, and they were piloted by the best-trained aviators in the world. Yamamoto had personally captained aircraft carriers and knew they could carry an overwhelming force in great secrecy across an open ocean.

The Imperial Navy had also developed a torpedo it called "Long Lance." The Long Lance was faster and more accurate, had greater range (twenty miles), and packed far more punch than anything in the U.S. arsenal. In fact, the U.S. Navy's torpedo would prove to be one of the biggest embarrassments of the war; after World War I, tight budgets had caused the U.S. Navy to skimp on testing. When war broke out again, it was discovered the torpedoes only sometimes detonated on impact and had a nasty habit of turning back on their users. Before the navy solved the problems, which took two full years, its submarines fired almost four thousand of the faulty torpedoes against enemy shipping, with only marginal results. On one patrol, the *Halibut* (SS 232) fired twenty-three torpedoes—only one exploded!

Given the Imperial Navy's powerful new weapons, and the success of the British torpedo attack in the shallow waters of Taranto Bay, Yamamoto elected to conduct a surprise attack on Pearl Harbor. He established two objectives for this attack: sink the American aircraft carriers based at Pearl Harbor and then destroy as many capital ships—battleships and cruisers—as possible.

Yamamoto planned his attack for a Sunday morning, as the Pacific fleet was in the habit of returning to its Pearl Harbor anchorage for the weekend, where it would stand down for Sunday services.

Yamamoto assembled a task force of six heavy aircraft carriers and twenty-four supporting ships commanded by Admiral Chuichi Nagumo. Nagumo sailed north from Hiroshima Bay on November 28 into the deserted waters of the Pacific. On December 6, the task force would run down to a point two hundred miles north of Oahu, where it would launch two waves of airplanes led by Commander Mitsuo Fuchida.

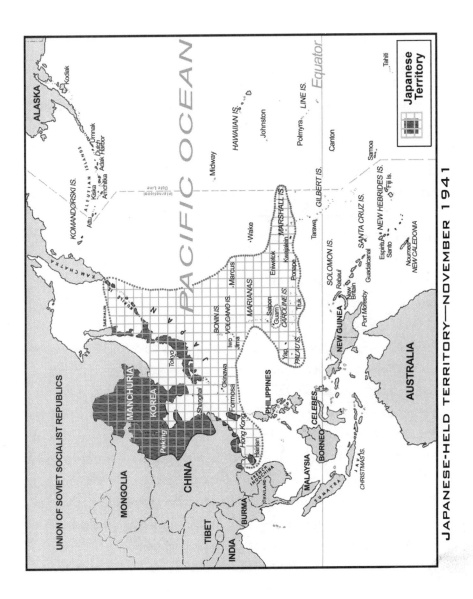

JAPANESE-HELD TERRITORY—NOVEMBER 1941

NOVEMBER: PEARL HARBOR, HAWAII

Pearl Harbor is an extensive, shallow embayment near Honolulu on the island of Oahu. Called Wai Momi ("Water of Pearl") by native Hawaiians, the harbor teemed with pearl-producing oysters until the late 1880s.

In the years following Captain Cook's explorations, Pearl Harbor was not considered suitable as a seaport because it was too shallow. Nevertheless, the U.S. Navy desired a permanent base in the Pacific and so leased the harbor from the nation of Hawaii in 1887. By 1908, the harbor was improved to the extent the U.S. Navy was able to establish its Pearl Harbor Navy Shipyard.

When tensions between Japan and the United States increased in the late 1930s, President Franklin Roosevelt ordered the U.S. Pacific fleet to Pearl Harbor. The USS *Dale*, and her sister *Farragut*-class destroyers, were included in this fleet redeployment, and took up residence at Pearl Harbor.

Cliff Huntley: You could tell who the new guys were. They were the ones who were always confused and out of step. The problem was a dreaded tropical disease called "lacanookie." Their only cure was to get acclimated as fast as possible.

USS *Dale* was only about six years old when we first arrived at Pearl Harbor. At that time *Dale* and our sister *Farragut*-class destroyers were the cutting edge of the U.S. Navy's Pacific fleet. Our job was to get in front of the nation's trouble, and we tin can sailors were mighty proud of that fact. Those of us who had been on *Dale* for a while walked with a swagger the new guys just couldn't step into right away.

Honolulu was a lot different back then. It wasn't the big city you see today. It was small, quiet, and orderly. Flowers grew just about everywhere, and only a few cars were on the roads. There were places we enlisted men could go and places we could not go. So long as you knew which was which, you could get along pretty well.

I had the best duty on the *Dale*. I was an electrician's mate first class and the ship's movie operator. Whenever we tied up at Pearl, Machinist Mate Stoddard and myself would head out to chase down movies for the crew. They gave us a car and driver's licenses. We had the car all weekend and could go wherever we wanted. The ship even paid for a room in town for me, so I could pick up the officers in the morning and [take] them back to the ship.

I met this beautiful gal in town who was half Hawaiian and half Chinese. She had lots of money, more than we could ever find a use for. She was very good to me, and I never did suffer from that dread "lacanookie."

Alvis Harris: Along about mid-November, we got orders to go out west of Pearl a couple of hundred miles with our sister tin can, the *Aylwin*, to pick up the SS *Komikura Maru* with Japanese Ambassador Nomura aboard, who was on his way to Washington, D.C., for peace talks. We escorted the ambassador into Pearl, where he disembarked from the *Maru* and embarked on a Matson liner for the States and his meeting in Washington, D.C.

Herman Gaddis: While the Japanese ambassador was boarding the Matson liner, we took up an anti-submarine patrol off Diamond Head. Our orders were to pick up the Matson liner when she left Pearl and escort her to the States. We were all looking forward to liberty in San Diego. But almost immediately, we picked up a submarine on sonar that we could not identify and nobody in the fleet would claim. While we were engaged with that sub the Matson liner left Honolulu with another ship as its escort. We missed our trip back to the States, which made us all very unhappy.

We sat on top of that submarine for about three days, waiting for something to happen. The sub would move here and there a little bit, but mostly it just sat on the bottom just off Diamond Head and did nothing. We didn't know who that sub belonged to, and, as we were not at war or anything, there really was nothing we could do. So finally we just backed off and let it go.

Author's note: When war with Japan became inevitable, the American government sent warnings to all of its military commands and political posts in the Pacific, including those of the army and navy in Hawaii. The Americans knew the Japanese were preparing to attack, but had convinced themselves the attack would be in the Philippines.

The first warning was sent November 27:

This dispatch is to be considered a war warning. Negotiations with Japan looking toward stabilization of conditions in the Pacific have ceased and an aggressive move by Japan is expected within the next few days. The number and equipment of Japanese troops and the organization of the naval task forces indicates an amphibious expedition against either the Philippines Thai or Kra Peninsula or possibly Borneo. Execute an appropriate defensive deployment prepa[ra]tory to carrying out the tasks assigned in WPL 46. Inform district and army authorities.

A second warning was sent throughout the Pacific on December 3:

Warning! Categoric and urgent instructions were sent yesterday to Japanese diplomatic and consular posts at Hong Kong, Singapore, Batavia, Manila, Washington and London

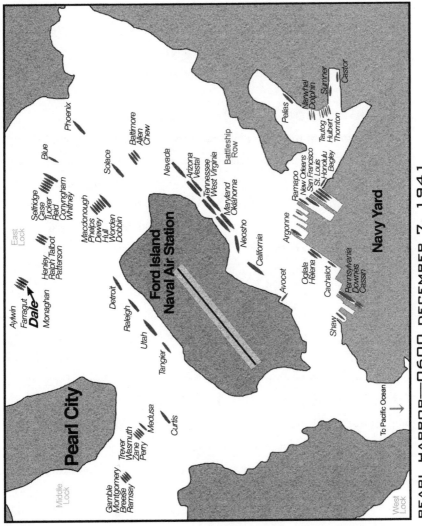

PEARL HARBOR—0600 DECEMBER 7, 1941

to destroy most of their codes and ciphers at once and to burn all other important confidential and secret documents.

Certain that Japan was on the move, America held fast to its belief the move would come in the Philippines. Most certainly it would not come at Pearl Harbor! This wishful thinking provided the perfect cover for Nagumo's carrier strike force, which arrived at a point two hundred miles north of Pearl Harbor early on the morning of December 7.

DECEMBER 7 TO 8: JAPANESE ATTACK

Pilots aboard Nagumo's six carriers awoke very early from what surely must have been a nervous sleep. Yet, despite all of the anxiety, Flight Commander Fuchida found Lieutenant Commander Shigeharu Murata, leader of the torpedo bombers who would soon strike Pearl Harbor's battleship row, hungrily wolfing down a hearty breakfast. Murata called out, "Good morning, Commander Fuchida. Honolulu sleeps!"

"How do you know?" Fuchida asked.

"The Honolulu radio plays soft music," Murata responded. "Everything is fine!"[1]

At 0600, Nagumo's six carriers began launching the first wave of airplanes. At 0630, Commander Fuchida turned south in command of forty Kate torpedo bombers, fifty-one dive-bombers, forty-three fighters, and forty-nine Kate high-level bombers. Months of training were about to culminate in an operation that would commit Japan to a war with the industrial might of the United States.

Though most of Honolulu slept, a few were being made aware that something was up. In the early morning darkness, the destroyer USS *Ward* (DD-139) spotted the periscope of an unidentified submarine near the entrance to Pearl Harbor. The *Ward* attacked the submarine, sank it, and then reported the incident up the chain of command.

Then, at approximately 0700, an alert army radar operator saw the approaching first wave of Japanese airplanes on his scope and called in a report to his superior. Both reports, however, fell on deaf ears and nothing was done to increase Pearl Harbor's readiness for what was about to come from the sky.

Harold Reichert: Some mornings, the waters of Pearl Harbor would be so still the seaplane pilots could not see where to land, and so we'd have to send out the motor whaleboat to stir up the water a bit. On mornings like that, you could always pick up the smells of fuel oil mixed with tropical flowers, and after a week or two at sea those smells were mighty inviting. My Sunday morning ritual at Pearl was to sit out on the fantail with a cup of coffee and a newspaper and enjoy the early sun and those tropical airs.

Cliff Huntley: In the peacetime navy, it was customary to give weekend liberty to two-thirds of *Dale*'s crew when we were in port. Three of us had gone together and purchased a much-used 1935 Chevrolet. The two-thirds rule meant that on any given weekend, two of us owners would have the car. On that weekend, Ensign Vellis and I drove the car into town to spend the night in some nice rooms across the street from the Moana Hotel. It was always great to get off the ship and get into Honolulu, a beautiful place with many small homes and maybe one-third the population of today.

Harold Reichert: There were ninety-six ships in Pearl Harbor that morning and no reason to expect any trouble. After all, the *Honolulu Advertiser* I was reading told how Japanese Ambassador Nomura was going to meet with the Secretary Cordell Hull in Washington that very morning to talk about peace.

0700 to 0755

As the first wave of attacking Japanese airplanes approached the north shore of Oahu, two reconnaissance planes launched earlier reported the U.S. fleet to be asleep at Pearl Harbor. While there was no sign of an alert, there were also no aircraft carriers tied up at the moorings on the north side of Ford Island. This piece of news greatly frustrated Commander Fuchida, as the carriers were his primary objective. But the battleships were lined up like bowling pins along battleship row. Fuchida radioed in code to Nomura, and all of Japan, "To . . . To . . . To . . . [attack, attack, attack] Ra . . . Ra . . . Ra . . . [success, success, success]." At the time, American radio operators translated the two separate syllables as the single word *tora*, Japanese for "tiger."[2]

Fuchida's fighters were the first to arrive in the air over Oahu. They fanned out over the island, established air superiority, and then commenced strafing the American airplanes parked wing to wing on the ramps of various air bases around the island. Next came his dive-bombers, which dove on ships and facilities. Then came the lumbering Kate torpedo bombers, which headed straight for battleship row. Finally, above it all, flew the level bombers with 16-inch armor-piercing naval rounds specially adapted for dropping from on high.

Dellmar Smith: I was sitting on a forward torpedo tube with a cup of coffee, talking with Humphrey. We saw a big bunch of airplanes coming in over the mountains and got to wondering which carrier they belonged to.

They could not be coming from the *Saratoga*, because she was in dry dock in Bremerton; nor the *Enterprise*, because she was participating in an exercise way down south somewhere. And the *Lexington* had just gone to sea Saturday, so it was doubtful her planes were flying back already. It just didn't make any sense. So we watched as they flew in from the mountains. Then, when they got to about a hundred yards away, Humphrey jumped up and said, "Goddamn! They're Japanese!"

Don Schneider: I had the messenger duty that night, which meant I didn't get to sleep until four in the morning. I was working as a mess cook, so my bunk space was down in the mess hall, where there were always a lot of guys coming and going. Mess cooks were at the bottom of the ship's totem pole, and sleeping mess cooks were fair game for whoever happened to come through. When someone came by yelling that the Japs were attacking, I yelled back, "Go to hell!" and rolled over for more sleep.

Warren Deppe: We were eating breakfast down in the mess hall. At the time, we had aboard this chief torpedoman we called "Sailor Boy White," who was the ship's practical joker. One of his favorite gags in those days, when everyone's nerves were on edge, was to sneak into a compartment when nobody was looking and yell, "The Japs are coming! The Japs are coming!" And so, when Sailor Boy White came running into the galley with a terribly frightened look on his face that morning, nobody paid him any attention, even when he started pleading that he was telling the truth. Then we heard the explosions!

Harold Reichert: Just then, a plane flew by at about thirty feet. I could see the pilot plain as day. He wore a leather helmet with straps under his chin and a pair of goggles. I could see the whites of his eyes, and he was totally fixed on the old *Utah*, which was an old battlewagon the navy had stripped down and converted to a target ship. She had a big wooden deck on her, so dive-bombers could practice bombing her with sandbags. She looked a lot like an aircraft carrier and was even anchored in the same berth the *Lexington* had vacated the previous day!

I did not realize what the plane was until I finally got focused on the big red rising sun painted on the fuselage. And then I saw the torpedo drop and watched as it ran up on the old *Utah*. The explosion sent a huge fountain of water shooting way up high into the air. I remember dropping my newspaper and yelling, "We're being attacked!"

Johnny Miller: I had the radio duty and was sitting at my desk reading the Sunday morning funny papers when I heard some unexplained explosions. Just then one of the fellows came by the radio room yelling, "The Japs are attacking!" I ran outside just as a torpedo plane came across our bow and let go his torpedo at the battleship *Utah*. I even noticed the smile on the pilot's face he was so close. Heck! I could have hit him with a rock!

Ernest Schnabel: I was absorbed in my Sunday morning crossword puzzle when I heard some aircraft flying real close. I looked up and saw two planes flying by at about masthead height. Then I heard explosions on the light cruiser *Raleigh* and the old *Utah*.

J. E. McIntyre: I had just finished breakfast when the GQ alarm went off. To get to my station in number one fire room, I had to go topside. When I did, a Japanese torpedo bomber flew by so close I could have hit it with a potato—if I had one. I then went below to the fire room and didn't come up again until the next day.

Jim Sturgill: I was sleeping in when the general quarters alarm clanged away and sailors began throwing gas masks, helmets, and elbows everywhere. I jumped out of bed, got dressed, and ran topside. When

I stuck my head out the hatch, I saw explosions throughout the harbor and burning ships. My stomach fell and I knew in an instant that we were at war.

Alvis Harris: I was down below, brushing my teeth and getting ready to visit a neighbor from back home who was stationed aboard the battleship *West Virginia*. There was a huge commotion, so I ran outside to see what was going on. The first thing I saw was a Japanese bomber dropping its torpedo, which then ran right up into the old *Utah* and exploded.

Mike Callahan: I was to have the duty at twelve noon and so went to early mass. While the service was going on, we heard a tremendous amount of gunfire, and I wondered why they were having exercises so early on a Sunday morning. Then someone burst into the church and yelled, "We're being attacked!" I ran outside and knew in a second it was true.

Ernest "Dutch" Smith: I ran up to the OOD, who was a young ensign, and said, "Sir, the Goddamn Japs are attacking!"

He said, "Ah, you're full of baloney!"

Then I said, "Well, go back and take a look at the *Utah*, if you don't believe me." He went back and looked at the *Utah*, which had just been hit with a torpedo.

Harold Reichert: My general quarters station was at gun two, which was up forward. So, when that torpedo hit the old *Utah*, I took off as fast as I could. As I was moving along the length of the ship, I passed the ward room, where a frightened-looking ensign was standing in the hatchway. "We're being attacked, sir," I said without slowing down.

John Cruce: A young ensign was standing in the hatchway with his jaws wide open. I ran past him yelling, "We're at war, sir!" I kept right on a-running until I reached the galley, where I pulled the general quarters alarm.

Cliff Huntley: We heard the bombing in our rooms across the street from the Moana Hotel, clear up in Honolulu. We dressed as fast as possible, jumped into the Chevrolet, and raced off toward Pearl Harbor, where we abandoned the car at the gate. It was the last any of us ever saw of that old Chevrolet!

0755 to 0820

With no aircraft carriers to attack, the Japanese pilots focused their attention on battleships, seven of which were tied up along battleship row on the north side of Ford Island. The remaining one, the USS *Pennsylvania* (BB-38), lay in dry dock across the channel.

`Within the first two minutes of the attack, all of the battleships along battleship row had taken hits from dive-bombers. The torpedo attacks took longer, as many pilots took two or three runs before actually launching their torpedoes. The anchored U.S. fleet was at a low state of readiness, and a few of the ships' machine guns were manned. The *Nevada* (BB-36), for example, had machine guns manned in her fighting tops, and consequently suffered only one torpedo hit, as compared to the six that hit *West Virginia* (BB-48), four on the *Oklahoma* (BB-37), two on the *California* (BB-44), and one on the *Arizona* (BB-39).

As the attacking planes sent torpedo after torpedo slamming into the battleships, *Oklahoma* rolled over onto her side and sank into the bay. *West Virginia* also took on a severe list, but counterflooding by daring seamen prevented her from rolling over and allowed her to settle onto the bottom on an even keel. The *California, Maryland* (BB-46), and *Tennessee* (BB-43) also suffered varying degrees of damage in the first half hour of the raid.

Despite the explosions that filled the harbor area with fire and smoke, the Japanese pilots, well trained from months of practice, maintained discipline. Most of their attack runs were made in coordinated groups of three to five planes. Many of the strafing fighters came in very low, sometimes passing within a few feet of the ground in pursuit of targets, which often included cars or people.

At about 0810, the *Arizona* was hit by one of the modified 16-inch armor-piercing naval rounds dropped by a level bomber. The round penetrated the *Arizona's* deck near turret two and ignited in the ship's forward ammunition magazine, mortally wounding the ship. The resulting explosion and fire killed 1,177 crewmen. Those serving on ships near the exploding *Arizona* that day would say, "It rained sailors!"

Harold Reichert: I got to my general quarters station at gun two before anyone else and even before the GQ klaxon sounded. By then, there were explosions everywhere, and I looked around for what to do next.

Each of our 5-inch guns needed a powderman, shellman, pointer, gun captain, and phone talker. Trouble was, most of our crew was ashore, including the older married guys, who were the ones who knew how to do everything. And that was not the least of it either, because we were tied up at Berth X-14 with three other cans. The order was *Aylwin, Farragut, Dale,* and *Monaghan,* which meant we were sandwiched tight between two other cans, and none of our forward guns could bear without shooting up our sister ships!

Johnny Miller: I dashed down to the radio shack and started the ball rolling. We came up on every important frequency I could think of. The Harbor frequency was the one on which all the important messages were coming over. The first message I copied was, "Air raid on Pearl Harbor. This is no drill!" Next was a message for all ships to get under way. Then the frequency became almost useless due to the Japs causing interference and sending out messages for all to cease fire.

John Cruce: We had no gunnery officer, no firing pins, no powder, no first-class petty officer to install the firing pins—if we could ever find them—and no orders to fire!

Herman Gaddis: The Officer of the Deck up on the bridge, Ensign Radell, hadn't been in the navy more than a year and was shaking like a leaf because he was now the acting captain of a U.S. Navy ship at war. But we also had a thirty-year chief petty officer up there, and he said, "Relax, son. We'll make it out of here just fine!" So they worked things out together and soon put out orders to set material condition Affirm and light off all the boilers!

J. E. McIntyre: When I got to my GQ station in number one fire room, the only person there was Lead Fireman Schnabel. I asked, "What are we supposed to do now?"

"Get the hell out of here as fast as possible!" Schnabel answered.

"Get out of this fire room, or get out of Pearl Harbor?" I replied.

"Let's light her off and get her out of Pearl Harbor!" he said. Luckily, we had the ready duty Saturday, and our boilers were still warm. Otherwise, we were cold iron.

But then I said, "We can't fire the boilers because they're full of water!"

"You take care of the fire, and I'll take care of the water," he ordered, and then opened the drain valves and started to drain the warm water straight into the bilges. Usually we lowered the water levels gradually by pumping the water overboard, but that morning, time was not allowing.

Harold Reichert: I looked up and saw a guy climbing way up to the top of the stacks. I watched him for a moment and realized he was trying to cut loose the stack covers. Whenever the burners weren't lit, the stacks would be covered to keep the rain out. But when the stacks were covered, there was no way to light off the burners because they couldn't get enough air. The bosun mates that had covered the stacks were all ashore when the Japanese attacked. So someone had to climb up there and cut the stack covers free, and all he had was a small pocket knife!

Herman Gaddis: Up on the bridge, things became pretty intense when we found ourselves looking straight down the muzzle of one of the *Farragut*'s 5-inch guns. Now the *Farragut* was tied up directly to our port side, and they were shooting wildly about at anything that moved. Ensign Radell ran out on the flying bridge yelling, "Point that damn thing the other way!"

Ernest "Dutch" Smith: I was the pointer on the forward 5-inch gun. But there was no place to point because the *Farragut* was tied up to port, the *Monaghan* was tied up to starboard, and the Japanese torpedo bombers were flying real low.

Herman Gaddis: We had this black mess attendant aboard named Dixon who was very popular with the crew. He came running up to the bridge and said, "Our five-inch guns can't fire because they don't have firing pins!" We then realized all the firing pins were in the gunner's mate's locker, and the gunner's mate was ashore somewhere. While the rest of us froze with the impossibility of the situation, Dixon ran down to the locker, broke in, grabbed up all the firing pins, and handed them out to the gun crews.

John Cruce: I asked for permission from the bridge to open fire, but no one answered. Since there was nobody up there to say "No," we went right ahead and blasted away at the next Jap plane to fly by. Our ammo was really bad, and our shots kept going off way behind the targets. I kept yelling down to the fuse cutter, "Cut the fuses! Cut the fuses!"

A. L. Rorschach, Captain's Log: The presence of ships on either side of *Dale* prevented the use of all forward guns. The forward twenty-four-inch searchlight made it impossible to bring the [gun] director to bear in the direction of the level bombing attacks on the battleships. The 5-inch guns operated in local control with very poor results, the shots bursting well behind and short of the targets, a squadron of level bombers flying at about ten thousand feet above the battleships on alternately northerly and southerly courses. 0815 an enemy dive-bomber attacking the USS *Raleigh* from westward came under severe machine-gun fire from all the ships in the nest, nosed down, and crashed into the harbor.

Jim Sturgill: Back aft on gun five, we had enough clearance from the other ships in the nest to aim and shoot, but our ammunition was locked up tight and no one could find a key. So I took a hammer and broke open the locker. The gun captain said, "You're going to be court-marshaled for this!" I just shrugged him off and started shooting just as a big torpedo bomber came lumbering by. We blasted him and he went down in flames.

Author's note: Two army P-40 fighters managed to take off and shoot down five Japanese planes. One of the pilots, Lieutenant George Welch, was recommended for the Medal of Honor, but was denied the honor because he had taken off without orders.[3]

Alvis Harris: In the radio shack we were up on the Air Raid, Harbor, and Channel frequencies. Orders and information came in fast and furious like, "All ships get under way immediately" and "DesDiv Two, establish offshore patrol. Enemy submarines sighted inside and outside Pearl Harbor!" I was running messages back and forth to the bridge and got to see a lot of the action. I saw the *Utah*, *Raleigh*, and *Detroit* being bombed, torpedoed, and machine-gunned. I saw the *Raleigh* settle down on the bottom, and the *Utah* turn upside down. The sky was a mass of exploding AA with Japanese bombers flying in and out of them.

Johnny Miller: The next time I dashed up to the bridge I saw a horrible sight. The USS *Utah* had turned over and was lying with only her bottom showing. I could see the big bomber hanger over on Ford Island alive with flames. The USS *Arizona* was afire and sinking fast. The *West Virginia* was hit with six or seven torpedoes and was afire. The USS *Nevada* was hit by a torpedo and was heading for the beach so she wouldn't sink.

J. E. McIntyre: While tied up in the nest with the other tin cans, we got all of our steam and power from the *Monaghan*'s boilers. So when she cast off, we were "cold iron." Under normal conditions, it took us about a hundred and fifty minutes to fire up our boilers. But there was nothing normal about that Sunday morning! After Schnabel flushed the water, I lit off all four boilers and began pumping the crude oil. Since our boilers were still warm, we were able to get up enough steam to get under way in nineteen minutes!

Don Schneider: When I got up to gun one, things were moving real fast. Someone handed me a fire axe and told me to chop the line to the *Monaghan*, which was tied up to starboard. When I finished chopping, they sent me to the ammunition handling room. Someone was down below in the magazine, and they were sending up powder and 5-inch rounds as fast as they could. Trouble was, we weren't shooting at anything yet, so the ammunition was piling up and crowding us out of the handling room, and whoever was down there wouldn't stop. I started stacking some of the rounds out on the deck, but someone running by bumped into my stack and sent a couple of the 5-inch rounds rolling across the deck and over the side.

Harold Reichert: The *Monaghan* had the ready duty that Sunday morning and so was ready to go first. I was happy to help throw off her lines, because it meant that gun two would finally have a clear field of fire to the east.

Johnny Miller: The *Monaghan* backed away from the nest and headed for the channel entrance. A Jap submarine periscope was sticking up out of the water, and the USS *Curtis* was firing into the water with her guns, trying her best to sink the sub. The *Monaghan* let out a blast on her horn to signal she was making a depth charge attack. She had to have a lot of speed on to clear the area of the explosion or be damaged from her own depth charges, and this caused her to run aground.

Ernest "Dutch" Smith: Immediately after the *Monaghan* cast off, it made a high-speed run on a midget Japanese submarine it had spotted and dropped two 600-pound depth charges. The explosions lifted the rear end of the *Monaghan* clean out of the water. If I close my eyes, I can still see her screws spinning wildly in the air!

A few moments later, we cast off, and as we were backing out, I happened to look up through the open turret of the gun and saw two white torpedo streaks coming straight at us just under the surface of the water. Luckily for us, *Dale* was due to tie up at the tender on Monday, and so we were low on everything and only drawing about nine feet of water. Those torpedoes streaked right underneath us and blew up on Ford Island.

Don Schneider: We figured out later how the miniature Jap submarines managed to sneak past the submarine nets into Pearl Harbor. That Saturday we escorted the *Lexington* out to sea, picked up the old *Utah*, and then followed her back into the harbor. There was quite a bit of room between the *Utah* and the *Dale* going in. Those little subs must have just jumped in line between the two of us and followed the sound of the *Utah*'s screws as she worked her way up into the harbor.

Johnny Miller: One torpedo came whizzing by our bow, but missed us by a few feet. Another came from the stern and went under us, hit the beach, exploded, and tore the beach up for yards around.

Harold Reichert: It usually took hours to get under way, but on that Sunday morning, it only took minutes. The interesting thing about being in battle is that you don't get to see much of it, even when you are in the middle of it!

0820 to 0855

By 0830, the first wave of attacking Japanese airplanes had spent themselves and were winging their way north to the carriers. A lull settled in over Pearl Harbor as sailors and soldiers prepared for further attacks.

During this lull in the action, the *Nevada*, the one battleship capable of getting up steam, got under way and began moving slowly down the channel toward the harbor entrance and open sea. The sight of this towering battleship moving along amid the flames and smoke brought hope to those trapped in the flaming hell of Pearl Harbor. But before the *Nevada* could move very far, she was jumped by the second wave of Fuchida's attackers. Pilots of this wave, which consisted of 170 airplanes, found *Nevada* to be the opportunity for which they had been looking. If they could sink *Nevada* in the channel, they could bottle up Pearl Harbor for months to come. In a few frenzied moments, the Japanese pilots dropped five armor-piercing bombs onto the lumbering giant. The *Nevada*, under the command of a junior officer, then received orders from the harbor control tower to stay clear of the channel. This left the young officer with one course of action, and that was to beach the *Nevada* and thereby prevent her from sinking.

While the *Nevada* was attempting her sortie, more dive-bombers and fighters appeared in the skies over Pearl Harbor. Unlike pilots of the first wave, whose attack had been carefully choreographed by Nagumo's planners, pilots of the second wave were given free rein to attack targets of opportunity.

Groups of airplanes circled high in the sky looking down through the smoke for good targets, which were quickly found tied up in Pearl Harbor's dockyards and dry docks. The battleship *Pennsylvania* (BB-38), sitting high in a dry dock, was hit by an armor-piercing bomb dropped from a level bomber, while destroyers *Cassin* (DD-372), *Downes* (DD-375), and *Shaw* (DD-373) were completely destroyed by bombs and fire. Still, the most important target of all for the attackers would be the one they could catch trying to sneak out of the harbor.

Alvis Harris: When we got under way, the first ship we passed was the *Monaghan*, which was stuck in the mud after making a high-speed depth charge run on a Japanese submarine. She was just moving too fast to avoid running aground, so she got stuck in the mud. Eight Jap planes were attacking her, and she was shooting back at them like mad. We could see her screws backing furiously trying to get her off that mud.

Johnny Miller: As we passed the *Monaghan*, guys on both ships waved a friendly goodbye.

Alvis Harris: Then we passed by the old *Utah*, which was rolling over and going under. She had just tied up at the *Lexington*'s berth the day before! All this time I was just a-standing there in the hatchway of the radio shack, a-gawkin' at all this like some old country boy.

Ernest Schnabel: As we left our berth and got under way, the deck force was still engaged in getting ready for combat. One young bosun named Fuller had the job of clearing the deck of all the wooden objects that collected in port. And there was a lot of it, because in port we had all these awnings rigged to keep the tropical sun off the decks. You also had to get rid of all the wooden swabs, buckets, and boxes, because if a machine-gun bullet from a Japanese plane were to strike any of it, slivers would fly all over the place just like shrapnel.

So Fuller was making his way aft, just tossing stuff like a madman when he came to the wooden ice cream gedunk. He grabbed it and was just starting to push it over the side when one of the guys said, "Hey, wait a minute!"

Back in 1941, ice cream was a mighty precious commodity in the destroyer navy. Today you can find ice cream and sugar candy on almost any street corner, but back then, we tin can sailors had to get our ice cream off the bigger ships that had the equipment to make it. They almost always figured out ways to make us pay for it, too! So that young bosun struck a nerve when he made moves to toss all the ship's ice cream over the side.

In a matter of seconds, the lock was broken and the ice cream distributed among the crew. Then Fuller kicked the empty wooden gedunk over the side. So, what you saw was the USS *Dale* steaming hell-bent out into the channel, while the guys back aft were standing by their guns eating ice cream and watching World War II break out all around them.

Harold Reichert: Then we passed by the *Nevada*, which was backing down the other channel. Her crew was pumping water over the side like crazy with portable pumps rigged up with handy-billys. You could tell she was going to try and beach herself on the mud to keep the channel clear.

Ernest "Dutch" Smith: The minute we got around the *Nevada*, all hell broke loose. Before that, we were like spectators at someone else's fight. The Japs didn't pay us much attention, attacking the bigger ships instead. But when we rounded the *Nevada*, they came after us with just about everything they had. We were the first ship to head out of Pearl Harbor, and they wanted to sink us in the channel and bottle up the fleet.

Johnny Miller: We were in a select position to be the first ship in the channel, and the high-level bombers were waiting for us. If they could sink us, they would block up the channel and then have a field day with all the ships trapped in the harbor. The bombs they were using were 16-inch armor-piercing battleship rounds with fins welded to them. Being only thirty-four feet wide, the bombs straddled us and sank deep into the mud before they exploded and showered us with mud and rocks.

Ernest "Dutch" Smith: There were bombs falling all around. And they were armor-piercing bombs, which buried themselves deep in the mud on the bottom of the channel before blowing up. The explosions sent huge fountains of water and stinking mud up higher than *Dale*'s radio mast. That's when we really opened up with every gun we had.

Eugene Brewer: On the way out, I was stationed aft at the manual steering hatch cover in case we lost steering on the bridge. An enemy plane dropped two bombs at us. One hit to the starboard, and the other fell into the water right next to the boat davit where I was standing. The explosion sent up a huge fountain of stinking mud that fell all over us. But nobody panicked. It was like being in a movie where everyone was calm even though all hell is breaking loose.

Warren Deppe: Our depth charges and torpedoes were locked up in the magazines down below, and our job was to get them all up on deck and ready to use. We had to lift them up to the deck with chain falls, and then get their exploder mechanisms together. The exploders were little tubes about two inches long that contained fulminate of mercury, which was very explosive and could easily blow up in your hands. You had to load that tube of mercury into the torpedoes and depth charges while *Dale* was steaming full speed up the channel and the Jap planes were dropping bombs on us.

Harold Reichert: We saw a plane flying low and slow out in the sugar cane fields and started blasting away at it. Thinking back, I also remember seeing a few civilian cars on the road that were most likely out for a Sunday morning drive. Our ammo and our aim were so erratic I'll bet we scared the hell out of those drivers! Probably the safest place to be that morning was in that Jap plane!

J. E. McIntyre: We usually steamed out of Pearl Harbor at a very careful five knots. But on Sunday, December 7, 1941, we steamed out at twenty-five knots!

John Cruce: The big question on the way out was the sub net. Was it open or closed? The net was a barricade stretched across the harbor entrance to prevent submarines from sneaking into the harbor. It had a little tender that stretched it back and forth. If the net was closed, we were in big trouble because we'd be penned in and a perfect sitting duck for the Jap planes trying so hard to sink us. So everyone aboard was hoping to see it open. And it was!

Author's note: Japanese submarines played a big part in the attack on Pearl Harbor. In fact, their presence so unnerved the admirals commanding the fleet they allowed only their destroyers to leave, believing the harbor was still the safest place to shelter the capital ships from the hoards of U-boats they believed were lurking outside. Even as the *Dale* was making its escape, the harbor was being sealed up tight.[4]

Johnny Miller: When we passed the submarine nets, we were making thirty knots. Shrapnel was falling like rain around us as a result of all the antiaircraft fire. As we passed the first entrance buoy to the channel, we sighted a formation of silver bombers flying high in the clouds. Next a bomb struck close to the starboard side and blew mud and salt water all over the ship. Another skipper bomb landed close to the port side, barely missing us. Another passed our stern and still another crossed our bow. They were trying their best to sink us and block the channel. The *Dale* must have been wearing her good luck charm, for nary a thing touched us.

A. L. Rorschach, Captain's Log: At 0907, cleared the entrance buoys and by stopping the port engine and coming hard left rudder, caused a flight of three enemy dive-bombers to overshoot their mark. As they went by on the starboard side close to the water, machine-gun fire from *Dale* struck the leading plane causing it to burst into flame and crash into the water on the outer starboard side of the restricted area. The remaining two planes made a half-hearted attempt to attack again but were driven off by machine-gun fire.

John Cruce: We darned near took a bomb running out of the channel. We made a hard turn to port, and the bomb landed exactly where we would have been. The explosion threw mud clean up over the bridge and the entire ship. Though it missed us, the concussion did knock out a circuit breaker on our port lube pump. And nobody noticed it was out. This would cause us big trouble a little later.

Don Schneider: When we got out of the harbor, we got orders over the radio to look for the Jap fleet, as nobody knew where it was. We were all afraid the Jap battleships would steam in from over the horizon and finish off what the airplanes had missed. It would have been pretty easy for them to do, as Pearl Harbor was a complete shambles and unable to protect itself. They could have steamed back and forth ten miles off shore and just wiped us clean out with their big guns.

Dellmar Smith: My battle station was in the aft fire room, and so I didn't get to see much of the action. In fact, I was so busy with getting up steam, I figured all the explosions I was hearing were just us depth-charging that two-man sub the *Monaghan* was after. Later, I got to thinking about all those explosions and wondered if we ever got that sub, so I asked a bosun mate. "Depth charges, hell!" he said. "Those were bombs dropped by the dive-bombers that were trying to sink us and block the harbor!"

0910 to 1930

Fuchida's second wave of attackers did not escape unscathed, as most of the twenty-nine Japanese airplanes lost that day were shot down during this attack. Nevertheless, the attackers did manage to inflict major damage to ships and facilities, and especially to the Army Air Corps airplanes, most of which had been parked wingtip to wingtip in order to protect them from being sabotaged. By 1030, Fuchida's last attacker was flying back to Nagumo's carriers.

On board the carrier *Akagi*, Admiral Nagumo and staff nervously awaited Commander Fuchida's report on the attack at Pearl Harbor. They had an important decision to make as to whether to launch additional attacks. This decision was certain to be a hotly contested one.

When Fuchida's force returned, his undamaged airplanes were rearmed for possible action against the missing American carriers. The American carriers did not appear. After a brief meeting with his pilots, Fuchida met with Nagumo and recommended additional attacks to destroy the remaining facilities at Pearl Harbor. But the cautious Nagumo had had enough. He quickly dismissed Fuchida and turned his carrier force back toward Japan. There would be no follow-up attack and no attempt to find the missing American carriers. Nagumo's decision was a great stroke of luck to the Americans, as the tank farms and repair facilities of Pearl Harbor were left largely intact.

A. L. Rorschach, Captain's Log: 0911, the *Dale* established off-shore patrols in sector one. Due to repeated airplane attacks the ship was forced to make frequent changes of course and to run at high speed, thereby rendering the sound gear inoperative. It may be of interest to note that a great number of the bursts on the water were of the nature of exploding 5-inch shells rather than bombs. It is believed that either the fuses were not cut on many of our 5-inch projectiles, or that they were not operative.

Jim Sturgill: Outside, we passed some Japanese sampans running for Honolulu. They were flying white flags from their masts. And they were white flags, not rags or pieces of clothing! Without thinking, I grabbed a rifle and took aim. But before I could shoot, someone grabbed the rifle away.

A. L. Rorschach, Captain's Log: 1114, the USS *Worden* (Commander Destroyer Squadron One) sortied. The *Dale* formed on the *Worden* as the third ship in column. After investigating the falsely reported presence of the three enemy transports off Barbers Point, formed inner anti-submarine screen on the USS *Detroit, Phoenix, St. Louis,* and *Astoria.* The *Dale* was assigned station nine. The Task Force speed was twenty-five knots. At 1410, the L.P. pinion bearings on the reduction gear of the port engine wiped. An attempt was made to stay with the assigned Task Force, but as the maximum speed attainable with one engine was twenty-two knots, the *Dale* fell steadily behind. The starboard engine began heating excessively, forcing a further reduction of speed to ten knots. Retired to the southward at 1654. Stopped at 1930 and lay to attempting repairs.

Harold Reichert: When we lay to, things got real quiet, real fast. There were no other ships. We did not know where the Japs were. We did not know where our task force was. There was just us, stopped dead in the night under complete radio silence.

1930 to 0500

Nagumo's fleet was now on its way back to a triumphant reception in Japan. The American sailors and soldiers, however, were in the dark as to the location of the Japanese. Surely, the Yanks thought, the Japanese fleet is out there somewhere, getting ready for another attack. This time they will bring the big guns of their battleships! After all, we don't have anything left that can stop them!

Jim Sturgill: There were two crews aboard *Dale* that night. One crew was made up of all of us trying to fix the burned out pinion bearing. The other crew was made up of those waiting for the bearing to get fixed. I'm glad I was one of the fixers, because the waiters really had it tough that night!

Alvis Harris: We were under radio silence all night long, but that didn't keep us from monitoring the traffic. And there was a lot of it to monitor! All night long, we got plain language broadcasts out of Pearl. Some broadcasts said Pearl was being attacked again. Others said the Jap fleet was steaming in for another attack. It was all panic gossip, but since we were under orders not to use our radio, we just had to sit there and listen all night.

Eugene Brewer: We were the perfect target for the Japanese subs that seemed to be just about everywhere that day. Why heck, we had been dropping depth charges on them all day long, and now it was night, and we were dead in the water! But maybe even worse than the Japanese subs were our own ships, which were shooting first and asking questions later. Someone got the bright idea to drape our largest American flag over the torpedo tubes so our own forces wouldn't shoot us up. But that sure didn't solve our submarine problem!

John Cruce: *Dale*'s decks were crowded with crew that night, because nobody wanted to be caught down below if we were going to be torpedoed. The only sailors down below were those trying to fix the bearing. Everyone else stayed topside and watched for submarines.

Ernest "Dutch" Smith: I had been without sleep for thirty hours and was still too afraid to go below. Sometime, way deep in the early hours, I finally just curled up on the deck and fell asleep.

Harold Reichert: It hit me hard the night we were laying to outside Pearl Harbor. We were at war! And I just knew it was going to be a long, long war. Where would it take me? Would I survive? Would I ever get to see home again? And I knew the war was going to be just like that day, December 7th, had been. We simply would never know what was going to happen to us next!

Jim Sturgill: We pulled the pinion bearing out, saw that it was scoured pretty badly, and took it up to the machine shop. We had a lot of help up there. Too much help! Nobody liked being dead in the water with all those enemy subs out there, so everyone wanted to help fix the bearing!

We put the bearing, which was about seven feet long with an eight-inch journal, into the machine shop's twelve-inch lathe. We got it to fit between the centers okay, but couldn't get the tool arm back far enough to make it turn the bearing's surface. So we filed down the rough edges of the scoured surface by hand. Then we took emery cloth and wooden blocks and polished it the best we could. It wasn't the best job, but it was good enough to get us running again, to the relief of everyone on the ship!

Herman Gaddis: We caught sight of the task force returning in the pre-dawn light and were very frightened. We had no radar and were under orders to maintain radio silence, so we had no way to signal our position to task force. The chief quartermaster "suggested strongly" to Ensign Radell that we break radio silence and call out our position before the task force blasted us out of the water. Much to the relief of everyone on the bridge, Radell picked up the mike and called us in. We soon formed up on the task force. Boy, was that ever a good feeling after a night of being dead in the water!

DECEMBER 8: RETURN TO PEARL HARBOR

A. L. Rorschach, Captain's Log: Rendezvoused with task force at dawn but as full repairs to the engine were impossible without the assistance of the tender, the *Dale* could not maintain her assigned screening station. Under orders of Commander Destroyers, Battle Force, the *Dale* established offshore patrol in sector one until the entrance of Task Group 8.4.

Harold Reichert: When we went into Pearl that night with the task force, it was very dark. We could barely make out the fires still smoldering on Ford Island, but couldn't see much more. We'd move up the channel thirty yards, drop anchor, get our bearings, wait our turn, and then move up another thirty yards.

Cliff Huntley: The harbor was a mess. The battleship *Nevada* was partially sunk and grounded, nearly blocking the harbor entrance. As a result, the ships in the task force entering the harbor had to anchor in the neck and wait for orders to proceed. Everyone aboard and ashore was very nervous. Any sudden movement or flashes of light justified a few exploratory rounds of fire from the jittery guards posted all around the harbor.

My job that night was to let the bridge know when the anchor was free of the bottom. The job quickly became a nightmare, because every time I turned on my flashlight to check on the anchor, some nervous guard on the beach would send a few rounds of 50-caliber tracer bullets over our head.

Herman Gaddis: Ensign Radell had been in continual command of the *Dale* from the first moments of the attack and was plenty glad to see Captain Rorschach come aboard outside of Pearl that Monday afternoon. In appreciation, Captain Rorschach allowed Radell to keep the conn on the way back into Pearl that night with the task force.

I was standing watch up on the flying bridge when Captain Rorschach lit up a cigarette to calm his nerves. There was a lot of incredible maneuvering we had to do in the dark, so there was a lot for him to be nervous about. But when his match flared, we took a couple of rounds from one of the guards posted along the harbor. I quickly walked to the other side of the bridge, but the captain followed. He took a deep drag, his cigarette flared, and we took another few rounds. I walked to the other side of the bridge, the captain again followed, and several more rounds again smacked into steel behind us. "What the hell are those guys shooting at?" he exclaimed.

"I think they're shooting at your cigarette, sir!" I answered. He then flipped the cigarette over the side, which drew a few more rounds, and that was the end of Captain Rorschach's cigarettes for the night!

DECEMBER 9: BATTLESHIP ROW

Ernest Schnabel: Dawn brought a scene of unimaginable disaster. Fires smoldered and smoke rose everywhere you looked in the harbor. We tied up to the tender, which went right to work repairing our burned-out bearing. The crew was still very much on edge, and we went to general quarters many times throughout the day.

Harold Reichert: Looking up battleship row that morning, I couldn't see a single mast standing tall and straight. All of them were cocked sideways, which meant our battleships were either sunk or sinking.

Ernest "Dutch" Smith: You know, if the big battleships like the *Nevada* had their watertight integrity together, they would have been darn hard to sink. But it was Sunday morning, and all the hatchways were wide open. They just caught us with our pants down! There's one thing the Japanese didn't count on, though. By taking out all the old battleships, they increased the speed of the fleet from twenty-one knots to thirty knots!

DECEMBER 15 TO 31: CLEANUP

During the waning days of 1941, *Dale* escorted a fleet reeling from the attack on Pearl Harbor and steaming full-speed from one reported sighting of enemy ships to another. Admiral Husband Kimmel finally ordered the fleet to the defense of Wake Island, which had been under constant threat from the Japanese. However, Kimmel was relieved of his command by President Roosevelt, and his temporary successor, Vice Admiral W. S. Pye, recalled the fleet to Pearl Harbor. Said one dejected *Dale* sailor, "I wish we could have at least seen Wake. We got so close!"

Pye's decision would prove tragic for those on Wake; when the Japanese took the island on December 23, they captured 1,603 men, including 1,150 civilian contractors employed by the Morrison-Knudsen Company. Three weeks later most were sent to POW camps in China, but about 350 of the contractors, and 21 marines and sailors who were too seriously wounded to move, were kept on the island. The contractors were put to work on various military projects for the Japanese—against the Geneva Convention.[5]

Roy Roseth: I was one of the first *Dale* recruits to arrive in Pearl after the attack. *Dale* was out at sea so I was TAD (Temporary Assigned Duty) to the district with orders to help with the cleanup. We spent our days picking up dead bodies and broken equipment and you name it. We collected it all in big piles, and then took it all up into the hills, dumped it into a wash, and buried it. Boy, was I ever happy to see *Dale* finally sail into Pearl Harbor!

Author's note: Tactically, Yamamoto's surprise attack on Pearl Harbor was an unqualified success. At a cost of five midget submarines, twenty-nine aircraft, and sixty-four casualties, the Japanese navy sank or heavily damaged twenty-one ships, destroyed two hundred aircraft, killed 2,388, and wounded an additional 1,178. In the remaining days of December, Japan consolidated its victory by taking control of strategic assets throughout Asia and the western Pacific.

Though it was difficult for the Americans to see rainbows amid the fire and smoke of Pearl Harbor, they were there. One appeared when Admiral Nagumo rejected the argument for additional attacks on Pearl Harbor's tank farms and repair facilities. These facilities enabled the Pacific fleet to regenerate itself in a very short period of time. Of the eight battleships present during the attack, only two were permanently lost and four were back at sea in less than two weeks. Three years later, in October 1944, five of the old slow battleships dredged from the muddy bottom of Pearl Harbor would sink the last of the Japanese fleet during the Battle of Leyte Gulf.

Furthermore, the principal target of the Japanese attack, the American carrier force, had escaped unscathed. In less than six months, these carriers would meet the Japanese off Midway Island and sink four of the Imperial Navy carriers that had participated in the attack on Pearl Harbor.

The tally of Japan's attack on Pearl Harbor was surprisingly light. In the final analysis, Japan succeeded in bombing the U.S. Navy's old slow ships into the mud, forcing it to build a more powerful fleet based on aircraft carriers and fast new battleships.

Most importantly, Japan's "sucker punch" attack on Pearl Harbor forced the people of the United States together for a fight to the finish. American allies were elated. Said Winston Churchill, upon receiving news of the attack on Pearl Harbor, "So, we have won after all!"

1942

As the sun, rising up over America, brought a new year into the Pacific Basin, Japan's military conquest of the Pacific Theater rolled on like a giant tsunami. To the southwest Japan rolled into China, Vietnam, and Burma; to the south, into the oil-rich Dutch East Indies, Bismarcks, New Guinea, Philippines, and Solomons; and to the east, the Marshalls and Gilberts, from which they threatened the shipping lanes between the United States and Australia.

The Imperial Navy now had more than twice the firepower of the Pacific fleet in battleships and aircraft carriers, and, given the U.S. policy of a Europe-first war, little hope was seen for parity. To protect against further losses, and to screen Oahu and the continental United States from further attacks, what was left of the mighty Pacific fleet was ordered to patrol the triangle of waters between the islands of Palmyra, Johnston, and Hawaii. The navy's decade-old plan to fight Japan for control of the Pacific—Plan

Orange—was shelved and "defense, defense" became the order of the day.

Despite the gloomy beginning to the year, change was in the air. On December 20, 1941, Admiral Ernest King became the navy's commander in chief (COMINCH), and on December 31, Admiral Chester Nimitz took over as commander in chief, Pacific (CinCPac). During the early days of January, King and Nimitz planned how to use their limited resources to change the "defense, defense" strategy they inherited into the "defense, offense" strategy they needed to bring hope.

JANUARY: THE RECRUITS

Two kinds of sailors manned the USS *Dale* during the early months of 1942: those who enlisted before the Japanese attack on Pearl Harbor and those who enlisted immediately after the attack.

Many of those who enlisted before had done so to escape the grinding poverty of the Great Depression. As the supply of potential recruits exceeded the prewar demand, it was difficult for them to enlist and exceedingly difficult to advance in rank.

But on December 7, 1941, the navy's need for recruits became great; and on December 8, young men from throughout the nation put down their plowshares and joined. To accept the many thousands of young men pouring into its recruit pipeline, the navy hurriedly modified its enlistment and training programs.

Though a fully staffed destroyer on the front lines of the Pacific Theater, *Dale* quickly felt the impact of this massive recruitment effort. When many of her veterans were transferred off to new construction, their berths were filled with new recruits fresh off the fields of America's heartland.

Jim Sturgill: I was a farm boy from northern Arkansas. During the great depression of the thirties and early forties, nobody had anything, and we had even less than that. Oh, we didn't starve, but we just didn't have anything.

Warren Deppe: Wages were poor back in 1940—a buck a day if you could find it, but not many could find it. I decided to join the navy, but had one little toe that didn't quite touch the ground. The medics said the navy probably wouldn't take me because of that toe. And when I talked the navy into accepting my toe, the medics found a cavity in a tooth, which had to be filled before I could swear in down in St. Louis!

Bela "Shorty" Smith: Joining up in the U.S. Navy wasn't all that easy for me. I was a good half-inch too short for the navy's tastes and so had to do a lot of finagling to get in. When the war broke out, I was on my way from boot camp in San Diego to San Francisco, where I was to catch a troop transport out to Pearl Harbor. When I finally arrived aboard the *Dale*, they assigned me to the deck crew. I did whatever they told me to do, which was usually chipping paint or swabbing decks. My first GQ station was powderman on gun one. Later, I worked my way up to pointer.

John Overholt: My parents were Amish farmers. When the Japanese bombed Pearl Harbor on December 7, 1941, I was working on a farm about fifteen miles south of Iowa City, Iowa. I had to sign up. I had to get involved. I just didn't have any choice!

Robert "Pat" Olson: I grew up working for Dad near Molt, Montana. Our job was to pump crude oil out of the ground, refine it, and then sell the gasoline, tractor fuel, and lubricants to farmers and ranchers from the high prairie.

Those visiting farmers and ranchers were about the extent of my social circle, and I took a lot of pleasure in wheeling and dealing firearms with them. They would bring in a handgun or rifle, and we would haggle until a price was agreed upon, and then I would sell or trade it to the next farmer or rancher.

A few days after Pearl Harbor, Dad took all us boys aside and said, "Our country is at war and you are going to be called to serve. You can take what they give you or you can make your own choice and sign up before they send you the letter."

When I went to sign up with the navy I started hagglin' with the recruiter, just like I did with all the farmers and ranchers. As a result, I was able to sign up as a Third Class Fireman. Now, a lot of guys in the peace-time navy had to wait years for that rating, and I just walked in the door with one! You can imagine the animosity I ran up against when I finally met those real sailors!

Billy Walker: I had just turned seventeen and talked Dad into signing the waivers for me. I hitched a ride into Oklahoma City and signed up. At the end of the first month, I had twenty-one dollars in my pocket, whereas before I don't think I ever had so much as one dollar at a time during my entire life. From farm boy to sailor, I was rich!

Orville Newman: I had been working as a welder in a Tacoma ship-yard. One night I got an assignment to do some welding in a real tight space between the ship's frame and its skin. I crawled in with the welding stinger held out in front of me, as there was no room to move it around once inside. When I completed the weld, I discovered that my leg had cramped. I couldn't back out because of the cramp and so asked my co-worker, who was one of the woman welders that the ship-yard had just hired, to massage the cramp out of my leg so that I could get out. "I'm a lady," she said, "and ladies don't do that kind of thing!" Next day I went down and joined the navy!

Robert "Pat" Olson: I lived in dread all the way through boot camp because I had never learned how to swim. There just wasn't any water in the high prairies of Montana! And so I knew I was going to wash out when they gave us the swim test on the last day of boot camp. But when that day finally came, they canceled the swim test and my worries were over. I had made it into the navy!

After boot camp they hurried us aboard the *President Tyler* for the trip over to Pearl Harbor. The *Tyler* was a rusty old cruise ship that had been converted to a troop transport, and there were five thousand of us packed into tiny quarters like hogs in a possum-belly trailer.

I remember standing in line once for five hours to get lunch. The sea was rough and the ship was tossing back and forth and food was strewn all over the deck. When we finally got to the serving window, there were wieners and sauerkraut all over the deck, and you had to wade through a half-foot of them to get your tray!

When we finally berthed at Pearl, I transferred over to the *Dale*. She was clean, orderly, and beautiful—a dream come true compared to that old *President Tyler!* My first job aboard her was to light off the burners for Spagnoli's crew. But when Spag yelled, "Man number one boiler," and threw up some hand signals, I didn't have the slightest idea what he wanted me to do! When Spag figured that out, he yelled out over the blowers, "How can I fight a war with a crew like this?"

But I was at sea, and at sea I would live until the end of the war. The sea can be terrifying, especially if you can't swim and are afraid of water, like I was. But the sea gets into your blood and you learn to love it.

Harold Reichert: As for being a recruit aboard *Dale*, the job description was simple: If it moves, salute it; if it doesn't move, paint it!

Orville Newman: I arrived aboard the *Dale* late one afternoon, and within a few minutes of checking in, got a job chipping paint. I asked if there was another job I could do aboard the ship, as I thought chipping paint was a waste of my talents. The bosun mate in charge of the deck crew said, "Try the engineers." I did. The next day I reported to the fire room at 0800 and soon found myself along with another guy inside a boiler scraping scales. We had to stay inside that boiler all day, as we were simply too filthy to come out. They handed our lunch through the hatch, and we had to eat it with our filthy hands. We spent days scraping boiler scales. I think those boilers gave me a life-long case of claustrophobia, as the hatches we had to crawl through were really small and forced us to squeeze in and out.

Earl Hicks: *Dale* had many new crewmen aboard and us new guys didn't have the slightest idea of what we were doing nor what lay ahead. What we did know was that we were steaming off to war, and everyone's nerves were on edge.

Though *Dale* was one of the navy's newest destroyers, she still had a lot of the old style equipment aboard. Take the enlisted men's head, for example. Where the officers had individual stalls, enlisted men had a long wooden plank with a half-dozen round holes spaced a few inches apart from each other. Beneath that plank was a long metal trough with a continuous flow of seawater running through it. We lined up on the plank for our morning dump, which then flowed down the trough and out to sea.

The enlisted head did have one convenience that was much appreciated by all, and that was a porthole in the bulkhead right above the forward end of the plank. That porthole was almost always open for fresh air. To welcome us new recruits aboard the *Dale*, the old salts would sometimes wait for us to line our bare butts up on the plank. Then they would wad up a big bunch of TP, light it afire, and drop in through the porthole so that it would float down the trough right under our exposed bottoms. *"Hey! . . . Ouch! . . . Damn!"* We'd have a big whoop-dee-doo poppin' up all down the plank! They did it to me when I came aboard, but I got 'em back later!

JANUARY TO MARCH: CARRIER RAIDS

As Japan's conquest of Southeast Asia rolled on through January, February, and March, the morale of the Pacific fleet deteriorated accordingly. The need was great for Admirals King and Nimitz to send the fleet on an offensive, both to boost morale and to provide for some "on the job" training. The opportunity for such a change came when the Imperial Navy's fast attack carriers moved deep into the Southwest Pacific in support of the invasion activities of the army, and then on to the Indian Ocean for raids against the British fleet, leaving the rest of the Pacific only lightly defended.

Nimitz quickly built two carrier strike forces out of his three carriers and gave them orders. Task Force 17, consisting of the USS *Enterprise* and *Yorktown* under Admiral William "Bull" Halsey, was to strike targets in the Marshall and Gilbert Islands in the Central Pacific. Task Force 11, built around the *Lexington* under Admiral Wilson Brown, was to stock up on forty-two days' worth of provisions and head southwest into the waters of Australia and New Zealand.

Farragut-class destroyers, like *Dale*, were designed for long-range screening. *Dale* would test the limits of this design over the next two months as she screened Task Force 11 to the other side of the Pacific.

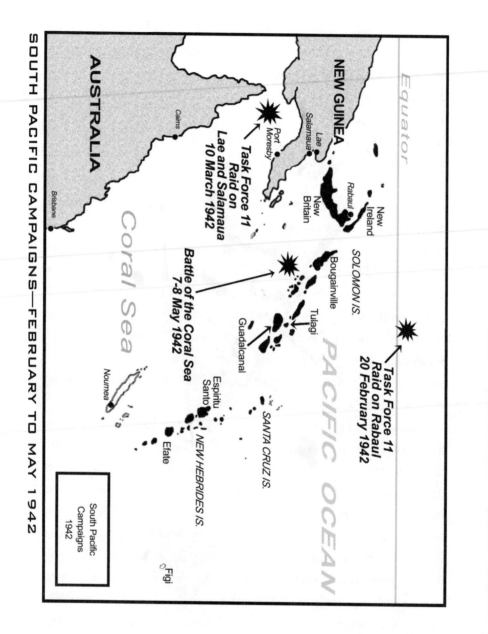

SOUTH PACIFIC CAMPAIGNS—FEBRUARY TO MAY 1942

AUSTRALIA

Brisbane

Cairns

Coral Sea

NEW GUINEA

Port Moresby

Lae
Salamaua

Task Force 11
Raid on
Lae and Salamaua
10 March 1942

New
Britain

Rabaul

New
Ireland

Battle of the Coral Sea
7-8 May 1942

SOLOMON IS.

Bougainville

Guadalcanal

Tulagi

Task Force 11
Raid on Rabaul
20 February 1942

Noumea

Espiritu
Santo

SANTA CRUZ IS.

NEW HEBRIDES IS.

Efate

Figi

Equator

PACIFIC OCEAN

South Pacific
Campaigns
1942

USS Dale War Diary, *January 31*: Underway with ships of Task Force 11 en route to South Pacific Area for air attack and shelling of Japanese installations on Rabaul, New Britain. Vice Admiral J. Wilson Brown, U.S.N. CTF 11 in USS *Lexington*.

Earl "Jitterbug" Pearson: *Dale*'s fire room was pressurized. To enter it we had to open one airtight hatch, climb into a pressure chamber, close and secure the hatch, open a second hatch, climb into the fire room, and then secure that hatch. Both hatches could not be opened at the same time because pressure would be lost and the fire would flare back and burn us up. We were literally sealed in!

Inside the fire room there was a maze of pipes covered in asbestos insulation. Our boilers burned bunker crude, which is the crudest form of petroleum there is. To get that crude to burn it had to be superheated, atomized, and then sprayed under pressure into the burning chamber.

The fire room drew air down from the main deck with big blowers, so there was always a big wind blowing. Brother, we had asbestos blowing everywhere! And there were loud noises from blowers and reduction gears, and no way to protect our hearing. But you got used to all that after a while.

Robert "Pat" Olson: We steamed south at flank speed, all the while testing our guns and conducting various practice drills. Each time one of the 5-inch guns would go off topside, we'd be showered by asbestos down in the fire room. But what really scared me were the steam lines that flopped crazily each time the guns fired. Back home the steam lines were brittle and broke easily. *Dale*'s lines were pressurized to four hundred pounds and the steam was superheated to seven hundred degrees. Why, an invisible little pinhole leak in one of those steam lines could slice you in two like a hot knife through butter!

Armor plating? Now there's a joke! *Dale's* hull was only three-eighths inch thick and the boilers themselves were covered with a Christmas foil-like insulation. That fire room was like a high-pressure balloon filled with superheated steam that just about anything could pop, much less a 5- or 8-inch Japanese naval gun!

Rabaul, New Britain

Given the Imperial Navy's superiority in capital ships, the Yanks were forced to leave many areas of the Pacific with little or no protection. The supply line from the United States to Australia was one of the most vulnerable.

To exploit this vulnerability, the Japanese invaded Rabaul. Rabaul was a small settlement with a magnificent natural harbor located on the Gazelle Peninsula on the northern tip of New Britain (now Papua New Guinea). In January 1942, Rabaul was garrisoned by fifteen hundred Australians, who were overwhelmed by the Japanese invasion toward the end of that month. The Japanese built Rabaul into their largest base south of Truk, with five airfields capable of holding more than five hundred aircraft, a float plane base, submarine base, huge numbers of naval vessels, and up to two hundred thousand Japanese armed forces personnel. POWs captured in Singapore were forced to dig more than three hundred miles of tunnels in the hills surrounding Rabaul. These tunnels housed fifteen hospitals capable of treating twenty-five hundred patients. Rabaul was employed as a staging area for Japanese military operations in Australia, Bougainville, Coral Sea, New Guinea, and the Solomon Islands—a domineering position overlooking the Hawaii-to-Australia supply lines. When Admiral Wilson Brown suggested his Task Force 11 raid the Imperial Navy's newly acquired prize, Admirals Nimitz and King readily agreed. (Although initial plans called for Allied forces to capture Rabaul sometime in 1943, the fortress instead was surrounded, isolated, and bypassed, leaving well over one hundred thousand Japanese soldiers with little or nothing to eat.)

Alvis Harris Diary, February 20, 0530: General Quarters. The plan is for the cruiser *Chicago*, *Dale*, and another tin can to dash within firing range of Rabaul Harbor, shoot up the place, and then get the hell out of there as fast as possible. Ammunition is ready and all the guns are uncovered. We are well within the range of Jap patrol planes— about 400 miles from Rabaul. All hands are in top shape, as if the big game is coming off. We have our gas masks, protective clothing, and lifejackets close at hand. The weather is in our favor, with intermittent rains and poor visibility.

0830: Two Jap patrol planes were picked up by the *Lexington*'s radar. The *Lex* launched five fighters, which destroyed the bombers. The admiral, knowing that the Japs had been alerted and would be ready and waiting for us at Rabaul, cancelled the attack and ordered the task force to a rendezvous for refueling. All hands were very angry at the cancellation.

1645: Lookouts report a group of planes flying in formation on starboard beam, low and far off. General Quarters. Setting "Condition Delta." *Lex* is launching aircraft and we all have ammunition in hand. The fight is on!

Author's note: The military's five threat levels—normal, Alpha, Bravo, Charlie, and Delta—each carry a set of increasingly restrictive security precautions. Condition Delta, the most serious, is normally declared when an attack is imminent.

Dellmar Smith: When general quarters sounded, I ran to my battle station, which was ammo hoist number one. I heard the gun captain on number four yell, "Run out to starboard." Then, "Load." Now, you don't load unless you are going to shoot! I looked up and saw nine Japanese bombers flying towards us in a V formation.

Cliff Huntley: This was so early in the war that we still had the WWI pancake helmets. I remember being on the foredeck, and every time one of our guns would go off my helmet would fly off the back of my head from the blasts. I would carefully put it back on, only to have it blown right back off again in a few seconds.

Mike Callahan: I didn't know much about gunnery when they made me the gunnery officer. In fact, our gun director was one of the first computers ever made, and not many people knew how to use it. We didn't even have proximity fuses in those days, just the old-fashioned time fuses. We had to estimate the time it took for each round to reach the target, and then set the fuse.

Though I didn't know much about gunnery, I knew something was wrong with our shooting, because all our shots were going off behind the enemy planes! I yelled down to the men, "These goddamn guns aren't hitting anything!" But that just made them really mad! I tried making some corrections on the gun director input knob, but even that didn't seem to do much good.

Alvis Harris: The *Lexington* sent only two fighters up to meet the formation of Japanese bombers because the rest of her fighters were away somewhere. Though we didn't know it at the time, one of those two fighters was Butch O'Hare. Butch had not been able to take off with the earlier flight because of equipment problems, and so he and his wingman were the only ones left to fight off the Jap bombers. I watched out the back door of the radio shack as Butch and his wingman took on the formation of Japanese bombers.

Cliff Huntley: All of the ships were blasting away with every gun they had when the Japs came over and dropped their bombs. It was thrilling to see our ships disappear in a spray of water when bombs hit on both sides of them, and then steam safely out the other side of the falling water! The black puffs of our antiaircraft fire filled the sky from horizon to horizon, but I don't think we ever hit a thing. In fact, outside of Butch O'Hare and his wingman, I think the safest place to be that day was in one of those Japanese bombers!

Author's note: Edward H. "Butch" O'Hare was born on March 13, 1914, in St. Louis, the son of "E. J." O'Hare, a wealthy businessman and attorney. After graduating from the Naval Academy and serving two years of sea duty aboard the USS *New Mexico* (BB-40), O'Hare began flight training at Naval Air Station Pensacola. During this time, his father was gunned down for providing the government with information leading to the prosecution of Al Capone. After flight training O'Hare served in various fighter squadrons aboard the USS *Saratoga*, *Enterprise*, and *Lexington*. In 1941, O'Hare shot down the five Japanese airplanes trying to bomb the *Lexington*, as described by the *Dale* sailors herein. Interestingly enough, when O'Hare landed back aboard the *Lexington*, it was learned that he had used only sixty rounds of ammunition to shoot down each bomber. For this act, O'Hare was promoted to Lieutenant Commander, awarded the Congressional Medal of Honor, and became one of America's first World War II heroes. As commander of the *Enterprise* air group in 1943, O'Hare was instrumental in developing tactics to fight the Japanese Betty tor-

pedo bombers raiding American shipping at night during the invasion
of the Gilbert Islands. During the first operational night mission
against the enemy, O'Hare disappeared, quite possibly shot down by
the friendly fire of a pilot from his own air group.

Dellman Smith: We watched as one of our two fighters came down
through the formation of Jap bombers, but nothing happened! Later
we learned his guns had jammed. Then Butch came down through
them and one of the large bombers caught fire, lazily rolled over, and
spiraled down into the water. Butch just kept after them, shooting up
one plane on the way up through the formation, and then another one
on his way back down. He shot down five enemy bombers before he
ran out of ammunition.

Then, right in the middle of all the action, when the air was blue
with steel, the *Lexington* turned into the wind to land her returning
aircraft. One of the Japanese bombers flying overhead caught fire and
started spiraling down toward the *Lex*. You could tell it was going to
crash into the *Lex*! Every gun on every ship was blasting away at that
bomber, but nobody could hit it! Then one of our returning fighters
flew down through that curtain of steel and shot the bomber out of the
sky when it was only about 150 yards away from the *Lex*. His plane
was all shot up and he had to bail out. When we pulled him out of the
water, someone asked why he flew into the firestorm. He said, "The
Lex is my home! If that guy had crashed into her, I wouldn't have had
any place to land!"

We shot down sixteen of the eighteen attacking bombers that day.
I watched the whole thing happen, sitting there on my capstan, like it
was some giant show put on just for me! Whenever I fly into Chicago
to visit the relatives, I think about Butch O'Hare and the pilots of the
Lady Lex.

USS Dale War Diary, *February 20:* Ship's position 02 degrees 35 minutes South, 157 degrees 50 minutes East. At 1643 a flight of nine Japanese twin-engine bombers were sighted on port beam, others shot down by fighters. The remaining planes scored no bomb hits on formation. Some of [the] enemy planes jettisoned bombs. At 1707 a flight of seven similar planes approached formation from astern and passed directly over formation, but no ship was struck by bombs. Suffered a steering casualty during attack at 1714 and backed full astern to avoid hitting USS *San Francisco*. Ceased fire at 1718. Task Force steamed on easterly course to clear area and then retired to southward.

Alvis Harris Diary, *February 30, 1845:* The fireworks are just about over. It's getting kinda dark. Secured from GQ. Ate supper and turned in, as I have the mid-watch.

Lae–Salamaua, New Guinea

By early March, Admiral Wilson Brown had put together one of the largest forces the U.S. Navy's Pacific fleet had yet been able to muster in the Southwest Pacific. This force consisted of eight heavy cruisers, fourteen destroyers, and the carriers *Lexington* and *Yorktown*. *Yorktown* was the progenitor of the *Yorktown*-class of U.S. Navy aircraft carriers that included *Enterprise* and *Hornet*. Though smaller than *Lexington*-class carriers, the *Yorktown*-class became the model for all future U.S. Navy carriers and garnered more battle stars and decorations than any other class of ship during World War II. After Pearl Harbor, *Yorktown* was shifted from the Atlantic to the Pacific to bolster the decimated Pacific fleet. In early 1942, she participated in the carrier raids on the Marshall and Gilbert Islands, under Admiral Halsey, and then steamed into the South Pacific. Brown took his force deep into the waters of the Coral Sea with the intent of raiding the Japanese fleet anchorage at Rabaul.

Before his plans could be carried out, however, the Japanese invaded Lae and Salamaua on the north coast of New Guinea. This invasion put the Japanese directly opposite Port Moresby, which was on the south side of the island and the last allied position left on New Guinea. In fact, the only obstacle preventing the Japanese from marching into Port Moresby was the Owen Stanley Mountain Range, the backbone of the southeastern tip of New Guinea.

Brown immediately drew up new plans to attack the Japanese while they were still exposed on the beaches at Lae and Salamaua.

USS Dale War Diary, *March 8–10:* Steaming as before in company with Task Force 11, with Task Force 17 nearby.

Cliff Huntley: Our chance to strike back at the Japs finally came when they invaded Lae and Salamaua on the northeast coast of New Guinea. Our side put together a big strike force built around the carriers *Lexington* and *Yorktown.* After sneaking around the South Pacific so long with just the *Lex,* it was great to have so much company! The plan was to sneak up into the Gulf of Papua, which is on the south side of New Guinea, and then fly over the Owen Stanley Mountains to attack the Japs on the north side. Those mountains were so high the Japs figured we wouldn't attack from the south.

After the planes left the carrier, they circled above us until everybody had joined up, then they flew off toward the mountains. Some of our old torpedo planes couldn't fly high enough to make it over those mountains, until one of the pilots figured out how to catch a thermal. The rest of the pilots followed him, and the thermal carried them all up and over the mountains. Our pilots sank a few Jap ships and shot the invasion beaches up really good. We didn't lose a single plane on that raid!

MARCH TO JUNE: CARRIER BATTLES

With their conquest of Southeast Asia completed in half the allotted time, and with far fewer casualties than anticipated, the Japanese military debated its next course of action. The aggressive, flush with their successes, argued for continuing the offense. The cautious, anticipating a counteroffensive from the United States, argued for the hardening of the defense. The aggressive won and invasion plans were developed for Port Moresby on the southwest tip of New Guinea and the island of Midway fifteen hundred nautical miles west of Honolulu.

Coral Sea

A successful invasion of Port Moresby and Tulagi would allow Japan to threaten closure of the sea-lanes from the United States to Australia.

The Imperial Navy had two distinct advantages in pressing home such an invasion: a battle fleet built around three aircraft carriers and a vast network of island bases stretching south from the home islands to New Guinea. This network of island bases allowed the Imperial Navy to island-hop aircraft from the home islands to the scene of battle.

To counter, the U.S. Navy would bring *Lexington* and Task Force 11 together with *Yorktown* and Task Force 17 under Admiral Frank Jack Fletcher. These ships would have to fight many thousands of miles from their base at Pearl Harbor. The extent to which the admirals could operate their task forces over this vast distance was determined by the availability of tankers. Tanker ships were developed at the beginning of the twentieth century and were soon plying the world's trade routes carrying liquids such as gasoline, oil, and molasses. During World War II, many tankers were built or taken over by the U.S. Navy and named after the Native American names for rivers and lakes (e.g., Neosho, Mississinewa, Truckee). These fleet oilers made 6,500 voyages to carry sixty-five million tons of oil and gasoline from the United States and the Caribbean to war zones and allies. They supplied 80 percent of the fuel used by bombers, tanks, jeeps, and ships during the war.[1] In a very real sense, tankers became the most important ships in the fleet, and screening them as they steamed back and forth across the broad seas became the job of tin cans like the USS *Dale*.

USS Dale War Diary, *March 16–17*: Screened USS *Kaskaskia* while she left Task Force 11 and fueled units of Task Force 17. At 1939 on 16th USS *Dale* was detached from Task Force 11 and proceeded to escort USS *Kaskaskia* to Pearl Harbor via Suva, Fiji.

Elliot Wintch: Sometimes the smooth sailing could be as dangerous as the heavy fighting! After washing my clothes one day, I was hauling them down to the engine room in a bucket to dry them out. The water that day was as smooth as a tabletop! Suddenly, the ship heeled over in a sharp turn and a four-foot wall of water came washing over the deck. I grabbed for the torpedo tube, but the water caught me before I could get a hold and I was washed over the side. Luckily, I managed to grab a cable on my way over the side and held on. I lost my bucket and clothes but somehow saved myself!

Alvis Harris: In the tropics the temperature was always hot, and sleeping below decks was intolerable because you would drown in your own sweat. A lot of guys would find a place on deck and sleep in the fresh air. I did, too, until one night I had this dream that a giant wave came over the deck and carried me away to be drowned. I woke up from the dream but kept working the idea over in my mind until I could no longer sleep on deck!

Earl Hicks: In the tropics it was so hot you couldn't sleep with any clothes on. One night someone noticed that a big seaman fresh off the farm had his wing-ding a-hanging out of his skivvies and decided to play a little practical joke. So he signaled for everyone still awake to quietly gather round. He took out some string, made a lasso, and slung it over the exposed wing-ding. Then he tied off the end of the string to the bunk above and yelled, "Fire!" I swear, that big seaman leaped out of his bunk but never did touch the ground! We all ran for it because he was huge and he was going to kill us all!

USS Dale *War Diary,* *March 18:* Arrived Suva Harbor in afternoon—the first port visited since leaving Pearl Harbor on 31 January, 1942.

March 20: Escorting USS *Kaskaskia* from Suva, Fiji Islands, to Pearl Harbor.

Alvis Harris Diary, March 23: The Captain turned the ship over to the shellbacks for a crossing-the-equator initiation. Though we polly-wogs had the shellbacks outnumbered, they really turned things up for our initiation. They clipped our hair and smeared oil, paint, jam, and sand all over us. They also beat us on the rear pretty good with clubs. The initiation lasted until 1300. The ship is still a mess with oil and paint everywhere. It took me two and a half hours to get myself cleaned up!

Earl "Jitterbug" Pearson: How did I get the name "Jitterbug"? Well, when we steamed across the equator, *Dale* had a big crossing cere-mony for all us pollywogs. Now, a bunch of shellbacks had me and another pollywog in a circle, and they were standing around with pad-dles ready to give us a good whack. One of them said, "Okay, we want to see you dancing, and whoever does the best dance won't get whacked on the bottom with these paddles!" Man, I put on a dance like you never seen before, and the pollywog in the circle with me was laughing so hard he couldn't even stand up! He got the whackin' and I got the nickname "Jitterbug."

K. G. Robinson: We were at sea for a long time and had run out of all sorts of food, cigarettes, and other PX supplies. I conned Hank Haneke, the cook, out of his last two pounds of butter, cocoa, milk, sugar, and coconut, and with the help of Ensign Callahan and two cooks, whipped up about 100 pie tins of fudge. Trouble was, the daily temperature was about ninety-five degrees, so the damned fudge would not harden. We put all those tins of fudge into our empty refrigerators and then handed them out to the boys. Not a great success, but it did provide a little satisfaction!

Dellmar Smith: We lived on chili con carne for breakfast, lunch, and dinner for days. By the time we finally got to Pearl we were fifty-three days on forty-two day's worth of rations. All we had left was one case of black pepper and three cases of tomatoes!

Alvis Harris Diary, *March 24*: Early morning off Oahu with *Kaskaskia*. Sure a lot of ships off Pearl. Saw *Enterprise*. She's the carrier that's seeing more action than us! Task Force 11 is in Pearl! We moored at buoy X-3 about 1130. Received mail and fresh stores. Nice!

USS Dale War Diary, *April 16–26*: Steaming in company with Task Force 11 on general SSW courses. Task Force fueled on the 26th and USS *Dale* was detached late in afternoon to escort USS *Kaskaskia* back to Pearl Harbor. A short while after leaving Task Force 11, USS *Dale* made underwater contact and dropped charges; no apparent results. After a search of approximately 30 minutes, proceeded to join USS *Kaskaskia*, who was without escort.

Author's note: On May 3, the Imperial and U.S. Navies began a series of engagements that came to be known as the Battle of the Coral Sea. The Imperial Navy's objective was to occupy Tulagi in the Solomon Islands and Port Moresby on the southern coast of New Guinea. The U.S. Navy's objective was to prevent both occupations.

The Battle of the Coral Sea opened with Japan landing troops unopposed on Tulagi. A subsequent attack on their beachhead by aircraft from the *Yorktown* did little damage, but did alert the Japanese to the presence of an American carrier. The two fleets then maneuvered cautiously through the Solomon[s] and Coral Seas for the next two days, trying to find the other without revealing themselves.

On May 7 and 8, the two fleets engaged in history's first carrier battle, during which the engaged ships did not come into visual contact with their opposition. Japanese aircraft damaged the light carrier *Yorktown* and sank the fleet tanker *Neosho*, its escort destroyer *Simms*, and the fleet carrier *Lexington*, while losing only the light carrier *Soho*. However, American aircraft did inflict severe damage on fleet carriers *Shokaku* and *Zuikaku*.

Though Japan had won a tactical victory by sinking three ships while losing only one, the American forces denied the Japanese their strategic objective of occupying Port Moresby. It was, in fact, the first time Japan had been denied territory in the still very young war. In addition, fleet carriers *Shokaku* and *Zuikaku* were rendered impotent for the looming Battle of Midway.

For security reasons, information regarding the American losses at the Battle of the Coral Sea was not forthcoming. In fact, crewmen of the USS *Dale*, which had screened the *Lady Lex* since the beginning of the war, did not learn of her sinking for more than a month!

Alvis Harris Diary, *June 12*: Dear Diary: As you know, this is the first time that I have commenced a day this way, but you are the only one that I feel and would DARE sing the blues to. TODAY the NAVY DEPARTMENT announced the sinking of the LEXINGTON, an aircraft carrier with the loss of planes and about eight percent of the crew. Knowing the LEX as we were and have been operating with her since the OUTBREAK OF THE WAR. But fortunately we were detached before the CORAL SEA BATTLE in order to escort the tanker that fueled the task force back to PEARL HARBOR. I think it's a DAMN shame the way the PERSONNEL (enlisted) have been deceived up to date as to her status. When I heard the News Flash it was tearing my heart out. I swear, repeat SWEAR, that if I am fortunate enough to struggle (and it is a struggle with the HS the enlisted men have to put up with) thru this War and ever have any boys—I'll do my damn[e]dest to keep them or him out of the SERVICE. OH YES the Navy announced the sinking of the NEOSHO AND THE SIMMS but this had been rumored throughout the ship. Some of the BLUE-BLOOD had let it slip. Thanks for the broad shoulders, Alvis Harris.

Midway

Japanese Fleet Admiral Isoroku Yamamoto saw a need. Having studied at Harvard, and served as the Japanese Naval Attaché to the United States, he understood the extent of America's industrial might and knew that, in a very short period of time, the U.S. Navy would replace the ships it had lost at Pearl Harbor and then catch, and surpass, the Imperial Navy in strength. To thwart this industrial might, the Imperial Navy needed to lure the U.S. Navy into a decisive battle

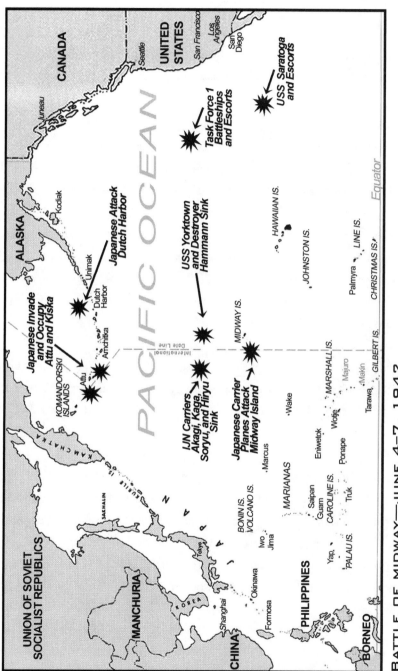

BATTLE OF MIDWAY—JUNE 4-7, 1942

while it still possessed superior firepower. Yamamoto believed he could lure the Americans to this battle by invading the tiny island of Midway. And, motivated by Jimmy Doolittle's daring April 18 raid on Tokyo from the deck of the carrier *Hornet*, the Japanese admiralty acceded to Yamamoto's plan.

To ensure victory Yamamoto would bring together an overwhelming fleet of 147 warships, including four fleet carriers, four light carriers, four seaplane carriers, eleven battleships, twenty cruisers, sixty-one destroyers, and nineteen submarines. His counterpart, Admiral Chester Nimitz, could muster only forty-seven warships, including three carriers, eight cruisers, seventeen destroyers, and nineteen submarines. Though Nimitz would be thoroughly outgunned in the looming battle, he would employ another weapon that would carry the day: Station Hypo.

USS Dale War Diary, *May 11*: Underway at noon in company with USS *Clark* acting as escorts for Convoy #4098 from Pearl Harbor to San Francisco. USS *Dale* granted ten days restricted availability at Navy Yard, Mare Island.

Lester Dailey Diary, *May 22*: Sighted land! About 0830. Boy does the old USA ever look good to me. Tied up at Mare Island. I get four days leave eight days from now, but have to give up all other liberty! . . . Ship went into dry dock today around 1100. Started in scraping bottom of hull below water line. The *Boise*, that's the heavy cruiser that got in the battle by Australia, is in dry dock right next to us. Boy she sure is torn up!!!

Author's note: Actually, the *Boise* had received her damage en route to battle. On January 12, 1942, she struck an uncharted pinnacle in Sapeh Strait, the narrow body of water separating Sumbawa and Komodo Islands, tearing a hole in her bottom. She was underway to intercept a large Japanese invasion force bound for Balikpapan, an important oil field in southeastern Dutch Borneo, but was forced to turn back to Java, keeping destroyer *Barker* as her escort.[2]

Alvis Harris Diary, *May 24*: San Francisco. First leave party went ashore. 1500 went on liberty to Oakland and San Francisco. It's good to be in the States, but for some reason, I am not too enthusiastic about it today.

June 3: 0800. Underway from dry dock at Mare Island Navy Yard to Frisco. Alongside *Fanning* at dock. Assigned to Task Force 1. JAPS RAIDED DUTCH HARBOR around noon. Two attacks!

June 4: Dutch Harbor under air attack. West Coast on alert. Task Force 17 under attack off Midway. 1830. *Fanning* and *Dale* moved from alongside dock to anchorage in stream.

Author's note: The Battle of Midway set opposing ships in motion across the most extensive battlefield the world had ever seen—the Pacific Ocean from the Coral Sea to the Bering Sea, and from the United States to Japan.

Yamamoto's battle plan was the model of complexity and cunning: he would open the battle far to the north with an attack on the American base at Dutch Harbor, Alaska, and then invade Kiska and Attu in the far western Aleutian Islands. He hoped this action would lure the American fleet north from Hawaii. While the American forces were steaming north, Yamamoto's main battle groups would invade and capture Midway. If all worked according to plan, the U.S. fleet would be trapped between Yamamoto's northern and southern battle groups and wiped out, Midway and the Aleutians would be occupied, and nothing would stand between the Japanese fleet and the U.S. mainland but the old slow battleships of Task Force 1 based in San Francisco.

To counter Yamamoto, Nimitz had only the wounded *Yorktown* under Admiral Fletcher; *Enterprise* and *Hornet* under Admiral Raymond Spruance; their screens; and the assorted navy, marine, and army aircraft stationed at Midway. However, despite repeated attempts and many claims to the contrary, the aircraft based at Midway did not inflict any damage on the attacking Japanese fleet.[3] Though Nimitz also commanded the battleships of Task Force 1, these old ships were nine knots slower than the Japanese fast carriers and, therefore, of little value in a fleet action.

Though vastly outgunned by Yamamoto, Nimitz brought to bear the most important weapon of all—intelligence.

After the surprise attack on Pearl Harbor, the U.S. Navy focused on breaking the Japanese JN-25 communications code at cryptography stations in Melbourne, Pearl Harbor, and Washington, D.C. Significant advancements were made at breaking the code and, in early May, Pearl Harbor's Station Hypo, under Lieutenant Commander Joseph Rochefort, predicted the Japanese would attack and invade a place called "AF." Rochefort and his team thought AF was Midway. To verify their hypothesis, Midway was ordered to make a plain language broadcast that it was low on fresh water. The Japanese dutifully noted that "AF" was low on fresh water in their coded traffic. During the month of May, Rochefort and his team managed to decrypt scores of coded messages every day.

The Battle of Midway opened at 0300 on June 3 when Rear Admiral Kakuji Kakuta's Aleutian Strike Force launched a carrier strike against Dutch Harbor. Despite having been apprised of the

Japanese intentions by Nimitz, the American forces were caught by surprise, and the Japanese successfully occupied Attu and Kiska in the western Aleutians.

Fully aware of the Japanese intentions, Nimitz focused his three carriers to the northeast of Midway at the exact point in place and time where they could attack Yamamoto's four fleet carriers at the moment of their greatest vulnerability.

The carrier battle began in the early hours of June 4, when *Akagi*, *Kaga*, *Hiryu*, and *Soryu* from Admiral Nagumo's First Mobile Force launched 108 aircraft, about one-half the total complement, against Midway's defenses. Though the Japanese quickly disposed of the American aircraft that rose to meet them, Midway's antiaircraft fire knocked down thirty-eight Japanese planes. When the surviving planes returned to their carriers, the lead pilot expressed the need for an additional attack. Nagumo then ordered another attack on the island. However, just as he was rearming for this attack, word came of the American carriers, and he ordered his planes to be rearmed with armor-piercing bombs.

Planes from the *Enterprise* and *Hornet* caught Nagumo's carriers turning into the wind with decks loaded with munitions-laden aircraft. First on the scene were the low and slow-flying Devastators of *Hornet*'s Torpedo 8, which were promptly slaughtered by Nagumo's combat air patrol. But their sacrifice left the skies clear for the high altitude dive-bombers from the *Enterprise* and *Yorktown*, which planted bombs on *Kaga*, *Akagi*, and *Soryu*. Within six minutes, three of Nagumo's four fleet carriers were afire and sinking.

As yet undiscovered, *Hiryu* launched an attack on the *Yorktown* and succeeded in setting her afire with three bombs. But within moments of retrieving her aircraft, *Hiryu* was caught by dive-bombers from the *Enterprise* and sent to the bottom to be with her sisters.

Though the Battle of Midway would continue through June 6, when a Japanese submarine would polish off the mortally wounded *Yorktown* and her destroyer screen *Hammann*, the damage had been done. At the cost of a carrier, a destroyer, 147 planes, and 307 men, the U.S. Navy destroyed four fleet carriers, a heavy cruiser, 322 aircraft, and 3,500 men, inflicting upon the Imperial Japanese Navy its first decisive defeat since 1592. (In August of that year, one hundred thousand Japanese troops in eight hundred ships had attempted to invade Korea. Admiral Yi Soon-Sin confronted the Japanese invasion fleet with eighty "turtle ships," galleys covered with a shell of iron plating to protect the soldiers and rowers. Each turtle ship had large iron rams in the shape of turtles' heads, from which smoke, arrows, and missiles were discharged. Admiral Yi's turtle navy sunk 119 Japanese ships, forced many more to be beached, and routed the remaining fleet. This engagement is considered to be one of the greatest naval victories in history.)[4]

Though his battle group was still numerically far superior to the American ships, Yamamoto turned west toward Japan in defeat. Far to the east, the once-proud battleships of Task Force 1 wandered in the fog of the cold Pacific, with the USS *Dale* as its screen.

USS Dale War Diary, *June 5:* Underway at 0800 and sortied with Task Force 1, consisting of BatDivs II and III and IV, USS *Long Island* plus destroyer screen, in support of the task forces fighting the Battle of Midway. Task Force patrolled in the general area of 39° N and 147° W.

Lester Dailey Diary, *June 5:* We got underway this morning at 0730 and passed under the Golden Gate Bridge at 0800. At present we are with four other cans and are patrolling about twenty miles out of

Frisco. Five battleships and one carrier have just joined us. The BBs are the *Idaho, New Mexico, Pennsylvania, Mississippi,* and *Tennessee.*

June 6: About 0900 last night they set the clock ahead forty-three minutes. This is very queer because as you travel westward you set the clocks back! It is very queer and first our course will be north and then south. We don't know where we're going. I wonder if it's Dutch Harbor, Alaska? Two more BBs joined up—*Colorado* and *Maryland*—and four more cans. Our course now is due west.

June 7: Our course is still west, so I think it will be Pearl Harbor or maybe a raid on some of the islands west of Hawaii. Sea is rough again.

June 10: Still going!?? It's foggy and windy and cold today, and I'm going to quit trying to guess where we're going as our course is always different. In fact, I think maybe we are just out on patrol now.

June 13: Steaming as before. USS *Dale* detached from Task Force 1 at 1039. Noon position 38° 38'N and 146° 58'W. Proceeding independently to Pearl Harbor.

Alvis Harris Diary, June 15: Around 1900 this evening Switzer, a coxswain and captain of gun number one, was killed instantly while standing on a newly installed platform. The crew was slewing the gun to starboard when his head was caught and wedged between the top of the gun shield and the extreme forward part of the Hollywood deck.

Incidentally, for two days the officers have been shooting the albatrosses following the ship. There is an old naval superstition about killing these birds. Some of the older sea-going enlisted men *raised hell*, but who are they to say anything to the great officers in our navy!

This is my first time seeing something like this. Somehow I feel a great change coming over me. Switzer was such a good egg—always a smile on his face. The Exec had been giving him hell for the past week for petty stuff. Switzer's head was—well, I can't describe it—but it's another sight that I won't forget very easy!

JULY TO DECEMBER: SOLOMON ISLANDS

The carrier battles of the Coral Sea and Midway dramatically changed the strategic situation in the Pacific. Before these battles, the Imperial Navy, with its marked superiority in ships and men, was in command from New Guinea in the south to the Aleutians in the north. The U.S. Navy could only hit the Japanese and run.

But when the Japanese invasion of Port Moresby was turned back, and four of the Imperial Navy's fleet carriers were destroyed at Midway, the Pacific war entered a period in which neither side had the carrier strength to capture new ground. In fact, on New Guinea the Japanese decided to simply hike over the Owen Stanley Mountains on the Kokoda Trail and take the port "by hand." In some of 1942's most bloody fighting, the Japanese attack was thwarted by Australian militiamen, whose average age was just more than eighteen years. It is estimated that, of the sixteen thousand Japanese troops that hiked up the Kokoda Trail, only seven hundred survived the fighting, disease, and starvation.

Though the Imperial Navy was still far superior in ships to the U.S. Navy—both in overall number and in technological development—it would never again be dominant in carriers. And the U.S. Navy would not dominate until its *Essex* and *Independence*-class carriers made their appearance in late 1943. Therefore, any offensive action by land or sea would have to be covered by land-based aircraft.

This balance of power greatly limited the ability of the U.S. Navy to launch its long-planned offensive across the coral atolls of the Central Pacific. In fact, the only place the United States did have assets sufficient to encourage offensive operations was in the South Pacific. When Japan began building an airstrip on the malarial plains of

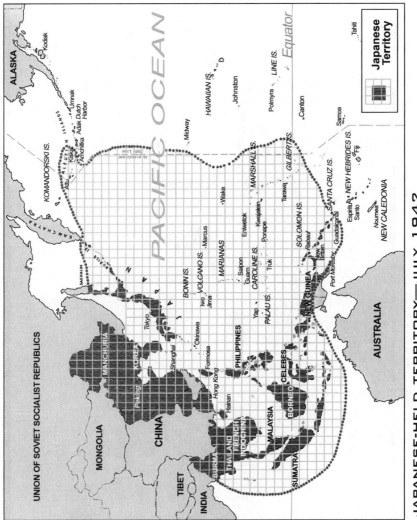

JAPANESE-HELD TERRITORY—JULY 1942

Japanese Territory

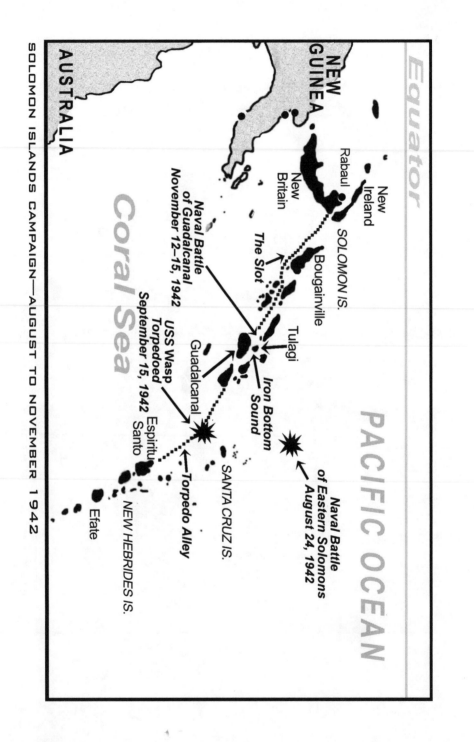

SOLOMON ISLANDS CAMPAIGN—AUGUST TO NOVEMBER 1942

Guadalcanal in the Solomon Islands, the United States was given all the encouragement it needed.

The Solomon Islands are a parallel chain of islands stretching shieldlike some nine hundred miles in a southeasterly direction off the northeast coast of Australia. There are six major islands (Choiseul, New Georgia, Santa Isabel, Guadalcanal, Malaita, and Makira) and approximately 992 smaller islands, atolls, and reefs. To the northwest of the Solomons, on the island of New Britain, lay the Japanese island fortress of Rabaul. To the southeast lay the undeveloped islands of the New Hebrides (now called Vanuatu).

Japan envisioned the Solomon Islands as a series of "island carriers" that would allow it to control the sea-lanes from the United States to Australia. The United States saw the islands as a means by which it could begin the long march north to the Philippines and Japan. The Japanese had established a Solomon Island seaplane base on Tulagi in May, and would establish an airfield on Guadalcanal in July. The Americans would invade both in August.

Espiritu Santo

The struggle for Guadalcanal and the Solomon Islands would find both Japan and the United States at the end of very long supply lines. Japan would have to move its aircraft, men, and ships southeast from Rabaul down the slot of water between the Solomon Islands to Guadalcanal at night. The Solomons consist of parallel chains of islands—totalling nearly a thousand—stretching southeast from Papua New Guinea toward Vanuatu. The distance between the most western and most eastern islands is approximately nine hundred miles. New Georgia Sound, the body of water that divides the island chains, became infamous as the "slot" because of the number of Japanese ships and airplanes that ran down from Rabaul to supply

Guadalcanal and fight the U.S. Navy ships occupying the waters off the island. The movements of Japanese forces up and down the slot were observed and reported by Australian coastwatchers, who were prewar residents of the islands that had taken to the jungles to avoid being captured.

The United States would be forced to build a base on the island of Espiritu Santo in the New Hebrides, from which they would move men and materiel north through Torpedo Alley during the day. Wherever ships are forced to concentrate in a predictable location—such as a straight or a cape—enemy submarines are certain to gather as well. These locations became known as "torpedo alleys" or "torpedo junctions" among those who served at sea. During World War II, one torpedo alley was located off Cape Hatteras in North Carolina's Outer Banks, where German U-boats enjoyed a "Great American Turkey Shoot" by sinking 397 ships filled with food, oil, and supplies. Other Atlantic torpedo alleys were located off Cuba, Iceland, and Ireland. During the fight for Guadalcanal, the U.S. Navy shipped men and materiel from Espiritu Santo to Guadalcanal through an open stretch of the Coral Sea. Japanese submarines concentrated in the area and, consequently, it became the Pacific Theater's first torpedo alley. The navies of each side would often meet during the ensuing months, and the waters north of Guadalcanal Island would become known as "Iron Bottom Sound" for the ships that would come to rest on its bottom. During this time, two battleships, nine cruisers, eighteen destroyers, seven submarines, plus numerous smaller craft, including destroyer transports, corvettes, patrol boats, PT boats, landing craft, merchant ships, coastal traders, motorized barges, native craft, and airplanes from Australia, Japan, and the United States were sunk in this relatively small body of water.[5]

The island of Espiritu Santo lies at the northern end of the New Hebrides (Vanuatu) archipelago. When the U.S. Navy surveyed the island for an advanced base, it found very little development. "These islands were primitive," said author James Michener, who was sent to the island by the U.S. Navy as part of an information-gathering mission. "They are at the beginning of history, and that's what made them exciting. This was the real frontier of human living." While on the island, Michener discovered a Tonkinese woman nicknamed Bloody Mary, who would become a character in his first book, a collection of short stories called *Tales of the South Pacific*. U.S. Navy sailors, including those from the USS *Dale*, would also find themselves captured in the pages of Michener's Pulitzer Prize–winning work.

USS Dale *War Diary*, *July 6:* Underway from Pearl Harbor at 1534 to await sortie of SS *Oliver Wendell Holmes*. Took station ahead of SS *Oliver Wendell Holmes* as anti-submarine screen at 1807. En route to Suva, Fiji Islands, and set course accordingly. SS *Holmes* carries a valuable cargo of steel landing mats, which are needed for newly constructed flying fields in South Pacific Area.

July 28: Passed between Malekula and Ambryn Islands at 1000. At 1350 SS *Oliver Wendell Holmes* proceeded independently to Segond Channel while USS *Dale* anchored in Palekula Bay, Espiritu Santo, at 1500.

D. J. Vellis: We were given orders to escort a merchant vessel to "Button." No one knew what "Button" was, but some suspected it was Espiritu Santo, which was soon confirmed. When we got to the island we couldn't figure out where to go, so we just cruised slowly around the island. Finally the lookout spotted some mast-heads sticking up above some palm trees and we rounded a point to find an entrance to a little bay. We went in and anchored along with our merchantmen. A boatload of Seabees came out to inspect their cargo.

When they opened the hatch they almost died. Instead of finding the heavy equipment they were so desperate for, they found a hold filled with landing mats! They were trying to build an airport out of a coconut plantation so our bombers could go against Guadalcanal, and were desperately fighting a time schedule.

USS Dale War Diary, *August 7–8:* All hands have been enjoying stay at Palekula Bay, although vigilant watches are kept, as it is thought that Japanese on Guadalcanal might try to impede construction of airfield on Espiritu Santo but no raids have been forthcoming. Some of the crew are sent to the beach each day and they return with boxes of coconuts, oranges, grapefruit, and tangerines of a succulent nature, thus adding to the ship's larder. Several rated men including a welder are sent to shore each day to assist in construction of makeshift dock and crane for unloading as there are no facilities.

Lester Dailey Diary, *August 15:* The volcano on Ambryn Island is active and the smoke rolls out in billows of black and white smoke for thousands of feet into the air. Sure pretty. The Island of Espiritu Santo is a low island with lots of trees and shrubbery. This destroyer is the first to put in here. There is swimming, bananas, and coconuts, but no recreation of any kind! The water here in Palekula Bay is very clear. You can see forty or fifty feet down. We saw several big sharks swimming around.

K. G. Robinson: I will never forget Palekula Bay in Espiritu Santo. Everyone went ashore and came back with marine sandbags filled with goods they traded with the natives for—wild tangerines, spears, war clubs, and [other] kinds of things that Chiefs Stedman and Porter threw overboard as soon as we got to sea. We even built an outrigger canoe that Ensign Vellis tested safely.

Robert "Pat" Olson: I was walking along a beach when I came to a coconut grove and decided to pick some up off the ground and take them back to the ship. Suddenly, I saw right before me a pair of the biggest, blackest feet I had ever seen in my entire life. Man, oh man! I studied those feet wondering what kind of person was attached to them. I looked slowly up to see a giant of a man, arms folded, chest puffed out, looking out to sea. I decided right then and there that I didn't need any of his coconuts!

Cliff Huntley: I think Espiritu Santo was the island James Michener wrote about in *South Pacific*. Michener's description fits perfectly, especially with outlying islands, one of which could have been Bali Hai. It was quite primitive at that time with just about nothing there other than a coconut plantation and some native villages. The water was blue and clear and there was swimming; however, many of us quit swimming when the others who were fishing caught some big sharks! We found the island to be especially interesting, especially the natives, who wore few if any clothes. The men only wore a small box containing their penis, which they considered to be the organ that is the source of life.

Earl Hicks: One of our officers built a homemade outrigger canoe, so one day a shipmate and I "borrowed" it and paddled over to the leprosy island, which was strictly off-limits. We hit the beach and moseyed around for a while before we got to thinking about the big trouble we could catch if someone discovered us. Luckily nobody did, and that's how I came to visit "Bali Hai"!

D. J. Vellis: While we were at anchor a field of mines was laid in a second channel leading in to Palekula Bay to keep the Japanese from sneaking in. But, before the information about the mining was put out, the *Tucker* (DD-374) ran right into the mines, blew up, and sank—with the loss of six men.

Author's note: The destroyer *Tucker* was not the only ship to run into a mine and sink in Espiritu Santo's Segond Channel. Three weeks later, on October 26, the U.S. army transport *President Coolidge* was making its way into the channel loaded with 5,092 officers and troops of the 172nd Regiment, 43rd Infantry division. The *Coolidge* also carried all of the soldiers' equipment and weapons. These soldiers, and their equipment, were desperately needed as reinforcements for the beleaguered American garrison on Guadalcanal. Lacking knowledge of Segond Channel's protective minefield, *President Coolidge*'s merchant captain steamed directly into two mines, mortally wounding his ship. Though only two lives were lost in this sinking, the army lost its big transport, as well as all of the equipment and weapons destined for Guadalcanal. (*Tucker* and *President Coolidge* now attract sport divers from around the world to Espiritu Santo's tropical waters.)

Guadalcanal

Guadalcanal Island is 2,200 square miles of forbidding mountains, dormant volcanoes, steep ravines, and deep streams. The island has no natural harbors and is protected by miles of coral reefs. The only beaches suitable for invasion were those found along the north coast. The U.S. Marines took those beaches on August 7 and 8, thus precipitating six months of intense battles in the air, on land, and at sea.

For this great struggle, the Imperial Navy would have more ships and men, a major base at Rabaul, superior night fighting skills, and the deadly Long Lance torpedo. Given its weakness and distance from home, the only advantages the U.S. Navy could muster were a determination not to lose and its radar-equipped ships. The Imperial Japanese Navy equipped some of its ships, including the light cruiser *Kitagami*, with experimental radar sets as early as 1941, but did not equip its fleet until late 1943. (Ironically, the technology had originated in Japan; Professor Hidetsugu Yagi of Tokyo was granted a 1932 U.S. Patent for an antenna that could send and receive radar signals. This patent was then purchased by the RCA Corporation, and the Yagi antenna is still in use today.) However, the tactical advantage radar gave the U.S. Navy was often diminished by the lack of experience with its use and by the confusing images of radar signals bouncing back from the thousand-odd islands, atolls, and reefs that make up the Solomon Islands.

The ensuing naval actions began shortly after midnight on August 9 and continued apace until the Japanese secretly evacuated the island on February 9, 1943. Between those dates, naval guns would thunder in the battles of Savo Island, Eastern Solomons, Cape Esperance, Santa Cruz Islands, Guadalcanal, Tassafaronga, and Rennell Island.

The struggle for Guadalcanal, the Pacific war's longest and most bitterly fought campaign, would provide much work for the tin cans of the U.S. Navy, and the USS *Dale* would get her fair share. She would escort capital ships, tankers, and supply ships through Torpedo Alley into Iron Bottom Sound; screen task groups as they moved back and forth to fuel and patrol; rescue downed pilots; and escort wounded ships from battles to safe harbors. The campaign included six major naval engagements and nearly fifty ship-to-ship and air-sea fights that were not given battle names. Many of these were night surface battles, where the weapons and tactics of the Japanese navy were at their finest. Unfortunately for the Japanese, they were faced with a foe willing to accept heavy losses in order to prevail. During this epic struggle, *Dale* would see twenty-four of her sister tin cans sunk in action, leaving the surrounding waters thick with bunker crude and tin can sailors swimming for life.

Earl Hicks: We were anchored between two islands and some of the guys were chumming the water off the fantail with galley scraps. You could see huge sharks swimming around, so I threw a couple of wooden crates over the side and the sharks went into a frenzy over them. The old man came on the squawk box and said, "You guys better not fall over the side because I don't want to pick up what's left!"

USS Dale War Diary, *August 19–22*: Steaming as before. USS *Long Island* launched aircraft on afternoon of 20th. Friendly planes reported twelve enemy aircraft but no attack materialized. After planes launched, Task Group changed to southerly course to return to Efate Island, arriving in the early afternoon of the 22nd.

August 24–25: Joined Task Force 2 consisting of USS *Enterprise*, USS *Saratoga*, and escorts which were covering Guadalcanal on afternoon of 25th. Task Force fueled from *Sabine* and other tankers present.

Author's Note: On August 24, the USS *Dale* was escorting Task Force 2, built around the carriers USS *Enterprise* and *Saratoga*, when the task force engaged the Japanese in the Battle of the Eastern Solomons.

At the time, an uneasy parity existed in the eastern Solomons. Each afternoon Japanese bombers flew down from Rabaul to bomb the Marines' position at Henderson Field on Guadalcanal Island. At night Japanese cruisers and destroyers of the "Tokyo Express" steamed down the slot to continue the harassment. Japan owned the night and the waters north of Guadalcanal. During the day airplanes from Henderson Field escorted U.S. Navy destroyer-transports through the waters of Iron Bottom Sound so they could deliver supplies to the beleaguered Marines. America owned the day and the waters south of Guadalcanal.

Determined to end this stalemate, and take back Guadalcanal, Admiral Yamamoto ordered an all-out assault that included a raid by two fleet carriers—*Shokaku* and *Zuikaku*—and an escort carrier—*Ryujo*. Correctly estimating the intentions of Yamamoto, Admiral Nimitz ordered Task Force 2 to a position off the Solomon Islands where, when the opportunity presented itself, it would attack the Japanese carriers.

Scouts from both carrier groups searched for each other across the broad expanse of ocean. Finally, on August 24, the escort carrier *Ryujo* was found and a flight of bombers from *Enterprise* vectored out to the attack.

As the *Ryujo* was being bombed to the bottom, flights of Japanese bombers flew south to take on the *Enterprise* and *Saratoga*. American fighters met the Japanese bombers at eighteen thousand feet to the north of the task force and shot down twenty-nine of them before the aerial battle drifted over the American carriers. The Japanese bombers dove on the *Enterprise* and planted three bombs on her flight deck within a matter of seconds. Though severely damaged, *Enterprise* steamed on and by evening was again landing airplanes on her flight deck.

The Battle of the Eastern Solomons was a tactical and strategic victory for the American side. The Japanese lost the *Ryujo*, seventy-one airplanes and crew, and their first attempt to wrest Guadalcanal back from the Americans.

Earl Hicks: One of the *Dale*'s jobs was to plane guard for the carriers. We'd follow along behind and, if one of the carrier's pilots had to ditch for some reason, we'd stop and pick him up. Deep-draft ships like carriers could never stop, because if they did, they would be torpedoed by a submarine. So the big boys never stopped for anything; they were always on the move. Only little boys like the *Dale* stopped.

Lester Dailey Diary, *September 5*: Underway at daylight with four men missing. Pounded my sack all morning. Sea very rough. At times the waves break clear over the bridge and the bow dips under every wave. Sure nasty! We are heading toward the Solomon Islands to make a raid, I think.

Jim Sturgill: The *Dale* was screening the *North Carolina* and the *Wasp* through a secure area south of Guadalcanal. The seas were calm and it was a day of rest. Everything was supposed to get aired out, so we had brought our bedding topside. I imagine the boys on the *Wasp* were doing the same. I was sitting out on the fantail with McIntyre when I spotted a mop in the water. Now, when a navy mop falls overboard the head will sink and the wooden handle will stick out of the water about fourteen to sixteen inches. "Mop hell!" McIntyre said. "That's a periscope!"

Lester Dailey Diary, *September 14*: At noon today we were called to GQ as unidentified planes were sighted. A fighter plane from the *Wasp* shot down a 4-engine Jap patrol bomber 18 miles from us. We must have been spotted. Well, at 1451 "it" happened. Our position at noon was 12° 23" 00" S. Lat/164° 37" 05' E. Long, course 280 true. I'll try to tell just how I saw it all. The sound operators including me were all on the bridge getting instructions on the gear. I heard Mr. Shaffer say, "There is a splash up forward!" Then the fireworks began! The *Wasp* was forward of us when three torpedoes hit her amidships, starboard side. She started blazing and the smoke was pouring out of her up forward. The planes could not be launched as they were aft. The destroyer *O'Brien* intercepted a torpedo meant for the *Wasp* and it hit her forward starboard side. We tried to take one but it went right under our bow. The *North Carolina* took one well forward portside. Mr. Robinson sent me after his life jacket and tin hat. When I returned the *Wasp* was down by the bow and a mass of flames. The whole fleet was swinging around and we dropped two 600-pound depth charges on a contact but do not know what happened. Two destroyers were detailed to remain with the *Wasp* to pick up survivors. The rest of the fleet was steaming south at full speed. The last I saw of the *Wasp* she was burning fiercely. All this happened in about fifteen minutes and there was no unnecessary excitement on board at all. Everyone remained very calm. It all happened so quick it's hard to describe just what did happen.

Cliff Huntley: The *Dale* was in a port-quarter position astern of the battleship *North Carolina*. She was a new, fast battleship and had just joined the fleet with the *Wasp* and some tin cans. We were happy to see them as our fleet was badly depleted. I was off duty and sitting up forward on a capstan when I saw the *Wasp* blow up. Someone called out, "Torpedo off the port bow!" I watched it streak right under the *Dale*'s number two gun and continue over to the *North Carolina*.

Author's note: The U.S. Navy's pre–World War II battleships, the newest of which were built at the end of World War I, were too slow to operate with fast carriers, and, for the most, were relegated to defensive patrols in the early years of the war. In 1936, two new battleships of thirty-five thousand tons were ordered into production. *North Carolina* and *Washington* were commissioned in April and May 1941, respectively. With speeds up to twenty-eight knots, they would become two of the navy's ten fast battleships. Next to be built was the *South Dakota*–class, of the same tonnage as the *North Carolina*–class, but of a smaller length, which allowed for more extensive armor. USS *South Dakota* (BB-57) became the first fast battleship to be adequately armored against 16-inch fire. (Read Morison's account of the Naval Battle of Guadalcanal to see what *adequate* meant!) Last to be built was the magnificent *Iowa* class, with newer and better 406mm guns and speeds of up to thirty-three knots.

Warren Deppe: When the *North Carolina* was hit she signaled, "Increase speed to thirty knots!" The *Dale* could barely keep up with her! I'll bet those old battlewagons that sunk at Pearl would have been proud of the *North Carolina!*

USS Dale War Diary, *September 15*: At 1451 the USS *Wasp* of Task Force 18 was struck by two torpedoes. The USS *Hornet* had just launched planes and several minutes later the USS *North Carolina*, who was about 1,000 yards on starboard bow of USS *Dale* was torpedoed as was the USS *O'Brien*, about 1,500 yards on the port quarter of the USS *Dale*. Dropped two charges at 1500 as the Task Force was putting on speed to clear area. At 2023 USS *North Carolina* screened by USS *Anderson* and USS *Dale* left formation to proceed to Tongatabu Island.

Lester Dailey Diary, *September 16*: Three GQs before noon today! Periscope was sighted twice. Once by us and once by the *North Carolina*. News today about southern Oregon being bombed by Japs. No news on the *Wasp*.

September 18: GQ at 0230! Ship would not answer challenge so we fired a shot across their bow and boy did they come to life!

Eugene Brewer: We never became complacent! We were always alert, not like some other ships! While we were escorting the *North Carolina* to Tongatabu we came upon a ship lollygagging along at about eight knots in the middle of the night. We challenged it three times but it never did respond, so the captain ordered us to lay a star shell right above its bridge. Boy, did that ever wake them up! Later, after the war, I told the story to a bunch of guys on a golf course. One of them said, "Hey, that was my ship, the *Majaba!* I was asleep on the flag bag when that star shell went off! Boy, you should have heard our captain. He was pissed!"

USS Dale War Diary, *September 19:* Arrived Nukualofa Bay, Tongatabu Island and fueled from USS *Hunter Liggett.*

Robert "Pat" Olson: How hot? Plenty! *Dale* was a fighting ship and her boilers were always burning crude and making steam. But when we arrived at Tongatabu, we shut her down and the boilers and fans went quiet. I couldn't go ashore on that beautiful tropical island, so rather than sitting around doing nothing, I went back down to the fire room to clean the burner tips on the boilers. I'll probably get a lot of flack from the deck crew for saying this, but those burner tips were the heart of the *Dale.* Atomized crude was injected through them into the firebox. If they were to get plugged up, the *Dale* would go dead in the water. Cleaning burner tips was a dirty, filthy job, but it had to be done, so I went down and scrubbed them with a wire brush and solvent. But after a while I got to feeling a bit strange—like I was going to pass out. I secured the burner tips and headed for the hatch. On the way out I glanced at the thermometer and saw the needle resting at 150 degrees. That was about as hot as I ever got!

Lester Dailey Diary, *September 21*: Underway at 0630 with the *North Carolina* and *Aylwin* headed for Pearl Harbor, at last! Been almost three months since we left there. School this morning on signals. Bulletin on board saying that keeping a diary is prohibited now, so don't know how long I can keep writing this one.

USS Dale War Diary, *September 21–30*: Underway in company of USS *Aylwin* to escort USS *North Carolina* from Tongatabu Island to Pearl Harbor. Investigated unidentified radar contact in early morning of 24th, which proved to be SS *Paul Revere*. Crossed equator morning of 26th entering northern latitudes at 158° degrees 35° West longitude. Arrived Pearl Harbor on 30th and moored to USS *Aylwin* alongside Merry's Point dock M-3.

Lester Dailey Diary, *October 6*: This morning I put in for the Royal Hawaiian Hotel and got it. Ferguson and I checked in and then went over to Hotel Street, had a few drinks and then went back to the hotel. The bed was too soft, and it was too quiet, so I couldn't sleep very well!

October 27: Got our orders to get underway about 1400. We are escorting the aircraft carrier *Kitty Hawk*. Our destination is Palmyra Island, then Noumea, New Caledonia. Got word of the severe damage to another carrier, which might have been the *Enterprise* as she left Pearl about 9 days ago. They also got the *Porter* (DD-356) who was picking up a downed pilot. [*Author's note*: The damage tentatively attributed to the *Enterprise* and the mistaken reference to the sinking of the *Porter* actually both refer to a single ship, the *Hornet*, during the Battle of Santa Cruz Islands on October 26. During this battle the mortally wounded carrier *Hornet*, the first U.S. Navy ship to launch an attack on the Japanese home islands, had to be abandoned and was subsequently sunk by torpedoes from Japanese destroyers.[6]] The

Kitty Hawk is loaded with planes and the morning orders say this is our most important mission and that we must get these planes [through] at any cost as they will decide the fate of Guadalcanal. This is going to be a dangerous trip because the Japs will have planes, subs and surface ships to try and cut our supply route to New Caledonia so it'll be a wonder if we miss trouble and get [through]. Also it says if we make it [through] we should be back in Pearl in a month and we should all be where we want to be most on Christmas!

USS Dale War Diary, *October 27–31*: Underway on 27th to escort USS *Kitty Hawk* from Pearl Harbor to Noumea, New Caledonia via Palmyra Island at which place fighter planes were to be loaded aboard USS *Kitty Hawk*. AA firing exercises conducted in afternoon of 27th. Arrived Palmyra Island morning of 30th. USS *Kitty Hawk* hove to off channel entrance to lagoon to await delivery of fighter planes. Patrolled off Palmyra Island awaiting departure of USS *Kitty Hawk*.

November 11–14: Underway morning of 11th; escorted USS *Kitty Hawk* to Espiritu Santo Island, New Hebrides. Arrived late afternoon of 14th and anchored in Segond Channel.

Alvis Harris: Those planes we hauled out to Espiritu Santo on the *Kitty Hawk* were gull-winged Corsair fighters. Our pilots flew them out over the fleet and teased the ships with loops, barrel rolls, and inverted fly-bys. It raised everyone's spirits to know these powerful new airplanes were on their way to Guadalcanal to raise some hell!

USS Dale War Diary, *November 15*: Underway in morning with Task Group 64.6 consisting of USS *Stack*, USS *Aylwin*, USS *Lardner* and USS *Dale* to rendezvous with battleships USS *Washington* and USS

South Dakota who were without escort, the USS *Benham*, USS *Walke*, USS *Preston* having been sunk as result of enemy action and the fourth escort, USS *Garvin*, damaged, and proceeded singly to port.

John Cruce: Late that night we picked up the *Washington* and *South Dakota* on our radar screen. It was so dark you couldn't see your hand in front of your face. Everyone was on edge because these battlewagons had just fought a huge battle off Guadalcanal and nobody knew what to expect from them. When ships get into a battle like that they are likely to be in a mood to shoot first and ask questions later! And they were armed to the teeth with big 16-inch guns, whereas we only had little 5-inch popguns. And so, with a great deal of uncertainty, we signaled them for recognition, and got recognition lights instead of gunfire!

Author's note: The Naval Battle of Guadalcanal was a series of air and ship engagements that took place between November 12 and 15, 1942, on and around the island of Guadalcanal. On the night of November 14, the *South Dakota* and *Washington*, together with screening destroyers, blocked a Japanese force of battleships, cruisers, and destroyers intent on bombarding Henderson Field. *South Dakota* was hit forty-two times by large caliber rounds from battleships and cruisers, and many more times by smaller caliber rounds from destroyers.[7]

Earl Hicks: When we anchored at Noumea, I was detailed to help clean up the *South Dakota*, and was it ever a mess! Her decks were stacked high with dead, and sharp, jagged edges from ripped steel were everywhere. A 16-inch round from one of the Jap battlewagons went right through the bridge and killed everyone. The hole it left was so big I could walk through it without bending over! Back aft another 16-inch round hit a gun turret and blew up the entire compartment, killing everyone there. I had to pick up their body parts.

Orville Newman: I was on the crew that helped clean up the *South Dakota* and it was a gruesome experience. Several of the guys I had joined up with had just been sent to duty on the *South Dakota*, and since they had not yet been assigned bunks down below they were sleeping topside when the shooting started. They just sat up there taking in all the action and became gun fodder! It was terrible cleaning up the mess because stuff would stick to your fingers and you just knew it was human flesh.

Earl Hicks: Things got to smelling pretty ripe down there along the equator, so personal hygiene became a matter of great concern to everybody. We had a pair of brothers fresh off the farm that refused to take a shower or wash their clothes. I don't know why, they just would not, and that was all there was to it! One night a bunch of guys got a hold of them, hauled them into the showers and scrubbed them clean with a kiyi brush. They were as red as a beet when they came out of those showers, and we never had to worry about anyone not taking a shower again!

Lester Dailey Diary, November 28: Whee! Boy oboy! Underway this morning en route Mare Island via Bora Bora, which lies 1,363 miles East of here. It lies just about 160 miles northwest of Tahiti. From Bora Bora to Frisco it is 3,663 miles.

December 4: Crossed equator into North latitude, which makes six times for me. We gave the new pollywogs a preliminary initiation this evening. What fun!

December 10: Fog was so thick we couldn't see any distance at all. When we did see the Golden Gate Bridge and land we were right under the bridge. We anchored for the fog was too thick to proceed. I rated liberty but it was cancelled as we did not go on to Mare Island. They cut my stateside leave to four days and it's the most dirty trick I ever had played on me! I want to go home and I don't know if I'll even get to see Max, only I hope and pray that I do get to see her. The lights sure do look good on the beach. It is very cold here!

USS Dale *War Diary,* *December 11:* Underway at 0900 to go alongside Hunter's Point Dock. As some of the bollards on the dock were set in fresh concrete and could not be used, considerable difficulty was encountered in getting stern in as tide was running also. Commenced navy yard activity.

Orville Newman: We had a great deal of difficulty docking in San Francisco. There was a strong tide running and we just couldn't get next to the dock. And that dock was filled with wives and girlfriends. Boy, did they ever look good! I heard a dock foreman yell out, "Stand back, girls! These boys have been at sea a long time!"

Alvis Harris: *Farragut*-class tin cans like the *Dale* were designed for the long range screening of capital ships. Trouble was, we had to steam twice as hard as those big boys just to keep up, so our engines and running gear were always in need of repair. In 1942 we steamed over ninety thousand miles, which is about four times around the earth at the equator!

Robert "Pat" Olson: I took leave to visit my brother, who was working in a shipyard up at Bremerton, Washington. On the way back

I was sleeping in a Pullman car when a conductor came back and woke me up. "Son, you are not on the road you thought you were on! A bridge washed out back up the line and we had to change tracks. You are going to be over leave!" He told me it wouldn't be a problem if he were to give me a letter of explanation. But when I got back to the ship the letter was not accepted and I was put on report. At the Captain's Mast there was a long line of sailors who had been AWOL and the captain was busting rates left and right. So I thought, 'By God, if I'm going to get taken down, I'm going to tell him what's what!' In fact, I was so distraught that I almost cried. "Captain," I said, "I gave myself an extra eight hours of travel to get back on time."

The Captain said, "Olson, your excuse is justified." I was in shock, and out of trouble!

USS Dale War Diary, *December 12–31*: Undergoing yard overhaul. In dry dock from 17–26 December, 1942. On 31 December received a message from CinCPac stating availability was to expire on or about 2 January, 1943.

1943

As ship bells rang in the New Year, the Imperial and U.S. Navies pulled back to staunch the wounds of 1942 and gather strength for the next round of fighting across a battlefield that now stretched from the Coral to the Bering Sea.

In January, Australian troops would turn back a final Japanese attempt to take Port Moresby, New Guinea, in hand-to-hand fighting through the jungles of the Owen Stanley Mountains. Though the fight for New Guinea would continue, it would no longer be a focal point of the Pacific Theater. Then, during a series of late-night runs down the slot from Rabaul in early February, the Imperial Navy would evacuate its troops from Guadalcanal, thus granting Americans the Solomon Island foothold they needed to begin the long climb north to the Philippines and Japan.

The carrier forces of the Pacific Theater, decimated by the head-to-head battles of 1942, retired to their respective corners to rebuild.

They would not go up against each other again until 1944. However, for tin cans like the USS *Dale*, there would be no time to rest, for there would be the call of the north to answer.

JANUARY: ALEUTIAN ISLANDS
AND THE BERING SEA

The American prewar contingency plan for war with Japan, code-named "Orange," called for an attack straight across the Central Pacific to the Japanese home islands. On planet Earth, however, the shortest distance between two points is the arc of a circle, and the arc of the great circle between the United States and Japan tracks north along the Aleutian Islands.

The Aleutians are a one-thousand-mile-long chain of islands stretching west like a highway from the Alaskan mainland toward the Japanese home islands. Because the Aleutian Islands were the shortest distance between Japan and the United States, they forced consideration of two strategic questions: Would Japan use this island highway to attack America? And, conversely, would America use it to invade Japan? These questions were formally placed on the table when Fleet Admiral Yamamoto ordered the capture of Attu and Kiska, the westernmost islands, during his Midway offensive of 1942.

Given their tactical situations in 1942, neither side had the resources for a protracted fight in the far north. Both were too far from home: Attu was 650 miles northeast of the nearest Japanese base in the Kuriles and 1,200 miles north of Tokyo. Kiska was 536 miles west of the nearest American base at Dutch Harbor and 1,957 miles from Seattle. Weather was of equal significance: Aleutian weather is dominated by thick, glutinous fog in summer and by freezing williwaw winds in winter. Williwaws—sudden, violent gusts of wind

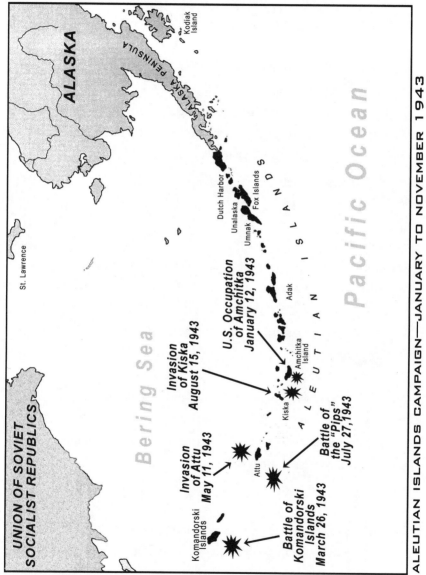

ALEUTIAN ISLANDS CAMPAIGN—JANUARY TO NOVEMBER 1943

UNION OF SOVIET
SOCIALIST REPUBLICS

St. Lawrence

Bering Sea

ALASKA

ALASKA PENINSULA

Kodiak
Island

Dutch Harbor
Unalaska
Umnak
Fox Islands

Adak

Amchitka
Island

Kiska

ALEUTIAN ISLANDS

Pacific Ocean

Invasion
of Kiska
August 15, 1943

U.S. Occupation
of Amchitka
January 12, 1943

Battle of
the "Pips"
July 27, 1943

Invasion
of Attu
May 11, 1943

Attu

Komandorski
Islands

Battle of
Komandorski
Islands
March 26, 1943

descending from mountains to the sea—are most common in high latitudes, especially in the Straits of Magellan and the Aleutian Islands. Winds may explode to well over 120 knots, creating tornado-like eddies in the lee of landmasses. Neither side had the wherewithal, nor inclination, to conduct a protracted fight in the world's worst weather so far from home.

Distance and weather notwithstanding, the political pressure to expel the Japanese from American soil was too intense for the U.S. military to ignore, and so, in the opening days of 1943, the USS *Dale* sailed north to take part in the only World War II battles to take place on American soil.

K. G. Robinson: Upon completion of our overhaul in San Francisco, which included removal of a 3- and a 5-inch mount, [and] installation of two 40mms plus several 20mms, and a new Sugar George radar, we were sent up to the Aleutians. A few days out nothing worked—the gyro tumbled, the radar went dead, and we sailed into a blinding snowstorm.

Author's note: SG ("Sugar George") radar was a microwave surface search radar fielded by the U.S. Navy in 1941. By 1943 most navy cruisers and destroyers had SG radar units installed, allowing viewers to "see" the position of land-based or low-altitude targets in any weather condition.

John Overholt: I was always seasick on the *Dale*, and there was never much to be done for it, so I just lived with it. But, when we headed up to the Aleutians, my seasickness became intolerable. When I went to the ship's doctor he handed me a bucket and a scrub brush and said, "Good luck!"

Robert "Pat" Olson: Down in the tropics we snipes were always sweating up heat rashes in the boiling-hot temperatures of the fire room. Boy, did we ever envy the deck crew their topside watches during those beautiful tropical nights! But all that changed the day we got to the Aleutians. We became the envy of the ship.

Lester Dailey Diary, *January 13:* Worst sea I've seen yet!! Bow is plowing clear under the surface! Very, very rough and cold. Foot is so bad I'm turning in today. The sea was so rough today we had a 38-degree roll. Foot is sure bad. It has a boil on it to boot! We hear our sister ship, the *Worden*, ran aground and sank up here.

Author's note: While escorting the transport *Arthur Middleton* (AP-65) to Constantine Harbor, Amchitka Island, on January 12, 1943, strong winds and currents swept the *Farragut*-class destroyer *Worden* onto a pinnacle rock that tore into her hull below the engine room, causing her to lose power. She then broached and sank with the loss of fourteen crewmen.

January 15: Sea is very rough again and visibility very low. It's so rough it's impossible to describe it. We were supposed to arrive this afternoon but at the present are lost as we can't see. Land was sighted once. We are lost—completely lost— and in danger of going on the rocks like the *Worden*. Just cruising around, hoping. Fog lying low.

K. G. Robinson: I had fleeted up to Exec and Navigator—I was having a hell of a time finding out where we were! When we arrived at Unimak Pass, between Alaska and the Aleutians, it was completely socked in. With fear and trepidation, Captain Rorschach headed for where we believed the opening would be. I nearly fell to my knees in thanks when the sun broke out and the lookout announced Scotch Cap Light on the starboard bow—just where it was supposed to be!

JANUARY TO MARCH: AMCHITKA ISLAND

Amchitka is a big island with a good harbor only seventy miles east of Kiska. If America could take the island, its aircraft could exploit small breaks in the interminable weather to harass the Japanese on Kiska. The United States opened its Aleutian offensive on January 12 with an unopposed landing at Constantine Harbor, Amchitka Island. Imperial Headquarters in Tokyo then resolved "to hold the western Aleutians at all costs" and thus began the struggle for Amchitka, Attu, and Kiska Islands. As the sunken *Worden's* replacement, *Dale's* first job in the far north was to protect the newly won beachhead at Amchitka.

Earl Hicks: When we first arrived on our patrol station off Amchitka, the navy sent mail out to us by plane and dropped it in a watertight bag at a predetermined time and place. The bag had a flag attached so we could see it floating from the ship. Pretty soon the Japs caught on, so every day a Zero would fly over and bomb us while we were pulling the mailbag out of the water! That pilot wasn't very good because he never did hit us. Captain got wise pretty fast and we cruised around until the Zero ran low on fuel and had to leave. Then we went in and scooped our bag out of the water and had mail call!

Lester Dailey Diary, January 24: GQ at 0900. At 1010 five Jap Zero float-planes attacked the ships in the harbor and dropped bombs but no damage resulted. We opened fire but did no good. Just one attack and they left.

January 25: Two Zeros attacked again, dropping bombs at the two merchantmen in the harbor, but missed both. Opened fire on them again, but missed.

January 26: Seas rough!! Wow! Worst yet!! GQ belayed!! Snow! Sleet! Hail! Wind! Another air raid this evening by more Zeros. Dropped bombs, but no damage resulted.

Hugh Melrose: Aleutian weather was much different from anything we had ever experienced before. Brief periods of calm would be broken by the freezing williwaws. It was like living on a roller coaster! But what really got to us were not the hundred-foot waves, because *Dale* could ride up and over them. What really got to us were the twenty-foot waves. *Dale* could ride up and over a twenty-foot wave, but then she would have to punch through the middle of the next one! I'd take the hundred-footers any day to punching holes in twenty-footers hour after hour, day after day, and week after week!

Bela "Shorty" Smith: One of the most important jobs the deck force had was to secure everything during heavy weather. If something broke loose it would thrash about the ship and raise all kinds of heck. The most dangerous things we had to secure were depth charges. One time we started taking huge seas over the fantail, which was where the depth charge racks were located. The waves were so big the officers got to worrying the pressure they created when they crashed over the depth charges might set them off. I was ordered to go out and set the depth charges on safe so they wouldn't blow up the ship. They tied one end of a line around me and the other end to a bulkhead where some guys were standing around watching. Then I crept out onto the exposed deck toward the depth charge racks. I reached the first rack and set the depth charges to safe. But, before I could move on to the next rack, I was swamped by a giant wave coming over the stern. I held on for dear life as it washed over me. Then I moved on to the next rack, only to be swamped by another wave. I don't know how many depth charges I set to safe, and how many waves washed over me, but somehow I managed to get the job done before I froze to death.

Orville Newman: The only way to get fore and aft aboard the *Dale* was on her deck. She simply didn't have internal passageways. Why the navy sent a ship without internal passageways up to the Bering Sea for nine months was beyond me. But they did, and I was aboard her! My quarters were aft, my work space amidships, and the galley forward. I had to cross open decks to sleep, work, and eat. There was no other way! When the watch came to wake me for the mid-watch, he would always tell me which side of the ship was lee, so I'd know which side of the deck to cross. If I crossed on the weather side, I'd get soaked. Well, up in the Bering Sea, leeward never stayed leeward very long. The wind up there shifted so fast it was scary. One minute I'd be walking forward leaning into the wind to keep from getting blown over. Then, all of a sudden, the wind would shift 180 degrees and hit me from aft! If you weren't on your toes all the time you'd get blown right over the side, because what was lee one minute might well be weather the next! I kept dry clothes in the fire room and in my quarters because I was always getting soaked.

Earl Hicks: *Dale* had no internal passageways, which meant we had to go topside to get chow or wash clothes or sleep in bunks. But up in the Aleutians you could never go topside for long because it was just too dangerous. The deck was coated with ice and very slippery, except right above the engine room where the heat kept the decks clean. Topside we moved fore and aft along the lee deck while holding on to guy wires, like a trolley. There wasn't much safe about it. One time a young redheaded mess cook was walking up the guy wire when a giant wave broke over the depth charges and washed a four-hundred-pound charge right square into this kid's face. It took out his right eye and smashed his face really good. He lay in his bunk for a couple of weeks before our supply ship returned and we could transfer him off. I have no idea what happened to him.

Robert "Pat" Olson: Sometimes the weather was so rough we couldn't get back to our bunks and so had to stay down in the fire room. But that could get frightening, too, because when you took rolls of forty to fifty degrees and more, toolboxes would pop open and loose tools would fly around. Our worst fear was that a loose tool would hit an electrical switch and short us out to where we'd be dead in the water. If you were dead in the water in those seas, you were dead in the water!

Bela "Shorty" Smith: We took some terrible waves in the Bering Sea. One time a big ground swell rolled us over so far I thought we'd never make it back. I still don't know why we didn't! I was on the lee deck when the ship went into that roll. Luckily, I was able to grab on to a bulkhead handrail when the ship went over because my feet left the deck. I hung there with nothing between my feet and the ocean but air. I was scared. No, I was plenty scared! She went way over on her beam and paused for a moment. Then she shuddered and shook because one of her propellers was out of the water and thrashing air. Slowly, she rolled back toward the vertical and my feet found the deck again. That wave scared the devil out of me!

Earl Hicks: When the weather calmed down a bit the old man would pull her into the lee of an island and order, "All hands turn to and break ice." We'd go out and break eight inches of ice off the rails with doggin' wrenches, because the extra weight made the ship top-heavy and less able to recover from steep rolls.

Bela "Shorty" Smith: I don't know how cold it can get up in the Bering Sea, but one day I was told it was fifty-four degrees below zero outside. On deck we wore five layers of clothes and a facemask to protect against frostbite. But nothing could keep that cold out. They didn't give us many outside jobs when it got really cold, but there was one job that always had to be done, and that was breaking ice. We got into a lot of different kinds of storms. Sometimes it would rain, other times it would snow. It seemed like whatever fell out of the sky froze the instant it hit the *Dale.* The only place there was no ice was right above the fire room. Up on the bow ice would be several inches thick. That ice weighed a lot and made us top-heavy, which increased *Dale's* rolling in heavy seas. I spent a lot of time breaking ice free with axes and picks. They wouldn't let us use blowtorches because of all the ammunition stowed around the decks. At least busting ice kept me warm.

Lester Dailey Diary, January 27: Zeros attacked again at 1000. No damage. Entered harbor and picked up landing party of eleven or twelve men to be landed on the West point of this (Amchitka) island about sixty miles from Kiska!! Too close to the Japs!

January 31: This evening just before dark two float Zeros attacked again, dropping bombs in the harbor. The *Aylwin* and the *Long* both opened up on them but missed all times. No aircraft protection provided for us at all.

February 1: Just after GQ at 0945 the alarm sounded again. Nine more Jap Zeros were reported. They split up and four of them came in on the *Dale* from the starboard quarter, strafing us as they came in. We opened fire with all our guns. They circled above, dropping bombs on us. The bombs all missed. There were six bombs dropped at us, the closest coming about 150 feet from our port beam. The attack lasted about one-half hour. They concentrated their attack almost entirely on the *Dale!* No casualties aboard ship. Boy, that was close and I do mean close!

Bela "Shorty" Smith: Several Jap Zeros came over and began strafing the *Dale.* I noticed that one of the powder cases for our 5-inch gun was lying exposed on the deck. If the Japs hit the powder case it would blow up and kill the entire gun crew, so I dove onto the deck and tucked the powder case beneath me so it wouldn't get hit. After the Zeros left one of my mates said, "You better get up. They've gone. Hey! Look at your life jacket. You've been hit!" Sure enough! When I took my life jacket off there was a big slash where a bullet had passed through. I didn't even know I'd been hit!

Lester Dailey Diary, *February 4*: Along before dark, five Jap Zero floatplanes attacked Amchitka and the ship. We opened fire and soon drove them off. No bombs dropped.

February 7: Our planes shot down four Jap Zeros between here (Amchitka) and Kiska. They will soon have the airfield done here then we'll have some air protection. (We hope.)

February 16: To west end of Amchitka Island again where we landed troops. Sub contact!

USS Dale Action Report, *February 16, 0904* C.C.A. operator reported contact bearing 180° True, range 450 yards. Ship swung to head for contact.

Earl Hicks: We had just sent a boatload of soldiers to the top (west) end of Amchitka so they could investigate a possible landing by the Japs. The water was smooth when we sent our motor whaleboat in filled with soldiers, but turned rough in a second as the boat was

returning empty. Before the boat got back we received orders to immediately investigate a sub contact, and so the race was on to see if the guys
on the boat could get back before *Dale* took off in pursuit of the sub.

Ernest "Dutch" Smith: We raced through heavy seas to get back to
the *Dale* because we didn't want to get left behind in the open boat.
You could never tell when a williwaw would hit, and if one hit you on
the open sea in an open boat your chances of making it were none too
good! When we finally caught up to the *Dale*, she was underway and
picking up speed. We hooked up to the davit on the run, but the seas
were so rough the boat was swamped by a wave. We managed to
scramble back aboard soaking wet, but couldn't lift the boat as it was
filled with water and the *Dale* was moving fast. We got orders to cut
the boat loose and sink it. So we cut her loose and shot her full of holes
to sink her. It was really sad to see her go because she was the only real
boat the ship had, other than lifeboats designed for the tropics that had
cargo net bottoms, and you can guess how much good they would do
you in those waters! They took us below to officers' country and
warmed us up with coffee and whiskey, but it took a long time to get
over the shakes!

Lester Dailey Diary, *February 16*: Skies cleared toward dusk. Jap
Zeros attacked again but were driven off by heavy fire.

February 17: Back on patrol again. Heavy seas. Boy! The field is
finished on Amchitka and they have eight P-40s. Tonight two Zeros
came over and our P-40s surprised them by dropping out of the clouds
on them. Both Zeros were shot down in flames.

February 25: Still on patrol. Wrote letters. *Lonesome*. Rough
seas. Snow. Sure tiresome! Wonder how Max and the folks are? Low
on grub.

John Overholt : We often ran low on food up in the Aleutians, so keeping the crew fed was real hard work. Whenever we ran short we'd radio for more and a cruiser or tanker would eventually deliver it to us at sea. Oh, we always seemed to have enough powdered potatoes and eggs, but try as I might, I could not figure out how to cook them so the guys would like them.

Lester Dailey Diary, *March 11*: On patrol at Amchitka. Sure no morale on this ocean-going tomato can.

March 20: Arrived Adak about 1500. Tied up to tanker and took on fuel, got one box of bait. Underway shortly in company of *Salt Lake City* and *Monaghan*. *Look out, Kiska here we come!* We hear five Jap merchantmen are headed for Kiska and we are going to intercept them??? Warships too??? Today is my first wedding anniversary. Wonder how many more of them we'll spend like this?

MARCH 26: BATTLE OF
THE KOMANDORSKI ISLANDS

A few days of calm, clear, cool weather can sometimes be found between the icy williwaws of the Aleutian winter and the glutinous fogs of its summer. March 26, 1943, broke as one such day.

In fact, the day broke so calm that sailors in Admiral Charles H. "Soc" McMorris's blockading fleet could actually hear the swish of water rush past the hulls of their ships; so clear, lookouts could see whales breeching miles away in the predawn light; and so cool, no sailor afloat was of a mind for a swim!

McMorris's task group of two cruisers and four destroyers was arranged in a north to south scouting line due west of Attu. His objective was to intercept Japanese transports reported to be on their way to reinforce Kiska and Attu. What McMorris, in flagship *Richmond*, did not know was that the transports were escorted by four cruisers and four destroyers commanded by Vice Admiral Boshiro Hosogaya, who had McMorris outgunned two to one, and outsailed by a full three knots.

The path of the northbound Americans intersected with the east-bound Japanese just south of the Komandorskis, a group of four tree-less islands east of the Kamchatka Peninsula, belonging to then-neutral Russia.

Author's note: The following timed accounts, unless otherwise credited, were taken from the USS *Dale*'s Action Report for March 26, 1943.

0700 Steaming on base course 020° in scouting line. Scouting distance 6 miles. Order of ships from north to south, *Coghlan*, *Richmond*, *Bailey*, *Dale*, *Salt Lake City*, and *Monaghan*. Zigzagging in accordance with plan No. 8. Sea smooth, visibility 10,000 yards, twilight.

John Cruce: The day broke still, with the ocean a flat calm, the air crystal clear and the cloud cover three to four thousand feet high. After what we had been sailing through for the past three months, you had to believe it was going to be a perfect day!

0735 *Richmond* reported radar contact 340° T (true), ordered full boiler power, all ships close *Richmond*, base course 078° T.
0825 Sighted smoke and masts of several ships, bearing 330° T, unable to identify, distance about 45,000 yards.

Eugene Brewer: We were just going to dawn GQ when the lead ships in the line called in a contact over the TBS. I was on the bridge with a pair of twenty-power binoculars and could see smudges on the northern horizon. *Richmond* then ordered *Dale* to take station astern of the *Salt Lake City.*

Author's note: TBS, or Talk Between Ships, was a short-range, very high frequency (VHF) radio. Prior to TBS, ships in a convoy were fearful of using radios to talk with one another as the signals might be picked up by distant enemies and their positions revealed by radio direction finders.

0828 Formed on starboard quarter *Salt Lake City*, about 160° relative, distance 1,200 yards.
0832 Identified superstructures of enemy ships as that of Cruisers bearing 340° T, distance 30,000 yards. Three ships appeared on easterly course.
0841 Closing enemy, identified as two heavy and one light three-stack cruiser. Enemy commenced firing.

Mike Callahan: I had the mid-watch and so was in happy dreamland when the GQ sounded. When I got up to the gun director's platform, which was up high above the bridge, I could see we were rapidly closing on a couple of ships on the northern horizon. The weather was absolutely perfect for seeing things, so I called Grace, who had incredible distance vision, over for a look. I once checked Grace out with the "Sugar George" and found him to be as accurate as radar! Just then the Japanese opened fire on us. Grace said, "Looks like a bunch of DDs at twenty-eight thousand yards!" I said, "Grace, who ever heard of a tin can firing at twenty-eight thousand yards! Cruisers shoot twenty-eight thousand yards; destroyers shoot eighteen thousand yards. Those guys are cruisers and we're in big trouble!"

0842 *Richmond* and *Salt Lake City* opened fire, bearing enemy 350° T, range 25,000 yards. Further identified enemy as one *Kuma*-class light cruiser, two *Nachi*-class heavy cruisers, and four destroyers. Enemy in column on easterly course, order of ships from right to left, two *Nachi*-class cruisers followed by *Kuma*-class cruisers, with four DD in line of bearing astern.

Author's note: *Nachi*-class heavy cruisers *Nachi* and *Maya* were longer, heavier, and three full knots faster than the *Salt Lake City.* The *Maya* was also three years newer. *Kuma*-class light cruisers *Tama* and *Abukuma* were slightly smaller than *Richmond*, and they carried seven 5 1/2-inch guns, as compared with *Richmond's* ten 6-inch guns.

Lester Dailey Diary: At first we thought there were only about three Jap men o war and were going right in for the kill. When we saw we were hopelessly outnumbered we turned and opened fire to the rear. The enemy cut us off by getting between us and Attu, which was about 180 miles to the west. We were not very far from Siberia. They gave chase and it became a running battle between our two cruisers and four destroyers and their four cruisers and four destroyers.

Eugene Brewer: The first three salvos from the Japanese straddled *Richmond,* and she turned away and ran towards the west.

John Cruce: When the *Richmond* spotted what she thought were Jap transports she took right after them like it was going to be a Roman holiday. I was up in the gun director and could see everything as plain as day through the range finder. But those "Jap transports" turned out to be cruisers and they opened up on us right away. The admiral turned to the west and we started running toward the Komandorski Islands. The *Salt Lake City* started firing back, because she was the only one that had the range, since the *Richmond* had turned tail and was way out in front of our formation.

Warren Deppe: The *Richmond* with the admiral aboard almost ran over everybody, trying to get first licks on the Japs, but when the splashes started showing up around her she plum turned tail and ran for it!

Lester Dailey Diary: Observed one hit on an enemy heavy cruiser, I think, for it started pouring out an immense billow of smoke. She kept on firing though. We could see the flashes of their guns and their accuracy and marksmanship were *very* good as their projectiles were striking all around our task force.

Ernest "Dutch" Smith: For a destroyer to be able to do its job, it had to be light and maneuverable, which meant that we had no armor to protect us from those Jap cruisers. Why, a 50-caliber machine-gun round would go right through us, and those Jap cruisers were shooting 5-, 6-, and 8-inch rounds! Every single man on the *Dale* knew what we were up against!

Mike Callahan: The first thing the admiral did in the *Richmond* was turn and run! The real commander of the battle was the skipper of the *Salt Lake City*. Funny thing about this war business is that you can send people to the Naval Academy and teach them to fight, but you can't make them fight when the time comes. Sometimes to save the body you have to lose a foot, and commanders who are afraid of losing troops should not be commanders. There is no substitute for leadership in combat. You can never be certain you are doing the right thing, but you have to make a decision and fight!

> **0846** Sighted another three-stack enemy cruiser ahead of two *Nachi* class, bearing 002° T, range 28,000 yards. Total enemy force now two *Nachi*-class cruisers, two *Kuma*-class cruisers, four destroyers (unidentified). Enemy continued eastward for reverse engagement. One enemy cruiser launched scouting plane.
>
> **0853** Enemy now bearing 040° T, range 21,000 yards. Enemy salvos falling just short of *Salt Lake City*, pattern very small, about 100 yards in range, 20 yards in deflection. Salvos falling 200 yards on starboard bow of *Dale*. Enemy laddering salvos up and down in about 300 yard steps, some salvos falling ahead and some on port bow from *Salt Lake City*.

Earl Hicks: The *Pensacola* and *Salt Lake City* were the only cruisers in the navy that had two turrets facing forward and two aft. They could charge and fight, and retreat and fight. Those two turrets facing aft on the *Salt Lake City* were the only things that saved our ass, because we were in full retreat! If the Japs got the *Salt Lake City*, we'd all be sunk.

Author's note: The *Pensacola*-class cruisers, *Pensacola* and *Salt Lake City*, were the first ships built by the U.S. Navy under the Washington Naval Treaty of 1923. This treaty confined the naval ships of signatory nations—United States, England, Japan, France, and Italy—to certain limitations on size and weaponry. *Pensacola* and *Salt Lake City* were the only cruisers in the U.S. Navy's fleet that could match the firepower of Japan's heavy cruisers. These cruisers also had a unique look, which earned the *Salt Lake City* the nickname "Swayback Maru."

Warren Deppe: Our four-stacker, *Richmond*, was running so far out in front of our formation that we didn't see her again until it was all over! We were cut off from our closest base in Amchitka and were running for the Komandorskis. The Japs had us cut off and they were three knots faster than the *Salt Lake City*, so they just kept herding us toward the Komandorskis. They would run up on us and then turn so their entire broadside would bear and then let us have it!

Ernest "Dutch" Smith: One thought kept going through everyone's mind: if we had been sunk down there in the South Pacific, we'd have just jumped into the water and swam for it. But that Aleutian water was so cold it would kill you as fast as the enemy's naval guns. When it got right down to it, our life jackets became a big joke!

Eugene Brewer: Guys were putting on their life jackets and I said, "Hey, no point in wearing a life jacket! You only get a few minutes in that water before you freeze to death!"

0906 Sighted enemy fleet type spotting plane bearing 159° T, range 15,000 yards. Plane kept just out of reach of five-inch fire. Enemy salvos falling about 300 yards short and then about 200 yards over *Dale* as ladder was walked up and down on *Salt Lake City*. Salvo interval about twenty seconds. Ships of our formation dodging salvos by constant maneuvering, heading toward last salvo, which was effective because next salvo was apparently spotted to hit. Plane spotting for enemy calling shots well, salvos getting closer to *Salt Lake City*. Enemy now on westerly course. Range now 23,000 yards, bearing 050° T. Enemy apparently not eager to close, as their cruisers are simply maintaining a firing position on the *Salt Lake City*.

Author's note: *Richmond* had pulled so far ahead that she was now out of range and ceased firing. All Japanese cruisers now focused their fire on the *Salt Lake City*. At 0907, fire from the *Salt Lake City* hit the leading Japanese cruiser several times amidships, setting her on fire. At 0910 the *Salt Lake City* took an 8-inch round on her mid-ship catapult, resulting in two deaths. She took another hit at 0920 on her quarterdeck. Despite these hits, the *Salt Lake City* was able to maintain thirty-three knots.

John Overholt: I was making sandwiches and coffee for the crew at their battle stations when word came down from the captain that the Japs were running us right into the Komandorski Islands, and that we should prepare to be interned in Siberia for the rest of the war. So that was the story. We were going to be POWs in Siberia for the duration, if we were lucky!

Darel Bright: I had just come aboard and as yet had no duties nor was I assigned a battle station. They told me to hang out in the wardroom during the battle, but there was nothing for me to do except feel totally helpless and wonder what the hell was going on!

Lester Dailey Diary: The *Richmond* was way out ahead of the *Salt Lake City*, which was doing all of the fighting. The crews' opinion of the *Richmond* is very poor. But we all give the *Salt Lake City* our highest praise. She was really pouring the gunfire out of her after turrets. We saw the enemy was gaining and the order to lay a smoke screen was given. The Jap spotter plane finally came too close and the *Monaghan* and *Dale* both opened fire on it and shot it down.

0922 Enemy salvos landing all sides of *Dale* and *Salt Lake City*. "Beautiful shooting" on part of enemy and a miracle that

Salt Lake City was able to avoid salvos.

0924 Enemy salvos falling 1,000 yards short of *Salt Lake City* and fire slacking off.

0927 Changed fleet course to 300° T.

0944 Changed fleet course to 320° T, speed thirty-two knots, closing enemy slightly. *Salt Lake City* still firing with her two after turrets. Range 21,000 yards, bearing 070° T. Enemy in same formation, making no attempt to use her light forces, concentrating on *Salt Lake City*.

0952 Changed base course to 000° T, closing enemy. Enemy resumed fire, concentrating on *Salt Lake City*. Salvos falling close.

1003 Changed base course 330° T, enemy firing very rapid and effective, salvos all around *Salt Lake City*, 100–200 yards away, some close aboard.

Author's note: McMorris turned his line north to bring *Salt Lake City*'s forward guns to bear on an apparently wounded enemy cruiser. That cruiser, however, quickly regained her speed and bored in on the *Salt Lake City* with three of her sister cruisers. With the enemy cruisers closing rapidly and the patterns of their shellfire moving ever closer, the *Salt Lake City* lost her steering and swung sharply to the left before rudder control was switched to steering aft. With the tactical situation deteriorating rapidly, McMorris ordered his line to again turn west. At 1010 the *Salt Lake City* took another hit, which produced flooding in several compartments. McMorris then ordered his destroyers to begin screening the *Salt Lake City* with smoke.

1007 *Salt Lake City* turned sharply to left, making smoke, reported steering casualty over TBS.

1018 *Salt Lake City, Coghlan,* and *Bailey* commenced laying smoke screen to cover *Salt Lake City.*

1023 *Salt Lake City* changed course to left and entered smoke screen, which consisted of two parallel columns of smoke laid by *Coghlan* and *Bailey,* one on each side of her. Enemy fire continued and salvos still landed close ahead, astern and on both sides of *Salt Lake City* in spite of smoke. Spotting plane was observed to west of formation where *Coghlan* and *Bailey* opened fire to drive it off. *Salt Lake City* still firing at enemy.

Earl Hicks: Down in the engine room Machinist Mate Toscano tied the throttle down wide open. *Dale* was running as fast as she could!

Roy Roseth: Up on the bridge the captain and exec were talking about how to deal with the Japanese gunfire, which was falling around us like rain. When a salvo would land close aboard one would say, "Let's go this way!" and the other would say, "No, no! Let's steer right into their last salvo!" And every time we would steer into their last salvo the Japs would correct and shoot right where we would have been, had we not outsmarted them! It was like calling "heads" on a coin flip and having it come up heads time after time all day long.

Charles O'Rorke: The *Richmond* took off and ran like hell. Never did help us a bit! That made it *Salt Lake City's* four 8-inch guns against the Jap's twenty 8-inchers! All the enemy had to do was lay back and lob in those 8-inchers until they put enough of them on the *Salt Lake City* to stop her, and then swoop in for the rest of us. It was our four against their twenty!

Bela "Shorty" Smith: I was a powderman on gun one, which was the first gun on the bow of the ship. The gun had a protective metal shield, but the only thing it protected you from was the spray off the bow. My job was to take the twenty-four-pound powder cases off the hoist and hand them to the rammerman. You could see the Jap ships as plain as day, and there were at least twice as many of them as there were of us. All they had to do was hit the *Salt Lake City*, and then they could swoop down for the rest of us. I don't remember how many times we fired, but we fired a lot because our powder magazine was way down by the time we finished. You have to remember that we were running from the Japs most of the time. Gun one was an attacking gun, not a retreating gun, so it couldn't be brought to bear most of the time. The guys on the aft guns got most of the action.

> **1044** Changed base course to 300° T. *Richmond* opened fire with her after turrets. Heavy smoke over sea between enemy and our formation, frequently preventing *Dale* from seeing enemy targets except through holes. All ships continued zigzagging at high speed to avoid enemy salvos. Salvos were aimed at *Salt Lake City* but overs and shorts were very close to screening DDs. Our formation at this time—*Salt Lake City* center, *Coghlan* and *Bailey* 2,000 yards on her port and starboard quarter, *Richmond* 3,000 yards ahead *Salt Lake City*, *Dale* and *Monaghan* just forward her port beam, respectively, dropping astern at 17 knots to lay smoke screen.
>
> **1050** *Dale* commenced laying smoke. *Kuma* class cruiser and four DDs now on starboard quarter at 16,000 yards. *Dale* commenced firing with aft turrets.

Warren Deppe: I was on number one torpedo tube and the gun director was running the numbers and angles for a possible torpedo attack. Then I got orders to go back and start the smoke generators on the fantail. Down in the fire room they sprayed bunker crude under pressure onto a superheated plate, and that made a real thick black smoke. On the fantail we used generators that mixed two kinds of chemicals together for a thick white smoke. We had black smoke pouring from the stacks and white smoke pouring from the fantail.

Ernest Schnabel: As "oil king," my job was to keep the *Dale* trim. During the Battle of the Komandorskis, we were burning oil like mad, not only because we were running hard from the Japs, but because we were also laying a smoke screen to hide the *Salt Lake City*, which was under intense enemy gunfire. My job as oil king was to keep the ship trim by pumping oil from tank to tank so the levels would stay equal.

Lester Dailey Diary: The smoke generators were started along with smoke from the stacks. I was on the after steering station in case the bridge got shot away and got black as can be from all the smoke boiling out of the stacks. The screen was very effective. All this time we were located on the port side of the SLC. The enemy's fire was landing so close we could see shrapnel flying through the air when it exploded after hitting the water. The *Salt Lake City* turned to the starboard at this time and opened up with a broadside [from] her main battery to chase away the light cruiser that was getting too close for comfort.

> **1053** Observed flash in hanger of *Salt Lake City*, believed hit by shell. Enemy still firing effectively through smoke.
> **1100** Changed base course to 210° T. *Salt Lake City* ceased firing.

Author's note: At this point, the *Salt Lake City* took her fourth hit, which caused flooding in her after engine rooms. She took on a five-degree list, but continued at full speed. McMorris then turned his line due south. Because of the heavy smoke, Hosogaya did not see this turn and continued west for nearly one-half hour.

1107 Changed base course to 180° T.

1110 *Kuma*-class cruiser commenced firing on *Dale*. Salvo landed about 100 yards short off port quarter. Shells yellow dye loaded. *Dale* commenced firing on *Kuma* class, range 17,400 bearing 010° T.

Robert "Pat" Olson: The only word we got down in the fire room was what came down from the captain, and he wasn't in the mood to talk about the scenery! It seemed like the battle was taking a month. Our machinery was shuddering like mad from the high-speed maneuvering, and the ship was leaning radically one way, then another. Sound travels clearly through water, so the near misses from the Jap gunfire sounded like we were being hit time after time after time. And when our 5-inchers went off, it sounded like you were inside a big metal barrel that someone was banging on with a sledgehammer. At one point we ran for so long and so hard that the asbestos insulation on our boiler casings turned bright red and the metal insulation started to melt.

1112 Several short salvos, port quarter. Salvos started about 1,200 yards short and walked up in range about 200 yards a step. *Dale* dodged by heading toward last salvo. Salvos crossed and one landed about 100 yards off starboard bow.

Earl Hicks: I was on the forward repair party and our battle station was in the forward machine shop. There wasn't much for us to do until we got hit, so we just hung around the machine shop. After a while we couldn't stand the suspense of not knowing what was going on so we went outside and lay down on the deck to minimize the chances of getting hit by shrapnel. I dogged the machine shop hatch down, but every time we'd get straddled the hatch would pop open and I'd have to dog it down again. Seems like this went on for hours!

> **1121** Changed base course to 160° T, smoke obscured *Kuma*-class cruiser and firing ceased. *Dale* ceased firing at it.
> **1129** *Salt Lake City* having trouble, slowing down. *Dale* and *Monaghan* reduced speed to keep smoke around *Salt Lake City*. Enemy closing fast, range about 18,000 bearing 330° T. *Richmond* now 6,000 yards ahead of *Salt Lake City*.

Richard Martinez: My job on the gun crew was to catch the hot shells being ejected and throw them over the side. And though we were about as busy as you could possibly be, every once in a while I would look up and see colored splashes all around us. Each of the different ships firing at us had different-colored dye markers in their rounds so they could see [the] difference between where their shots were landing from the other ships. The air was filled with a rainbow of smokes! And every time I looked up I could see that the Jap ships were getting closer and closer. After a while I just kept my head down.

> **1130** *Salt Lake City* slowed to about five knots, looked bad. *Richmond* ordered, "Destroyers prepare for torpedo attack, course 060° T." *Dale* commenced firing on heavy cruiser, which had closed to 16,900 yards, bearing 330° T. *Salt Lake*

City firing at cruiser.

1138 Destroyers ordered to attack. *Dale* came to 060° T.

Mike Callahan: The Jap cruisers had closed to nine miles, but at sea a mile is nothing. Why, some ships can't turn in less than a half-mile! When the order came down for us to launch a torpedo attack, I knew we were in big trouble, because I could see them as plain as day from the gun director. There wasn't going to be anything to protect us as we ran up to the launch point.

Eugene Brewer: When *Dale* received the order to commence a torpedo attack on the enemy heavy cruisers, the captain decided to roll a die to see where we would launch the torpedoes. If he rolled a "six," we would launch at six thousand yards, and so on. He rolled and it came up "two," which meant we were going to run in to two thousand yards before we would launch. Word spread like wildfire throughout the ship that we were going in to two thousand yards, and every single one of us knew what our odds would be at that distance.

John Cruce: When the order was given for us to commence a daylight torpedo attack on those Jap heavy cruisers, the gunnery officer came around shaking hands and saying, "So long, it's been good to know you!" But hell, I didn't want to give up! I was up on the range finder where I could see everything and I wanted to fight it out!

Roy Roseth: I was a gun pointer on one of the 5-inch guns. Word had just come down that we were going in for a torpedo attack on the heavy cruisers when the gunnery officer looked around the corner and yelled, "Well, boys, we're done now for sure!" When we heard that we all gathered around and got down on our knees and said a prayer.

Then went back to work. There were salvo splashes all around the ship!

Orville Newman: Our fire room section leader, Lonnie Massey, came back to us and said, "Boys, we're going on in for a torpedo run, and you all know what that means! I want you to tie up your pant legs with some clothes stops, because I don't want any of your crap splattered over the deck!" Needless to say, that took us all aback!

Billy Walker: I was scared, really scared. I was down in number two fire room when Massey, the first class petty officer in charge, came around and started shaking hands and saying, "Goodbye!" I was a kid just off the farm, with few contacts on the ship, and here was my boss saying we were going to die! I didn't know what to do, so I just kept firing those boilers to keep power up. If we quit, the ship would lose steam and wouldn't be able to maneuver. And if we were hit by one of those 8-inch shells raining down, we'd be sunk.

Robert "Pat" Olson: Our section leader in the fire room, Lonnie Massey, came around and said, "We are going on a suicide torpedo run and destroyers do not return from them. We are driving straight to death!" We were left wide-eyed and open-mouthed. He was totally distracted from his job of running the fire room, which in turn, distracted me from my fear of impending doom. I stopped Lonnie in a place where no one else could hear and yelled over the noise, "Look, let's give the captain all the steam he needs. We don't give a shit about dying! Let's just take two of them for every one they take of us. That's a good trade!" It was just he and I, shouting at the top of our voices over the roar of the machinery. My tirade startled and calmed him. He went back to work and ran his fire room and did a good job.

1144 *Dale* received an order via TBS to stay with the *Salt Lake City*, which was making about 10 knots. *Nachi*-class cruiser had closed to about 14,000 yards. *Dale* came about to 180° T to lay smoke astern of *Salt Lake City*. *Nachi*-class cruiser shifted fire to *Dale*. Salvos landed short and kept walking up. Came to about 30 yards short and then the cruiser shifted fire to *Coghlan*, *Bailey* and *Monaghan*, who were maneuvering to starboard of *Salt Lake City* for torpedo attack. *Salt Lake City* picked up speed. Torpedo attack cancelled.

1148 Enemy concentrated fire on *Dale*, which was closest target, about 13,900 yards range. Several close salvos but no hits.

Warren Deppe: Someone actually counted the guns firing at the *Dale* at this time and came up with twenty-eight! That's right! There were twenty-eight guns firing at us at the same time! The colored die markers from their rounds had turned our fantail into a rainbow of color. That's how close they were coming!

Mike Callahan: All the gunfire that had been aimed at the *Salt Lake City* was now coming directly for us. From my position up in the gun director atop the bridge I could actually see the rounds coming in from the cruisers. Captain would yell up, "Over or under?" I'd yell my guess back down and he'd give the helmsman his orders. Those Japs had their batteries lined up right, I'll tell you! They'd drop a dozen shots short and then walk right up on us as neat as you please. Their dispersion wasn't twenty feet, and that's what you want to see if you are the gunnery officer, except, of course, if you happen to be on the wrong end of that gunfire! Hell, even the men down in the fire room knew we were done for!

John Overholt: We were all frightened. Shells were dropping all around us and exploding. We were shooting back and saying prayers as fast as possible. Everyone on ship was down on their knees at some time during the battle. God was with us . . . no other way to describe it!

> **1154** Changed base course to 160° T speed 20 knots. Still maneuvering to dodge salvos and lay smoke screen astern *Salt Lake City.*

D. J. Vellis: The *Salt Lake City*, which was hit again by the cruiser 8-inchers, signaled, "My speed zero!"

Author's note: At 1150, engineers counterflooding to correct the *Salt Lake City*'s list accidentally pumped seawater into the fuel lines and extinguished her burners. By 1154, *Salt Lake City* was dead in the water. Captain Bertram Rodgers signaled, "My speed zero" with flags, but the flags were immediately shredded by Japanese gunfire. He then broadcast the *Salt Lake City*'s condition over the TBS and requested escorting destroyers to launch an immediate torpedo attack on the rapidly approaching Japanese cruisers.

> **1159** *Salt Lake City* reports another hit. *Coghlan, Bailey* and *Monaghan* came right to close *Nachi*-class cruisers for torpedo attack. Enemy cruisers are laying barrage on attacking destroyers. Destroyers zigzagging radically to avoid salvos and firing a heavy barrage at the two *Nachi*-class cruisers. The *Dale* remained astern of *Salt Lake City*, zigging to cover her with smoke. The *Richmond* was ahead of the *Salt Lake City* about 5,000 yards and the *Coghlan, Bailey* and *Monaghan* still closing the enemy cruisers.

Lester Dailey Diary: When the *Bailey*, *Coghlan*, and *Monaghan* were detailed to attack, we were ordered to stay and screen the SLC, which was dead in the water. When they attacked we lost sight of them in the thick smoke.

Ernest "Dutch" Smith: We were running and shooting. But what the Japs didn't know was that our air support was fogged in at Dutch Harbor. I'm sure they had heard us screaming for help over the radio. I was a rammerman on gun number four and we fired until there wasn't any ammo left on the ship. We were screening with smoke so the Jap fire controllers couldn't get a range on the *Salt Lake City*. The *Salt Lake City* was in the smoke but we were out in the open, and that's what a destroyer's job is, to get between trouble and the capital ships. We were just doing our job, but with all those straddles it was sure scary work.

Charles O'Rorke: I was watching the action from the engine room hatch and could see plenty. Colored salvos were splashing all around us and the air was filled with rainbow-colored smoke. Toward the end the *Salt Lake City* ran out of armor-piercing rounds and had to use antipersonnel rounds. These made an entirely different kind of splash near the Jap ships, which apparently befuddled them into thinking they were being attacked from the air, because they started shooting willy-nilly into the sky, which quickly filled with flak bursts.

Roy Roseth: We were very low on fuel and ammo and the *Salt Lake* ran out of ammo toward the end. I know because I saw her shooting star shells at the Jap cruisers.

1205 *Dale* ceased firing, all enemy ships obscured by smoke.

1212 Observed huge explosion in vicinity of enemy, too large to be a shell splash. *Salt Lake City* now making twenty knots, *Richmond* on her port bow about 4,000 yards. *Dale* still laying smoke screen on port quarter of *Salt Lake City*.

Eugene Brewer: We listened over the TBS as the *Coghlan*, *Bailey*, and *Monaghan* went in for their attack. *Bailey* was in the lead, and we heard her calling out a hit on the lead heavy cruiser. A few moments later *Bailey* said that she had received a direct hit in the galley.

Earl Hicks: When *Bailey* turned after dropping her torpedoes she received a hit from an 8-incher that killed the entire forward repair party. Never did find the head of the officer in charge!

John Cruce: When the *Salt Lake City* went dead in the water we figured we were all goners for sure. All the Japs had to do now was lay a few more 8-inchers into her and then swoop in for the rest of us. The only thing protecting her now was the smoke we were laying on the water, but they had a spotter plane up and would soon be able to see that the *Salt Lake City* was dead in the water. But then the Japs turned their fire on *Bailey*, *Coghlan*, and *Monaghan* as they ran in with their torpedoes. You could see the cans zigging like mad to avoid salvos from all those Jap ships. The *Bailey*, which was in the lead, took an 8-inch round that killed the entire forward repair party. Then another round went clean through because tin cans are so thin-skinned that the armor piercing 8-incher didn't even detonate. That water temperature was right at thirty-three degrees, which would give us about ten or twelve minutes before we froze to death. Just when things got to be about as bleak as you could imagine, one of our cans got a 5-incher right smack on the bridge of the lead Jap cruiser.

You could see it as plain as day. Then the Japs simply turned tail and ran. It was a miracle!

Mike Callahan: I was looking at them through the binoculars, thinking they had us cold turkey when I saw their lead cruiser take a hit right on the bridge. I looked up, thinking maybe our air forces had finally shown up, but no, one of our sister cans had nailed them right on the bridge! Then, all of a sudden, the Japanese turned away and broke off the fighting. Why? I'll never know! Everybody on the ship knew in an instant that we had been saved.

Robert "Pat" Olson: The relief was indescribable. Four ships had been throwing 8-inchers at us for well over three hours, and any single one of those 8-inchers could have sunk us like a stone. And right when it appeared we were goners, with the *Salt Lake City* dead in the water, word came down to the fire room that the Japs had turned and run. We just stood there in wide-eyed disbelief. But when Myers came down from his GQ at the 5-inch guns with a face made pitch black from the powder, we knew it was true.

> **1215** Changed base course to 090° T, enemy ships completely out of sight. *Bailey*, *Coghlan*, and *Monaghan* returning from torpedo attack under cover of own smoke screen. Enemy has apparently turned away. Movements not visible through smoke.
> **1217** *Bailey* reported hit, slowing her to fifteen knots. *Coghlan* remaining astern with *Bailey* to assist. *Bailey* reported probable torpedo hit on enemy ship.
> **1245** All ships ceased making smoke. Enemy out of sight, last reported by attacking destroyers who were returning as being about 42,000 yards astern.

Warren Deppe: When we turned off the smoke generators after the battle I went back to my torpedo tube. A fellow torpedoman was standing there holding a big chunk of shrapnel and said, "Look what you missed! I found this right next to your tube!"

Earl Hicks: The most frightening moment came when we realized the battle was over. During the battle we had been running and shooting for three and a half hours nonstop. During that time we were totally engaged—had to be! When you turn a tin can at flank speed you better hang on, because it won't lean into the turn like a speed boat; it'll lean away from the turn because it's so top heavy. Then a huge wall of water comes washing down the deck, and if you're not ready for it you'll get carried away. So during the fighting everyone was real busy fighting, but when it was over the realization came. Those Japs had been shooting 6- and 8-inchers at us for hours; must have been over a thousand rounds. If any one of them hit us, it would have gone through us like a hot knife through butter. The only life rafts we had were cork ones with a cargo net bottom—fine for the tropics but totally worthless in thirty-three-degree water. If the enemy rounds didn't get us, we'd have frozen to death in the water. You don't think about those things when you're fighting. But when the fighting ends you get to thinking about what might have happened, and then you start shaking.

1415 Enemy has evidently withdrawn completely.

Ted Palumbo: I was both powderman and shellman on number one gun because they had transferred the shellman off at our last port. To save time I was running under the barrel of the 5-inch gun to keep the gun supplied. After the shooting was over I went back to the radio shack and found that I could not hear anyone talking! I was completely deaf for three days. I was one happy sailor when my hearing finally returned because that was my job!

Ernest "Dutch" Smith: The *Dale* had been turned pitch black from the smokes we had been laying to protect the *Salt Lake City*. I mean, you could have grabbed a handful of that soot off a railing and used it for shoe polish.

Eugene Brewer: So many rounds had landed so close to the *Dale* that her longitudinal beam had cracked three-quarters of the way through. If that beam had broken, *Dale* would have fallen in two like a split log!

Earl Hicks: After the battle both the *Bailey* and the *Salt Lake City* went back to Seattle for repairs. I don't have the slightest idea what happened to the *Richmond*. We went into port and tied up next to a tender, where we spent time getting cleaned up.

Lester Dailey Diary, March 28: We arrived at Adak at 0330. The *Salt Lake City* went on east with the *Monaghan* and *Coughlan* as escorts. Early this morning we went alongside the *Bailey*. She was hit twice by eight-inch shellfire and once by five-inch. The hits flooded her engine room and killed five men. Sure a sight! Shrapnel also hit our stern and made big dents in it. I understand one of our longitudinal frames has cracked and we'll have to go into the yard to get it fixed. States? Pearl? Kodiak? Bremerton?

Jim Sturgill: After the battle we went into Cold Harbor for liberty. It was the first time I had set foot on land in months. The only thing there was a bar and a gedunk stand. The bartender had received instructions from the captain of the *Salt Lake City* to "Give that *Dale* crew whatever they want. If you haven't got it, get it, and bill it to the *Salt Lake City!*" When we bellied up, the bartender said, "You can't pay for this, it's on the house!" Most of the crew got pretty well lit that day, thanks to the *Salt Lake City.*

Author's note: Though the Battle of the Komandorski Islands ended in a tactical draw, it was clearly a strategic victory for the U.S. Navy. Hosogaya had allowed the vastly inferior McMorris to escape relatively unscathed; he had also failed to reinforce Attu and Kiska, leaving the troops on those islands little hope of fending off the increasingly aggressive Americans. Hosogaya was subsequently relieved of his command.

McMorris became the hero of the Komandorskis for "the magnificent manner in which all of the ships responded to his leadership"[1] and was subsequently appointed chief of staff to Admiral Nimitz at Pearl Harbor.

Many of the U.S. Navy ships that served under McMorris on the morning of March 26 were relieved of their dreary Aleutian duty and ordered off to warmer climes. During the three hours and twenty-four minutes of the Battle of Komandorski Islands, 5,462 rounds and forty-eight torpedoes were fired by American and Japanese ships. This equates to approximately one shot fired for every two seconds of the engagement.[2] But for the USS *Dale*—which had fired 794 5-inch rounds at the Japanese cruisers—the Aleutian campaign was just beginning.

APRIL TO JUNE: ATTU ISLAND

Though Japan had been turned back at the Komandorskis, it still occupied Attu and Kiska, and thus still occupied the highway from Japan to America. This presented the Americans with two possible courses of action: blockade or invade.

Given the Americans' newly won superiority in the air and on the sea, a blockade could have, at relatively small cost, sealed the Japanese positions in for the duration of the war—a strategy that would be used extensively during MacArthur's campaigns in the South Pacific. But Attu and Kiska belonged to the United States, and public opinion demanded the Japanese be removed forthwith.

Kiska, which lay a scant seventy miles west of the American base at Amchitka, was the obvious place to invade. However, after a long, hard look at the strength of the Japanese position on the island, American planners realized they simply did not have the firepower needed to retake Kiska without great expense, and so decided to bypass it for what they believed would be the softer Attu.

At this stage of the war in the Pacific, the U.S. military had but one successful amphibious landing to its credit, and that was the largely unopposed one on Guadalcanal. Attu would hopefully be the second. Because Attu lay nearly two thousand miles from the continental United States, it would take nearly three months before all the men and materiels could be brought together to do the job.

While the American invasion force assembled in the warmth of the California sun, *Dale* prowled the fogs of the Bering Sea to prevent the Japanese from reinforcing Kiska and Attu.

Lester Dailey Diary, *April 7*: Well, well! Liberty today after three months at sea and only setting foot on land twice!

April 8: Turned to and painted back porch, binnacle hoods, etc. Worked hard all day long, too. Today Captain Rorschach released his command of the *Dale* to Lt. Cmdr. C. W. Aldrich.

Eugene Brewer: Those endless hours of steaming around in circles watching for Japs got to us after a while, and everyone went a bit

Asiatic. [*Author's note: Asiatic* was a World War II adjective for crazy or eccentric behavior; it also provided individuals a way to escape intolerable conditions. For example, to frustrate their captors and stay alive, American prisoners in Japanese internment camps would "go Asiatic," or go blank, during interrogations and beatings and thus mentally escape the torture.] One way we blew off steam was by playing cops and robbers. Seemed like everyone aboard the *Dale*, including Captain Rorschach, had made themselves a wooden pistol to play along, and some of those pistols looked pretty real.

One night, just after Aldrich took over as captain, we were in port standing condition watches. The rule in port was that if you had one active lookout the rest of your section could slough off a bit. Two guys on the gun crew were sloughing with a game of cops and robbers when Captain Aldrich stepped out of the chart house, where he had been pouring over charts of the Aleutians. He was night-blinded when he stepped out into the dark and couldn't see much. One of the wooden-gun slingers thought Captain Aldrich was one of his buddies, and so ran up to him, stuck a wooden pistol in his belly, and said, "Pray, you son of a bitch, because this is where you get off!" Aldrich had no idea this kid was playing a game and just about lost it. When the kid figured out who he had cornered, he quickly disappeared into the darkness. Aldrich scrambled up to the bridge and said, "Someone just tried to shoot me with a pistol!" The OOD, Ensign Radel, was trying to explain about the *Dale*'s favorite pastime when the XO came into the bridge with a new wooden pistol to show off. Captain Aldrich said, "My God Robinson! Not you too!"

Earl "Jitterbug" Pearson: One thing you always had to remember in the Aleutians was the extreme tides. One day I led a work party ashore in the *Dale*'s new whaleboat to pick up some stores. The stores were waiting for us on the dock, but before we loaded them into the boat we decided to slip into the village and see what was going on. After all, we hadn't set foot on land in months! When we got back, we found that our whaleboat was now twenty feet below the dock! This meant that we had to tie ropes around the cases of stores and lower them into the boat, which worked out fine until we came to the egg cases. Now, these were not your common, everyday egg cases. They were navy ship–sized egg cases, and each case held at least two hundred eggs. By then it was getting dark and I guess I got in too much of a hurry. My noose slipped and the crate of eggs crashed down into the whaleboat! Every single one of those eggs broke in the bottom of that boat. When we got back to the *Dale*, I laid low in the fire room for a while because I knew whichever poor deckhand had to clean that mess was going to be gunning for me!

Lester Dailey Diary, April 12: Yesterday we took some new recruits to Adak and did they ever get seasick. Wow!

John Overholt: My Amish mom wrote me a letter about my seasickness and said I needed something to sour my stomach. So I made up sandwiches with dill pickles and bread, and lived on them for a few days. It worked. I no longer had any seasickness! My dill pickle sandwiches cured thirty-five other guys on the *Dale* of their seasickness, too!

Lester Dailey Diary, April 13: Well this is certainly a "suicide " mission as we only have two light cruisers and three destroyers. We are supposed to stop enemy shipping coming in from northwest of Attu. Some job! If we meet up with enemy forces like we did a couple of weeks ago, we won't have much of a chance.

April 15: Today we are sixty miles northwest of Attu and are expecting *anything*. Smoke was sighted and we chased fifty-four miles after it, but it was either false or they outran us. All hands were at their battle stations but GQ was not sounded. We got close enough to see the Komandorski Islands, which belong to Russia.

Earl Hicks: It had been months since any of us had seen a woman, and, next to food, they were what occupied much of our talk. One night, when we were steaming through some real thick fog, we raised an unidentified ship on the radar and went to investigate. When I say foggy night, I mean the fog was so thick we couldn't even see the water under the ship! We pulled up close to the mystery ship and challenged it with a signal light. It turned out to be a Russian fishing boat. We signaled, "What's your name?" The signal came back, "My name is Olga!" We asked, "How many women aboard?" Olga answered "Five!" Word spread quickly throughout *Dale* that women were out there, and soon the rails were manned with sailors hooting and hollering into the fog!

Lester Dailey Diary, *April 23*: We relieved the *Long* on patrol this morning. No dope (information). Nice weather. Had inspection today.

April 24: Still on patrol. No dope.

April 25: Still on patrol. No dope.

April 26: Still patrolling. No dope.

Earl "Jitterbug" Pearson: When we ran short of food up in the Aleutians we would get replenished from other ships at sea. I used to volunteer for the unloading detail because I could always figure out a way to slip a case of peaches or something down the fire room hatch to my mates. At holidays and special events they would hand out free cigarettes and cigars. I didn't want to give mine away, so I went down to the fire room where no one would see me and learned how to smoke them. And I've been smoking them for fifty years!

Warren Deppe: On my very first day on the *Dale*, I was in the chow line when the guy in front of me, a big Italian, took all the spaghetti in the tureen and left me nothing. I called him out and we fought on the fantail. After that we were great friends, and I never had any more trouble in the chow line from anyone!

Robert "Pat" Olson: When I grew up in Montana, there was nothing to restrict my wandering around under those big skies except for the prickly pear cactus under my feet. When I was assigned to the *Dale's* fire room, I found the constricted quarters to be incredibly stifling, so I volunteered for messenger duty, which meant I got to make my way around the ship to take readings and relay messages. Since I had all this freedom, my boss in the fire room often ordered me up to the galley to steal Overholt's fresh-baked bread and some jam. We ate so much of it guys started calling me "fat boy"!

Earl Hicks: We were always hungry up in the Aleutians. One way we dealt with this hunger was by stealing a bunch of potatoes from the galley. We'd cut them up and put them in a bucket with salt and pepper, take them down to the engine room, unhook a steam line, and stick it in the bucket. Presto! Potato soup! Seaman would come around at all hours for a ration of our soup. Once we looted the galley and came up with a bunch of raisins, and so made up some raisin jack. We stored it in coffee cans down in the engine room where we figured no one would find it. But our plan went down the tubes when the electricians discovered our hiding place.

John Overholt: We were always running short of food up in the Aleutians, and they never sent me anything good to fix—nothing but dried eggs, canned meat, and whatever else they could send in a bucket from a supply ship. I used to lay awake at night trying to think of ways to cook up this stuff for the boys, because they deserved the best. The biggest problem I had was that my leading chief always wanted me to cook things the navy way. But when I cooked things the navy way, the garbage cans would always fill up. Nobody liked the food so they just picked at it and threw the rest in the garbage. After I passed my test for Second Class Baker, I started using some of the recipes from my Amish mom. Take rice, for example. One of the navy's staples was dry white rice with chili con carne poured over it. The boys got real tired of that after a while, and the garbage cans were always full of it. So what I did was make rice the way mom made it for us kids, with raisins and cream and a little bit of brown sugar over it. Then I'd put the chili con carne over my homemade bread. The sailors loved it, and the garbage cans were always empty. But my leading chief didn't like it, because it wasn't the navy way. One day, when I was coming up through the hatch from the reefer, the chief stomped on my fingers and then looked down at me with a mean grin. I cursed him out in German so he wouldn't know what I was saying, but he wrote me up for insubordination anyway. The captain was so mad at him he asked if I would like to have him busted down to Seaman First. I said, "No, just transfer him off." He did, and after that we had navy cooking—the Amish way.

Lester Dailey Diary, April 28: We are getting underway with the *Monaghan* bound for Cold Bay up on the Alaska Peninsula to pick up some marine transports in order to take Kiska, as our job is to screen the transports as they land the troops. Nasty weather. Heading east through Amukta Pass into North Pacific.

April 30: Arrived in Cold Bay, Alaska. Quite a bit different than the last time! Our entire squadron is here. Also a tanker and three or four transports. It won't be long before we try to take Attu or Kiska. We were granted liberty tonight until 2400. Over on the beach and beer!!!! Did I ever get pickled!!! Wow, what a night! And then the mid-watch on top of that!! Some fun.

Bela "Shorty" Smith: There wasn't much to do in Dutch Harbor. They did have a base, but it didn't have much to offer in terms of entertainment. We'd just sip a few beers or whatever beverage we could get our hands on. There were a few pretty girls, but they were well protected. I was just a young squirt and wanted to associate with everybody. But I was told, in no uncertain terms by some very big guys, not to mess with the gals. So I left them alone. But some of the guys were older and had been around gals. They knew what to do and say. I think they had some adventures.

Lester Dailey Diary, *May 3*: Well, here we go!! At 0800 we got underway with the *Phelps, Farragut,* and *Abner Read.* I don't know if the rest of the task force is out of the bay yet as it is very foggy and miserable weather. I just can't help but wonder if we will be lucky like we were last time and survive all this and if we will succeed in taking Attu.

May 7: The morning orders said to get all the sleep and rest possible because at 0910 we would start landing troops on Attu. So I slept all day. Nasty rough weather today. We are making all preparations for going into battle tomorrow. Hope we make out okay. Around midnight Doc had to operate on an appendicitis. The sea was very rough so we left the task force to keep the wind astern.

Mike Callahan: Seemed like most of our supplies came in olive drab cans—milk, beer, even ether! The night we were heading into Attu, Dr. Tratenburg had an emergency appendectomy to perform in the *Dale's* tiny operating room. There were extremely rough seas as well, and the doc talked the captain into turning the *Dale* so as to minimize the pitching and rolling. The doc said, "Mike, I've never had to operate by myself before!" And I said, "Doc, I've never had to con a ship by myself before!" I watched over his shoulder and everything seemed to be going okay. About 0330 in the morning I ran back down to see how the doc was doing. As he was stitching the patient up, the guy woke up and began to panic. It took the doc and both his medics to hold him down. Doc yelled, "Mike, grab that can of ether and knock him out!" The poor patient was listening to everything and getting more frightened by the moment. I poured ether out onto some cheese-cloth, and was just about to slap it on the patient's face when doc said, "My God, Mike, you're gonna kill him with that much ether!" That poor kid just about died from fright!

Lester Dailey Diary, May 9: Today is Mother's Day. I can't send a greeting so will let her know I never forgot her when I get back!???

USS Dale War Diary, May 10: *1311* Received hose from *Nevada* and commenced fueling forward. *1430* Received notice of radar contact on unknown target. Wind caught bow, causing ship to veer from *Nevada,* parting fuel hose. *1440* Cast off all lines from *Nevada.* Received orders from *Nevada* CO to return two pairs of sound-powered phones used in conjunction with fueling operation. *1445* Commenced maneuvering on various courses at various speeds to go alongside *Nevada* to return phones.

Earl Hicks: When we refueled from the *Nevada* I was stationed at the forward hoses on a sound-powered phone. Those phones worked just like two cans connected by a string. Mine consisted of a headset and a large microphone, attached to a chest plate. The entire thing was attached by cord to the *Nevada* so we could talk back and forth. [*Author's note:* Ships prone to suffer damage in combat must have an internal communication system independent of electricity, and thus the phone system powered by voice.]

Those big battleships like the *Nevada* had blisters built around their hulls to protect them from torpedoes. But blisters create big waves, and one of those big waves suddenly forced *Dale* away from the *Nevada.* All the fueling hoses broke away, but I was still connected with the phones. A bosun mate quickly took out a knife and cut the phone's cord. I still wore the phones, but they weren't attached to the *Nevada* anymore!

The Old Man on the *Nevada* ordered us to send his phones back, so while *Dale* maneuvered close to *Nevada*, I went way forward and perched on the peak of the bow so I could toss them back. You can't imagine how cold, cold, cold I was, perched there in the wind and icy cold spray, waiting for the ships to come together. When I finally got the go ahead, I tossed those phones clear up to the bridge on the *Nevada.* But just then, another wave caught and lifted us up on top of the *Nevada*'s blister. There was a giant grating sound as our little tin can bounced up and down along [the] top of the giant *Nevada*'s blister. It ripped a hole in *Dale*'s mess hall real close to the water line. But *Nevada* got the worst of it because our anchor caught on her 20mm guns and ripped them right off the ship. The *Nevada* had to return to Seattle for repairs, and that's how [the] little *Dale* put [the] big *Nevada* out of commission over a pair of sound-powered phones.

Author's note: To avoid running up on rocks, an old rule-of-thumb of arctic fisherman was to never approach a fog-enshrouded island closer than the sound of barking sea lions. But to retake Attu, the Americans would have to ignore the old rule and brave treacherous currents, uncharted rocks, and glutinous fog to land soldiers on sand beaches secreted among jagged volcanic rock outcroppings. One landing was planned for the north side of Attu and one for the south. *Dale* was assigned to screen the southern task force to the beaches of Massacre Bay. Given what happened to the *Worden* during the invasion of Amchitka, everyone aboard would be on alert.

Lester Dailey Diary, May 11: Well I had the mid-watch and is it ever foggy. Worst I've seen yet. Visibility about 100 feet. The *McDonough* and *Sicard* had a collision but I don't know how much damage was done. [*Author's note:* *McDonough* and *Sicard* were approaching Attu in pea soup–thick fog with the rest of the invasion fleet on the evening of May 10. The *Sicard*, distrusting her erratic surface search radar set, relied on stopwatch dead reckoning to hold her station with the task group. The *McDonough*, maneuvering to conform to the transports she was screening, cut in front of the *Sicard* and was rammed. There were no casualties on either ship and both made it back to port safely. However, both had been assigned critical missions during the invasion and other ships had to take their places in the dense fog.] We are on course 190° T for Attu, coming in from the north, navigating by radar. At 0515 we had GQ as we are about twenty-five miles from Attu. As we got nearer we got one glimpse of it through the fog. We are south of Massacre Bay off Chirikoff and Alexai points and are covering the transports while they land troops by landing barges. Still very foggy and can't see over 500 yards. The landing started a little before noon and went on all day. The *Pennsylvania* and *Idaho* are shelling the beach where the main encampment is this afternoon on the north side of the island at Holtz Bay. The Japs have offered no resistance yet and our troops have already started landing stores. Pushover so far. At GQ until 1900. Sure tired but have the 2000–2400 watch. Still foggy.

USS Dale War Diary, *May 11: 2000–2400* Steaming as before off Alexai and Chirikoff points, Attu Island, Alaska, covering landing of troops from *Haywood, Zeilin, Perida,* and *Harris. 2011* Proceeded on various courses and speeds showing eight landing craft, lost in fog, way back to USS *Zeilin. 2107* Returned to patrol area. *2319* Proceeded on various courses at various speeds, leading another group of loaded landing barges, lost in fog, to the *Dewey*, who has pilot duties. *2359* Returning to patrol area.

Lester Dailey Diary, *May 13*: The *Pennsylvania* was attacked by a sub but the torpedoes missed. Fighting still going on. We got reports more Jap troops have been landed here up at Holtz Bay, where the main encampment is. Reports say we have got a number of captured Jap landing barges. We anchored in the main channel to Massacre Bay, too close to the beach. The Japs have already strafed the transports from the beach and you can even see the gunfire. I think the Battle of Attu is going to be another Guadalcanal.

Ernest "Dutch" Smith: Our job was to take the landing craft into the beach, but it was so foggy we couldn't see anything, much less the landing craft we were supposed to lead. Everybody was very nervous about all the uncharted rocks in the water. We had already lost the *Worden* on the rocks of Amchitka. If we ran up on some rocks it would mean almost instant death because the water was so cold a body just could not take it. On our second trip to the beach we brought back a bunch of soldiers from the first wave whose feet had already frozen.

Lester Dailey Diary, *May 24*: A PBY crashed into the bay close to where we were anchored. The depth charges it was carrying blew up and killed everyone aboard. They carried the dead aboard the *Dale* for the doctor to see. It was a pretty gruesome sight.

Author's note: On May 29, the approximately 2,000 Japanese soldiers still on Attu launched one of the biggest banzai charges of the war, which ended when the last five hundred, surrounded and without hope, blew themselves up with hand grenades. Second only to Iwo Jima, Attu was one of the most gruesome island battles in the Pacific Theater. The Americans listed 3,829 casualties, roughly 25 percent of the total invasion force, including 549 killed, 1,148 injured, and 1,200 cold-related injuries. Of the Japanese defenders, 2,351 were interred by American burial parties and 28 surrendered. Radio Tokyo declared the island had "little or no economic value" and was but "a small episode in the broad current of the war."[3] Radio Tokyo's claims notwithstanding, the invasion of Attu isolated the remaining Japanese stronghold of Kiska and provided the Americans with many lessons for invading Japanese-held islands.

JUNE TO AUGUST: KISKA ISLAND

The guns had not yet ceased firing on Attu when the Army Corps of Engineers began building new airstrips on the island. Kiska was now completely surrounded by air and sea, and attacked daily by bombers and ships. The impossibility of this position was not lost on the Japanese, and on June 8, Rear Admiral Akiyama ordered the island to be evacuated. Unaware of this intention, the Americans proceeded with their plans for a massive invasion. During this time, *Dale* steamed in endless circles through relentless fogs to prevent the Japanese from reinforcing their position on Kiska.

Lester Dailey Diary, *June 5*: No dope. Took on some second-class mail today but none was for me. Still around Attu. Sure disgusting.

June 15: There is really no use of keeping this diary as all we do is patrol and ships come and go—all except us. Very foggy weather now.

June 24: Expect to be here at Adak for five days. After tying up received mail. Oh boy, a letter from Max! Boy, I'd give anything I've got to see her and be with her again, but it looks like we'll be lucky to get back yet this year the way things look now. I think we'll take Kiska before we return, and after we take it, we'll be on patrol a long time till things are squared away completely! Saw movie. Liberty was granted but I didn't go. Ice cream and lots of it.

June 28: Well, well. Finally went ashore! It was the first time since we were in Cold Bay on April 30. That is fifty-nine days without setting foot on any earth!

Jim Sturgill: While ashore in Alaska a crewman came back to the *Dale* with a salmon. We took it down into the engine room and cooked it. It tasted so good! I went to the officer of the deck and asked permission to go ashore and get enough salmon for the whole crew. He balked at first, and then said, "All right, go ahead!" I enlisted some help and we went ashore and walked up the creek a way to where we met a soldier standing along the bank. I asked him if he knew where we could find some fishing gear. "How many fish do you want?" he asked. When we told him we were trying to feed the entire crew, he took out a hand grenade and tossed it into a big pool. And that's how we fed the entire crew of the *Dale* a dinner of fresh salmon!

Lester Dailey Diary, *July 14*: Liberty all afternoon. From 1300 to 2200. Ate ice cream, got boots re-heeled, visited Glenn, drank beer and saw U.S.O. show. Good time. Back aboard at 2200. Six letters from Max! Boy am I happy!!!!!

July 25: Above Kiska today. No Japs but all indications say they are here. Our cruiser group ninety miles south of Kiska reported they had picked up three targets. Also reported seven unidentified planes overhead but no more dope was reported.

Author's note: While *Dale* blockaded the northern approaches to Kiska on July 26, a task group of battleships, cruisers, and destroyers led by Rear Admiral Robert "Ike" Giffen guarded the island's southern approaches.

Early in the evening, a patrolling PBY called in a report of seven Japanese ships to the west of Kiska. Giffen immediately turned his task force to the west for a high-speed run on the reported ships. At approximately midnight, *Mississippi*, *Idaho*, *Wichita*, and *Portland* reported radar contacts with enemy ships at fifteen miles. When the range closed to eight miles, Giffen's ships opened up, pouring nearly a thousand rounds of 14- and 8-inch fire at the radar contacts, or "pips." No American ship was hit during this engagement.

At dawn, Giffen launched a search plane that circled the area but found nothing—no ships, no debris, no wreckage, nothing. It then became clear that Giffen's force had been firing at the radar reflections of distant islands, and thus the engagement became known famously as "The Battle of the Pips."

On July 28, while Giffen's task group was southeast of Kiska refueling and replenishing, a Japanese task force of two cruisers and six destroyers led by Rear Admiral Masatomi Kimura slipped through the island's unguarded southwestern approaches and into fog-enshrouded Kiska harbor. Within fifty-five minutes, Kimura evacuated the entire Kiska garrison of 5,138 men and steamed off into the fog without leaving the Americans the slightest notion of his maneuver.

Though Kiska was now a deserted island, the unsuspecting Americans went full steam ahead with plans to attack the island with a force of nearly one hundred ships and thirty-five thousand troops.

Lester Dailey Diary, *July 28*: Still West of Attu. No more dope and no Japs! Still foggy. The *Edwards* reported a torpedo wake today and later one passed directly beneath us early in the morning. It was set too deep. A shallower setting would have hit us below the bridge and sunk us like a rock!

July 30: Fog and rain. The tanker joined us shortly before noon and we commenced fueling operations. We also got mail! Yippee . . . eight letters from Max! They transferred a guy by the name of Kilgore to the tanker for transport to San Francisco because he went nuts! That's the Aleutians for you!

K. G. Robinson: The Aleutian theater was not my favorite place. And come to think about it, nobody else seemed to like it very much, either. We steamed around the Bering Sea for nearly six months before finally setting foot on land, and when we finally did, the crew got into some rotgut liquor in a native village. Boy, did that ever start a ruckus! And, as *Dale*'s executive officer, I had to deal with it!

I also had to deal with *Dale*'s mental cases. And we had a few! I remember one evening a seaman came running into the wardroom and asked Dr. Trachtenberg to come look at Kilgore, who supposedly had gone into a coma down in the galley. When Doc examined young Kilgore, he saw that he was conscious enough to be eating something, but not coherent enough to talk. Doc questioned the galley crew and learned that Kilgore had been hanging around asking for handouts. Investigating further, he found a note from Kilgore predicting that he would go back to San Francisco, get married, die, and then ascend to heaven where he would sit on the left hand of God! Doc came back to the wardroom and told us about Kilgore's condition. He speculated that Kilgore had gone nuts because he was starved as a youngster growing up in the mountains of Tennessee. When we sent Kilgore across to the supply ship in a bosun's chair, he called back over his shoulder, "Hey boys, I'll take good care of all the girls for you!" I recall a lot of the men asking me afterwards, "If I go nuts, will you send me back, too?"

Mike Callahan: We spent months up there groping around in the fog with our only eyes being *Dale's* primitive search radar. We lost five men for mental reasons. The lack of sun just drove them crazy. When we sent one of them, Kilgore, across to a supply ship in the bosun's chair, the executive officer turned to me and said, "I'm not so sure he's the crazy one!"

Earl "Jitterbug" Pearson: Up in the Aleutians there were long periods of time with not much to do. One night down in the fire room, I got to dreaming about getting a tattoo when we finally got back to civilization. The thought of getting that tattoo bugged me until finally I said to the guys, "When we get back, I'm going to get myself a tattoo!" Someone said, "Ah, you're too chicken to get a tattoo!" And so we made a twenty-dollar bet, and that was a lot of money back then!

Robert "Pat" Olson: It was pretty well known the Aleutians were no place to retire. It was always cold, wet, and overcast. We never saw the sun. Everything was cockeyed and depressing, so I learned how to gamble. It was my lifesaver. Oh, I didn't gamble for the money, but rather for the enjoyment of watching how different guys reacted to winning and losing. I never did take the money seriously, and because of that, I won more than I lost and was able to send a lot of money home to Mom. But some guys would start losing and just have to win it back. They would try and try until everything they had was gone. One of them was a young kid named Lyle. To make extra money he sold subscriptions to *Our Navy* magazine. I felt sorry for him and bought five subscriptions for the different members of my family. But nobody ever received a copy of the magazine, because Lyle lost all the money playing craps. I was ordered to report as a witness for his general court-martial. I felt sorry for the kid and passed a petition around to have him released. The XO called me in and said, "Olson, I advise you not to pursue this petition." Poor Lyle should have known better than to steal from his shipmates.

USS Dale *War Diary,* *August 2*: *1600–1800* Steaming as before. *1657* Took station 3025 on USS *Tennessee.* All ships adjusted stations for firing to Starboard. *1713* Commenced bombardment of Kiska Island, USS *Dale* on target No. 108. *1722* Ceased shore bombardment. 200 rounds of 5"/38 cal. AA common projectiles expended.

Lester Dailey Diary, August 2: Never been so close in to Kiska before. At 1530 we went to GQ. Kiska was then visible. We steamed down the East side at 18,000 yards from the enemy gun emplacements and let them have it!! We fired fifty rounds per gun, 200 rounds! The enemy returned some fire but very little!! The wagons sure opened up. No enemy planes or subs opposed us. When we had completed we headed northeast and then circled back to the north. [*Author's note*: Reports of the enemy, which had evacuated Kiska on July 28, were quite numerous. Some examples: air spotters flying over the island on August 2 reported "light flack" and tracers from enemy machine guns. One flyer even reported strafing a Japanese soldier and watching him "fall flat."[4]]

August 10: Adak Harbor. Went to the Beach today and got two teeth filled. Sure muddy and nasty. No army for me!!! Lots of ships are here, including eight new DDs fresh from the States. Everyone talks about going back to the States as soon as we take Kiska. It's supposed to be the straight dope, too! Sure hope so.

August 15: Went to GQ at 0635. Going in South of Kiska in Vega Bay. Very foggy. Visibility about 200 yards. PT boats are operating with us. We are going to fake a PT landing in Vega on the South Part of Kiska. Tomorrow we will really land the troops on the NW part of Kiska. This is just a bluff to draw the Japs. But we can't even see the beach, and I don't think the Japs can see our PT boats! This duty is sure getting the best of the crew for I really believe we are going a little insane. After all, we are going on eight months up here now. Don't know how much more we will have to take, either!! If I could only see and be with Max again!

Bill Ryan: As firecontrolman, I was stationed up in the gun director, which is above the bridge at the highest part of the ship. My job was to bring the gun director's diamond over the target and keep pulling the trigger. From what I could see, Kiska was just a bunch of big, old bald rocks with what looked like moss growing all over them. But it was really foggy. Over the radio I heard the soldiers talk about the thick fog and not being able to see the enemy. And then later they found the enemy and started shooting, but it turned out they were actually shooting at each other and were finally ordered to stop.

USS *Dale* steams through pre-war fleet exercises off San Diego. *U.S. Navy photograph*

Robert Olson (right) bellies up to the Honolulu photographer's bar with unidentified shipmate. *Robert Olson collection*

Farragut-class destroyers of DesDiv 2 in San Diego fleet exercises. Including, from left, USS *Aylwin, Monaghan,* and *Dale. U.S. Navy photograph*

USS *Dale* sailors Tom Martin and John Miller enjoy peaceful moments before December 7, 1941. *John Miller collection*

Equipment transfer from USS *Dale* to unidentified Task Force 1 battleship during the Battle of Midway in June 1942. *U.S. Navy photograph*

Swimmers enjoy the waters of Palikula Bay, Espiritu Santo, New Hebrides, during the 1942 campaign for Guadalcanal. *U.S. Navy photograph*

Captured Japanese photograph of attack on Pearl Harbor, looking eastward across Ford Island. USS *Dale* was anchored in the East Loch north of the island, with sister ships *Aylwin*, *Farragut*, and *Monaghan*. *U.S. Navy photograph*

USS *Wasp* torpedoed and sunk in Torpedo Alley off Guadalcanal by
Japanese submarine I-19 on September 15, 1942. *U.S. Navy photograph*

Robert Olson's
Shellback
Certificate, earned
by crossing the
equator and
participating in
the ceremony
initiating
"pollywogs" to
"shellbacks."
*Robert Olson
collection*

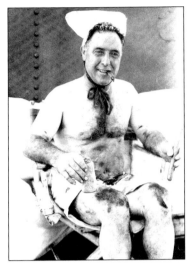

Chief Petty Officer "Pop" Maher plays the role of the Royal Baby for the initiation of *Dale*'s pollywogs. *Robert Olson collection*

Pollywogs, whether captain or mess cook, must crawl under one rope and over the next while getting swatted all around the ship. Note the poised paddle blade! *Robert Olson collection*

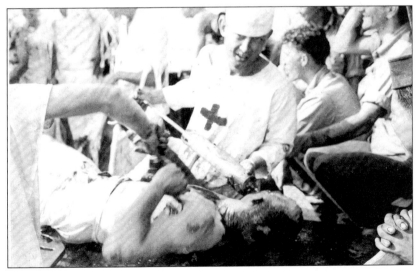

Shellback medics administer emergency drugs—most likely leftover slop from the enlisted men's galley—to pollywogs while crossing the equator. *Robert Olson collection*

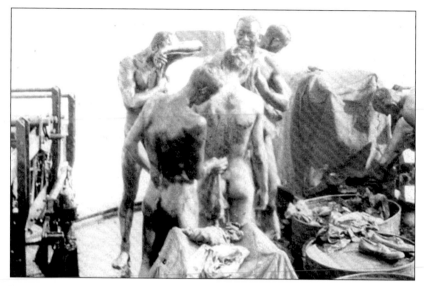

Newly minted shellbacks talk about what they will do for the next crossing of the equator as they clean up from the last crossing. *Robert Olson collection*

Crew abandons ship after USS *Worden* runs onto rocks off Constantine Harbor, Amchitka, January 12, 1943. Approaching landing craft rescued all but fourteen sailors, who drowned in the frigid waters as *Worden* broke up and sank. *U.S. Navy photograph*

USS *Salt Lake City* firing at Japanese cruisers astern in the Battle of the Komandorski Islands, March 26, 1943. Note smoke from accompanying destroyers. *U.S. Navy photograph*

USS *Pruitt* leads landing craft to fog-shrouded invasion beaches of Attu on May 11, 1943. *U.S. Navy photograph*

Earl "Jitterbug" Pearson, with unidentified sailor, shows off a new tattoo while at anchor in Pearl Harbor, December 1943. *Earl Pearson collection*

Earl "Jitterbug" Pearson loads 5-inch projectiles during operations against Eniwetok Atoll in the Marshall Islands. *Earl Pearson collection*

Robert Olson (right) and unidentified sailor model destroyer-at-sea attire while at Majuro Atoll in 1944. *Robert Olson collection*

USS *Dale* during the May 1944 Task Force 58 carrier raids, taken from the USS *Yorktown. U.S. Navy photograph*

USS *Dale* performing messenger duty in Saipan-bound convoy in June 1944. *U.S. Navy photograph*

USS *Dale* alongside USS *New Mexico* during operations against Saipan in June 1944. *U.S. Navy photograph*

Japanese plane shot down while attacking USS *Kitkun Bay* off the Marianas Islands in June 1944. *U.S. Navy photograph*

USS *Dale* comes out of a Puget Sound Navy Yard overhaul sporting a brand-new coat of camouflage paint in October 1944. *U.S. Navy photograph*

USS *Ward* hit and sunk by a kamikaze at Leyte on December 7, 1944, exactly three years after she had fired the first shot of the Pacific War while on patrol off Pearl Harbor. *U.S. Navy photograph*

Torpedo maintenance aboard the USS *Dale* in an unidentified South Sea port. *Earl Pearson collection*

Sole survivors of the 550 crewmen who served aboard the USS *Hull* and *Spence* during Typhoon Cobra in the Philippine Sea, December 1944. *U.S. Navy photograph*

Sailors look for some solid ground at Mog Mog, the fleet recreational island at Ulithi Atoll, January 1945. *U.S. Navy photograph*

Mog Mog became known as "Beer Island" for tens of thousands of enlisted men who would drink over 7.6 million cans of beer and soft drinks on its sandy beaches. *U.S. Navy photograph*

Herman Toscano (second from left) and Hugh "Okie" Nelson (far right) pose with two unidentified sailors for Earl "Jitterbug" Pearson's camera somewhere in the South Pacific. *Earl Pearson collection*

Fleet gathers at Ulithi Atoll for the invasion of Iwo Jima. *U.S. Navy photograph*

Ships in Kerama Retto anchorage spread an anti-kamikaze smoke screen, May 3, 1945, as seen from USS *Sargent Bay*. *U.S. Navy photograph*

USS *Bunker Hill* hit by two kamikazes within thirty seconds off Okinawa on May 11, 1945. *U.S. Navy photograph*

Kamikaze shot down near Okinawa on May 14, 1945, as seen from the USS *Randolph*. *U.S. Navy photograph*

Earl "Jitterbug" Pearson and Herman Toscano celebrate the end of the war by having their photograph taken with a Hotel Street hostess. *Earl Pearson Collection*

USS *Dale*'s last Plan of the Day.
John Miller collection

Secretary of the Navy's end-of-war thank-you letter. *Robert Olson collection*

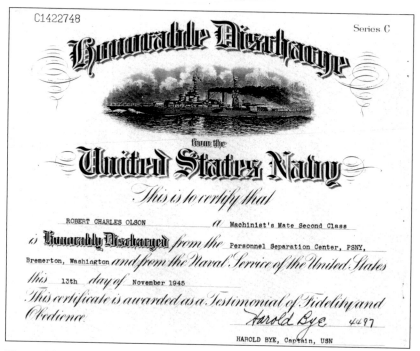

Honorable Discharge. *Robert Olson collection*

Lester Dailey Diary, *August 16:* When I went on watch early this morning we had moved to an area West of Wolf Point at the NW end of upper Kiska. The troops are landing today by a bunch of lakes on the West side of Kiska, about six miles from the main Jap encampment. We were at GQ a long time today. When the troops finally made it to the main Jap camp all they found was some booby traps, a pot of warm coffee and one dead Jap. Something funny!!????

August [18]: We were called to GQ at 0315. The *Abner Read* either hit a mine or got torpedoed in the stern. She has sixty-one men missing and twenty-six injured!!

At 0134 *Abner Read* (DD-526) had run into a Japanese mine off the coast of Kiska. The resulting explosion was so powerful it completely severed her stern. She lost seventy men, dead or missing, and another forty-seven were wounded. USS *Bancroft* (DD-598) towed what remained of her to Adak. *Abner Read* was repaired, returned to duty, and sunk by a kamikaze off Leyte Gulf in the Philippines.

Meanwhile, American army troops on Kiska had groped their way to the enemy's main encampment, only to find signs of a hurried evacuation. Nervous soldiers nevertheless shot at targets in the swirling mists before they were identified. As a consequence, twenty-five soldiers were killed and thirty-one wounded by friendly fire. The only live enemy found on Kiska was a mongrel dog. The Japanese, by then safely ensconced at Paramushiro, most certainly listened with glee to Radio Tokyo accounts of the landings on the deserted Kiska.

When the outlying islands of Buldir and Rat had been scoured for Japanese holdouts, the Aleutian Island campaign finally came to a close. With the Aleutians now firmly in America's hands, the question of what to do with the desolate islands had to be answered. Would the Aleutians be used as a staging area for an invasion of Japan? Although promoted by advocates in Washington, D.C., the plan was shot down by those who had served in the Aleutians and knew its conditions. The only suitable answer seemed to be "as little as possible." American bases were established, staffed, and maintained at Adak and Attu, from which occasional bombing raids were conducted on the Japanese base at Paramushiro. The Japanese returned the favor with occasional half-hearted raids on Attu and Kiska. For the most, however, everyone turned their backs on the frozen wastes of the north and steamed off for warmer waters.

SEPTEMBER: ALEUTIAN ISLANDS
TO PEARL HARBOR

Of the U.S. Navy ships that participated in the Aleutian campaign, some were conscripted to serve out the war guarding the Aleutians and Alaska; others would be sent back to the States for rest, recuperation, and overhaul; and others, including the USS *Dale*, would be sent south to help kick off the next great campaign in the Pacific war.

Mike Callahan: I got ashore once in eight and a half months, and that was for three hours! At one time up there, *Dale* was under way for eighty-nine days in a row. It was a terrible place. The sun either never came up or never broke through the fog. All I could think was that it was a God-awful place to die.

Gene Gould: Going home? Not after Kiska! All aboard the *Dale* were aware of newspaper stories stating that all ships involved in the Aleutian campaign would be returned to the continental U.S. for leave and recreation prior to Christmas 1943. We were all shocked and disappointed when we learned that *Dale* had been ordered to Hawaii.

Lester Dailey Diary, *September 5*: Still anchored but will get underway this afternoon for Pearl Harbor. Hooray!!! We've got almost nine months in this God-forsaken hole. We deserve it! We are really and truly going to Pearl Harbor!

September 7: Through the Amukta Pass and into the North Pacific early this morning. Heading 161° True. Speed ten knots. Late today we could just barely see the Aleutians. I'll bet it will be a long time before we see them again!

Darel Bright: After nine months we were finally relieved of duty in the Aleutians. But instead of going back to the States, like so many of the other ships, we got orders for the South Pacific! Though very dispirited about not being able to go home, we all loved the change of weather as we steamed steadily south toward Hawaii.

Lester Dailey Diary, *September 9*: Today it warmed up a bit. Nice day.

September 10: Hotter yet. Very nice day. It'll be getting hotter than this soon. We are all getting our whites ready for Captain's inspection and *liberty!!* in Honolulu.

September 11: Captain's inspection this morning. 900 miles to go. Hottest day yet!

September 12: Phew!! Hot day!! Turned in all winter clothing. 782 miles to go!

September 13: Hot. Phew!!

September 14: Should get in tomorrow. Hot.

September 15: Early this morning Kauai was visible. Later on Oahu. Sure looks good.

September 17: Wow! Liberty today! Mel and I went over. Got new dungarees and whites. Saw lots of women and had a drink or two.

Earl Hicks: We had been steaming around the Bering Sea for nine months without stop. When we finally got back to Pearl we tied up next to one of the new *Fletcher*-class cans fresh from the States. [*Author's note:* In 1941, the U.S. Navy began building a fleet of large destroyers to rival the Japanese "special types" then in service. By late 1943, these flush-deck "2100 tonners," which were fast, roomy, and capable of absorbing enormous punishment, displaced the *Farragut*-class 1500s as the mainstay of the U.S. Navy's destroyer fleet.] It was the first 2100 I had seen, and it was a lot bigger and had more guns than the *Dale*. It even had a flush deck with internal passageways and two engine rooms and two fire rooms. It was big and it was beautiful! When we tied up alongside, its crew gathered along the rails and looked down on us. You could see them whispering back and forth. Then I realized that we were solid rust from top to bottom, and they probably thought we were slackers. There just was no way we could keep *Dale* painted while steaming around the Aleutians!

Earl "Jitterbug" Pearson: When we finally got to Pearl I went down to the first tattoo parlor I could find and got me a tattoo. But by the time I got back to the ship to collect on my bet, I bled clean through the bandage and my uniform. The OOD took one look at me and confined me to quarters without pay until I healed! But I won that twenty-dollar bet!

Bela "Shorty" Smith: One of the happiest times aboard the *Dale* was when we pulled into Pearl Harbor after steaming around the Bering Sea for nine months. There was liberty for everyone, lots of pretty girls, and it was warm. Whatever you wanted was waiting right there for you. It was paradise!

Mike Callahan: As the executive officer, my job was to keep the guys from slacking, but after nine months in the Bering Sea, the tropical airs of Pearl had us all a bit lazy. One day the leading chief and I were making rounds getting the guys to put away their mattresses after a session of airing out the bedding. There were mattresses slung about everywhere. I could tell some slackers were up in the searchlight tub napping behind their mattresses and was about to yell at them when the new 2100 tied up next to us and took care of the matter for me. Two recruits on that 2100 were messing around with the twin 50-caliber machine gun when they accidentally cut loose with a burst that shredded the mattresses hanging on *Dale's* searchlight tub. I told the chief, "That ought to wake 'em up!" Sure enough, those slackers came flying wild-eyed out of that tub so fast their feet never touched the deck until they landed way down below on the mess deck!

Hugh Melrose: By late forty-three, *Dale* had become a second-stringer to the new 2100s, but that didn't mean they were any better. One day we steamed out of Pearl for some antiaircraft gunnery practice. *Dale* was at the end of a line of 2100s when a PBY came flying down the line towing a target sleeve. The line opened up and everyone missed until it flew by the *Dale*. We shot the sleeve to shreds. The PBY then turned around and came flying back up the line. We blasted the shreds to nothing, so the PBY had to go get another sleeve. When it came back up the line with the new sleeve, the order was passed, "All ships but *Dale* commence firing!"

OCTOBER: CENTRAL PACIFIC AND WAKE ISLAND
Admiral Yamamoto's worst fears about the industrial potential of the United States were being realized.

In 1940, the U.S. Maritime Commission began building five new shipyards throughout the United States. The 1941 Japanese attack on Pearl Harbor accelerated this effort into a national "emergency ship-building program," in which the nation's experienced shipyards built complicated navy ships, such as aircraft carriers, while the new ship-yards, which sprang up almost overnight around the country, built less-complicated ships, such as "Liberty" transports. Nicknamed "Ugly Duckling" by President Franklin Roosevelt, these ships were con-structed using a standardized mass production system in which a quarter million parts were prefabricated at plants throughout the country and welded together at shipyards in as little as five days. One Liberty ship could carry 2,840 jeeps, 440 tanks, or 230 million rounds of ammunition. Liberty ships were named after prominent Americans, beginning with the signers of the Declaration of Independence. By 1943, the emergency shipbuilding program included twenty-four large *Essex*-class carriers and nine of the light *Independence*-class carriers, which were built on cruiser hulls.

Carrier attack groups built around the new *Essex*- and *Independence*-class carriers included fast battleships, cruisers, destroyers, tankers, and submarines. These powerful attack groups raised many questions for the officers responsible for managing them: Can a carrier attack force stand up to the unsinkable island carriers of the Japanese? Can so many ships be made to work as a single unit? What is the most efficient way to use the task force? How can a task force rescue its downed pilots? To find answers to the questions, the U.S. Navy conducted practice raids on Japanese-held strongholds on Marcus, Tarawa, and Makin Islands during August and September. Then in early October, a massive task force was built around the carriers *Essex, Yorktown, Lexington, Cowpens, Independence,* and *Belleau Wood. Dale* would help screen this massive armada on a raid of Wake Island—finally getting a chance to go to Wake after being called back to Pearl Harbor in December 1941. After nearly two years of occupation, only a fraction of those captured when the Japanese took the island remained. The marines and sailors had been shipped off to camps in China in May 1942, and the following September 265 of the remaining civilian contractors had been sent to Yokohama, Japan; in late 1943, there were still ninety-eight American POWs providing labor for the Japanese.

Hugh Melrose: The new fast carrier task force bound for Wake was much bigger than anything we had ever screened before. It was divided into two groups. Each group had three carriers and three battleships, with thirty-two destroyers on an outside ring and six cruisers on an inside ring. By this stage of the war, *Dale* had become a second-stringer to the new 2100s, so we were expendable. *Dale*'s job was to get between the capital ships and the enemy to protect them from bombs and torpedoes. The idea was to take the torpedo in the bow and not in the boiler room. But you could never really count on taking a torpedo in the right place. Five other tin cans went down taking torpedoes in the wrong place.

Author's note: On October 5 and 6, planes from the fast carrier attack force made 738 sorties against Japanese-held Wake Island. Cruisers and destroyers also shelled the island. The Japanese figured this ferocious attack signaled an imminent invasion, so the commanding officer, Admiral Sakaibara, ordered the execution of the ninety-eight American civilians in order "to eliminate any threat they might pose." They were bound hand and foot, blindfolded, shot, and buried in a common grave in an antitank ditch on the northern tip of the island. The attack force had never intended to invade.[5]

The fast carrier attack force proved to be capable of standing up to the unsinkable island carriers of the Japanese. In fact, a raid on the Japanese stronghold at Rabaul by a task force built around *Saratoga,*

Princeton, Essex, Bunker Hill, and *Independence* withstood vicious counterattacks from all of the island's front-line fighters, without suffering a single blow to any of the carriers.

After these practice raids, the American carriers and their screens retired to rest before the opening of Operation Galvanic, the invasion of Makin and Tarawa atolls in the Gilbert Islands.

NOVEMBER: GILBERT ISLANDS

Operation Orange, the American plan for the conquest of Japan, consisted of a drive from the Marshall Islands straight west across the Central Pacific to the home islands. General Douglas MacArthur, however, objected to Orange because a full-force campaign in the Marshalls would divert resources from his drive on the Japanese stronghold of Rabaul in the South Pacific. By way of compromise, the Joint Chiefs of Staff gave its approval for Operation Galvanic, the invasion of the Gilbert Islands.

Admiral Chester Nimitz brought together a force of two hundred ships, thirty-five thousand troops, and six thousand vehicles from bases throughout the Pacific, and divided them into four task forces. Task Force 50, commanded by Rear Admiral Charles Pownall, consisted of three groups of ten fast carriers tasked with the suppression of enemy air forces. Task Force 52, commanded by Admiral Richard Turner in the *Pennsylvania*, would sail south from Pearl Harbor, cross the equator, then sail due west and attack Makin Atoll. Task Force 53, commanded by Admiral Harry Hill, would sail north from New Zealand and attack Tarawa Atoll. Task Force 57, commanded by Rear Admiral John Hoover, consisted of supporting land-based aircraft based on Funafuti and Canton Islands.

Though no longer the cutting edge of the U.S. Navy, the USS *Dale* would nevertheless find herself leading this entire fleet of two hundred ships into battle.

Gene Gould: After a quick overhaul in a Pearl Harbor dry dock, *Dale* received orders to proceed south to Canton Island to pick up some LSTs full of Marines. [*Author's note:* LSTs (Landing Ship Tanks) were amphibious vessels designed to deliver equipment and men directly from the high seas onto enemy-held beaches. Their relatively flat keels made them extremely slow sailers, and they were consequently called "Large Slow Targets" by those who sailed them.] From Canton we would sail west to Makin Atoll in the Gilberts. This resulted in our crossing the equator on the way down to Canton. The skipper author-ized an initiation of pollywogs by the shellbacks although he, too, was a pollywog. Among the shellbacks was a fellow junior officer from California who rejoiced in telling us all the things he was going to do to us during the initiation. It got to the point that we pollywogs joined together to stand up to his threats. We actually ganged up on him and cut all his hair off! So when it came time for us pollywogs to go through the shellback line, he had the "Royal Barber" shave the hair completely off each one of us. Though it was a bit humiliating at the moment, it would later turn out to be a very good thing!

Bill Ryan: When we crossed the equator on our way down to the Gilberts my buddy, Bob Nearing, wrote up my pollywog summons. He said I was employed by the Gainesville Chamber of Commerce and guaranteed no *Dale* shellback could lift my ass off the deck with a paddle! In those days, our produce came in wooden boxes, and shell-backs used the staves from those boxes as paddles. But I wasn't the only pollywog on the *Dale*. Captain Aldrich was one, too!

A bunch of *Dale* shellbacks were talking about how they were going to really tear up Aldrich's behind when he came through the ini-tiation line. When the chief heard them, he said, "You silly fools! Aldrich might be a pollywog today, but he's going to be captain again tomorrow. If you hit that man hard today, you will pay for it harder tomorrow!" The chief's wisdom seemed to get through, as the talk cooled down a bit. Now, I've never been one to kiss an officer's butt, but I'll tell you, I got right behind Captain Aldrich in that line and, as we crawled around the deck on our hands and knees, I stayed as close behind him as possible! I didn't get hit very hard, either; at least until I got up to where my buddy Nearing was stationed.

Hugh Melrose: At Canton Island we picked up some big box-shaped LSTs to screen. They were real slow, and our cruising speed went from twenty-four knots down to six, which made us extremely vulnerable. Since the LSTs were so slow, *Dale* was ordered to lead them to Makin Island several days before the rest of the fleet so all the ships would arrive at the same time. This meant we were out in front of the invasion force escorting some real slow LSTs. We were the perfect target for attacking aircraft and submarines, and it didn't take the Japs very long to find us.

USS **Dale** *War Diary,* *November 18, 1600–1800*: Steaming as before. *1705* Bogey contact bearing 090° T, distance 9 miles. All hands to general quarters. *1712* Sight contact bearing 010° T, distance 7 miles, identified as Japanese flying boat of Mavis Type. *1720* Lost sight and radar contact. *1730* Secured from general quarters.

1800–2000: Steaming as before. *1826* Had simultaneous radar and visual contact of Japanese flying boat of Mavis type, bearing 235° T, distance 8 miles, position angle 1°. All hands to general quarters. Closed LSTs in direction of contact. *1733* Plane came in toward LSTs flying very low, directly out of the sun. *1735* Commenced firing, range 8,000 yards.

Hugh Melrose: When that Mavis four-engine bomber came out of the sun we let loose with our 5-inch guns. In one minute we put out sixty-seven rounds! There were black smudges all around that Mavis, but it kept bearing in. We were using some of the new proximity fuses but they didn't appear to be working. Finally, the Mavis banked away and headed back over the horizon with two of its four engines smoking. One thing was for sure. We had been spotted!

Author's note: Proximity fuses emitted radio waves, measuring the Doppler effect of the returning radio waves to detonate projectiles when closest to the target. Before the invention of proximity fuses, detonation of projectiles was induced by direct contact with a target, time since launch, or altitude.

Bill Ryan: I was a lookout up on the bridge when some movement in the water caught my eye. Being new to the tropics, I thought it must be a fish. But as I watched, it grew into a torpedo that passed right underneath the ship. It must have been set too deep, because it went right underneath us clean as a whistle.

USS Dale War Diary, *November 18:* 1836 Plane turned radically to the left and proceeded to withdraw over the horizon. Ceased firing. *1855* Regained bogey radar contact bearing 180° T, distance 25 miles. Bogey proceeded to shadow task group remaining out of gun range.

November 19: 0800–1200 Steaming as before. 0908 Had bogey contact bearing 245° T, 28 miles. Closed LSTs. All hands to general quarters. *1004* Lost radar contact. Resumed normal patrol. *1030* Secured from general quarters.

1200–1600 Steaming as before. *1400* Had bogey contact bearing 255° T, distance 18,000 yards. Closed LSTs. All hands to general quarters. *1413* Sighted plane bearing 265° T, distance 15,000 yards, circling very low, identified as "Betty." *1433* Plane disappeared over horizon. *1445* Sighted "Betty" bearing 270° T, distance 15,000 yards. *1515* Enemy plane shot down by three U.S. Navy fighters. Proceeded to investigate wreckage. *1548* Arrived on scene, two dead bodies and miscellaneous wreckage. Proceeded to rejoin LSTs.

1800–2000 Steaming as before. *1830* Sighted enemy plane identified as a "Betty," bearing 010° T, distance 14,000 yards. Closed LSTs. All hands to general quarters. *1835* Plane disappeared. *1900* Sighted a Betty bearing 147° T, distance 12,000 yards, flying very low. *1929* Enemy plane commenced low level run on formation. *1930* Opened fire on plane. *1932* Ceased firing, expended 50 rounds of five-inch Mk 32 proximity projectiles, no casualties. *1949* Had simultaneous bogey radar contacts bearing 120° T, distance 10,000 yards and 270° T, 9,000 yards. *1950* Commenced firing at enemy plane bearing 270° T. *1952* Ceased firing. *1955* Float flares dropped by planes landed in water dead ahead and dead astern.

Earl Hicks: Some Jap Betties picked us up in the morning and tagged along just out of gun range throughout the day. We ran them off with gunfire but they kept coming back in. When night fell they came in for the attack. It was a dark, moonless night. You couldn't see a thing out there. I was stationed with the forward repair party portside and could hear their engines as they came in for us. I turned around and saw that someone had left a porthole open. Light was pouring out into the night and I'll bet those Betties were boring in on that porthole from a thousand miles away! I picked up a dogging wrench and threw it at the open porthole. Nothing happened so I threw another one. Finally, someone reached up and closed the porthole. I heard a Betty passing right over the top of us, and when I looked up I could see the blue flame from its exhaust stacks.

Elliot Wintch: It was a real frightening night because we were on our own way out in front of the task force. It was dark and there were torpedo bombers out there. They would fly up our wake and drop a floating flare. Then they would fly up ahead and drop one directly ahead of us. They had us boxed in by the flares and dead to rights for a torpedo attack on our starboard beam. The captain heard about a cruiser that had been sunk with this tactic and so maneuvered the task group away from the floating flares.

Hugh Melrose: The torpedo bomber came in from about 130 degrees relative to starboard. The captain ordered everyone to hold fire because he didn't want to reveal our position until the very last moment. I was plotting enemy plane locations on a big plastic board in CIC, which was right below the bridge. The captain repeated that he was to be the only one to give the order to commence firing, and if anyone opened fire before he gave the order there would be hell to pay. As the Betty came in on us we sent the captain a continuous flow of information about its position relative to the *Dale*, and frequently noted the target was approaching rapidly. We fed this information over the sound-powered phones to a phone talker who was standing right next to the captain on the bridge. Since words transmitted over a sound-powered phone tend to lose their emotional impact, I editorialized a bit: "Target is now within range of our 5-inch guns. . . . Target is now within range of our forties. . . . Target is now within range of our twenties. . . . "By then all aboard the *Dale* were certain the Betty would see the fluorescence of our wake and run a torpedo into us. Finally, when the Betty was so close you could see the flames from its exhaust, the captain ordered "Commence firing!" Our gunners lit up the night with their fire and set the Jap's port engine on fire. The flaming plane was then blasted by a 40mm on the LST.

Bill Ryan: When the plane came over our twenties and forties opened up. Man, I'll tell you, those guns lit up the night sky so I could see the pilot as plain as day. He wore a leather helmet and goggles and was hunched over intent on one of the LSTs. I never saw so much fire coming from anything in my entire life! He didn't stand a chance. His plane crashed and exploded on the other side of an LST. That was the last of our night visitors.

USS Dale War Diary, *November 19:* 2240 Secured from general quarters.

Mike Callahan: After we finished escorting the LSTs we were assigned patrol duty around Makin Atoll. On the evening of the 23rd we picked a young airman out of the water from the *Liscombe Bay.* He became frantic about getting back to his ship and said, "You've got to get me back because all my things are there. . . . It's my home!" He put up such a fuss I told Doc to give him something to knock him out for the night. So he did. Next morning at dawn, a Japanese submarine torpedoed the *Liscombe Bay.* Bright orange flames shot up a thousand feet in the air, and flesh and debris showered down on surrounding ships. Within a few minutes she went down. The young airman came up to the bridge to see what was going on. I said, "See, I told you you'd be better off spending the night with us!"

The *Liscombe Bay* (CVE-56) was one of a group of "escort" carriers built on top of cruiser hulls by the Henry Kaiser Company, manufacturer of the ubiquitous World War II jeep. The lightly armored carriers thus became known as "jeep carriers." Around the fleet, CVE came to stand for "combustible, vulnerable, and expendable." Escort carriers were tasked with fill-in jobs for which large fleet carriers were ill suited, including providing close air support for ground troops and anti-submarine patrols for convoys. *Liscombe Bay* was providing close air support to ground troops when she was torpedoed by Japanese submarine I-175 off Makin Atoll. She sank in twenty-three minutes.

Operation Galvanic was a costly first step in America's Pacific crossing. Tarawa was the first time the Japanese opposed an American landing on the beach, and ignorance of how to attack well-defended coral atolls surrounded by protective reefs led to costly mistakes. Approximately one thousand marines and one thousand sailors were lost in the invasions, and newspaper accounts of the losses created doubt and fear about the prospects for future invasions. But the road across the Pacific was now open and the lessons learned at "Tragic Tarawa" would reduce the costs of future landings. With the Gilbert Islands firmly in America's hands, the USS *Dale* turned north on November 24 to escort a task group of transport ships back to Pearl Harbor.

DECEMBER: PEARL HARBOR TO SAN FRANCISCO

Gene Gould: Following Makin and Tarawa, *Dale* was conducting training operations around Maui when an officer came with a request to accompany *Dale* on its forthcoming trip to San Francisco. The captain called for the communications officer and asked him if there were any messages he hadn't seen. The communications officer said, "Yes, there is one message that I've not been able to decode yet!" The captain sent for me with an order to get the message and get it decoded posthaste. I had done a lot of decoding and was pretty good at it. Sure enough! The message was an order for *Dale* to escort a damaged ship back to the States. We were all delighted. The navy had kept its word!

We arrived in San Francisco a day or two before Christmas with a South Sea tan and, thanks to our shellback initiation, very little hair. Our barhopping was a great success because it was obvious from our

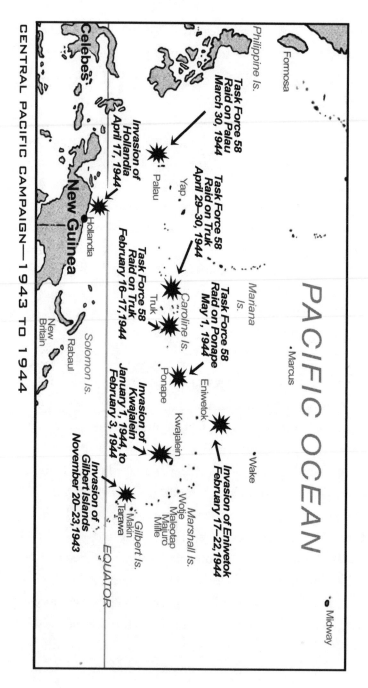

CENTRAL PACIFIC CAMPAIGN—1943 TO 1944

tans and short hair that we had just arrived from the Pacific. Everybody bought us drinks and the girls were all very friendly.

Earl Hicks: When we got to San Francisco I went to visit an old farm buddy that was running a theater. I saw him walking across Haight Street with a beautiful gal, who I thought was his date. It turned out she was just a friend, and we got to talking and I asked her out on a date. When the *Dale* went back to sea I wrote her letters. I guess you might say I left my heart in San Francisco, because somewhere out there on the Pacific I decided I wanted to marry her. I bought a ring from my old buddy Toscano, who had just received a "Dear John" letter and so happened to have an extra wedding ring in his locker. That was over fifty years ago. She's still wearing that ring today.

•

1944

After two full years of hard-fought preliminaries, the United States and Japan now faced off across the Pacific Ocean for a fight to the finish.

Japan, on defense, hunkered down behind a network of bases in the Marshall, Bismarck, Caroline, Philippine, Mariana, Bonin, and Ryukyu Islands. The Imperial Navy, secreted among this giant web of unsinkable island fortresses, lay in wait of one Tsushima-like battle that would win the war for the emperor.

The United States, on offense, plotted west from the Gilbert Islands and north from New Guinea with wolf-packs of submarines, land-based bombers, amphibious invasion forces, fast carrier attack groups, and the support units required to sustain all while far from friendly shores. The USS *Dale*, and her sister destroyers, were issued orders to protect this armada by standing in harm's way. For tin can sailors, the order of the day—every day—would be, *"Anchors aweigh, my boys . . . Anchors aweigh!"*

JANUARY TO MARCH: MARSHALL ISLANDS

Dale began her year by steaming from San Francisco to Hawaii, where she participated in training exercises. She then joined 295 ships of the Pacific fleet for Operation Flintlock, the invasion of the Marshall Islands, an archipelago of twenty-nine coral atolls and five islands about eight hundred miles northwest of the recently conquered Gilberts.

Situated like a tollbooth at the westbound entrance to the Great Pacific Highway, the Marshall Islands had always been planned as the first stop on the U.S. Navy's Pacific itinerary. This itinerary, Plan Orange, called for the invasion of the Marshalls' heavily fortified perimeter atolls— Jaluit, Maloelap, Mili, and Wotje. Very late in the planning process, Admiral Nimitz suggested the plan be changed. Instead of attacking the heavily defended perimeter islands, U.S. forces would simply steam right on by and go for the archipelago's heart—Kwajalein. Most senior planners objected, thinking it was simply too risky, given the powerful Japanese airbases located on the perimeter atolls. But Nimitz insisted his carrier forces, together with Gilbert-based fighters and bombers, could suppress the Japanese air forces, and overruled the objections.

The Americans had learned some very expensive lessons in wresting the Aleutians and Gilberts from the Japanese. Planners were determined to put those lessons to good use during the invasion of the Marshalls. This invasion began on January 30 when U.S. forces invaded the undefended Majuro Atoll and rolled on the following day when marines landed on the beaches of Kwajalein. Though the Japanese were surprised by the speed of the onrushing Americans—it had been only a month since the invasion of the Gilberts—and by the bypassing of their defended positions, they were prepared to fight.

Kwajalein

Kwajalein Atoll featured the world's largest lagoon and enough land area to build navy support units and Army Air Corp bomber fields. Though Japan had occupied the atoll since 1914, and had used it as an administrative center for the area, it had done little to develop it as a military base. By taking Kwajalein from the Japanese, and developing its military potential, U.S. forces could dominate the entire archipelago.

For the invasion, *Dale*, *Farragut*, and *Monaghan* were ordered to screen escort carriers *Sangamon*, *Suwannee*, and *Chenango* in Task Group 53.6. These relatively small, thin-skinned Jeep carriers would support the invasion with combat air patrols (CAP) and ground support missions from positions twenty miles offshore. Lacking armor and speed, the Jeeps would be sitting ducks in need of much protection from prowling Japanese submarines.

USS Dale War Diary, *January 25*: Cruising in company with TF 53 en route to Kwajalein Atoll. *1635* Carriers left the formation to recover planes, accompanied by carrier screen. *1657* A plane, landing on the USS *Sangamon*, crashed into planes parked on forward part of flight deck, starting a gasoline fire and knocking several planes and men into the water. USS *Dale* searched the area for survivors bringing aboard two at 1715. Search was continued until 1803.

Bill Eggenberger: *Dale* had a twenty-six-foot whaleboat that was always ready with a pharmacist mate and an engineer. When an airplane hit the water it usually had about twenty-two seconds before it started sinking, so we had to move real fast.

USS Dale War Diary, *31 January*: Steamed as before in company with TG 53.6 en route to carrier operation area 20 miles northeast of

Roi Island, Kwajalein Atoll, in formation 5LS. *0610* A plane from USS *Suwannee* crashed ahead of USS *Chenango* and USS *Dale* was assigned to search for survivors. Visibility was poor (due to darkness) and survivors were not picked up until 0705. Two of the crew of the TBF were taken aboard. William A. Proctor, ARM2c, went down in plane. *0735* Abandoned search and rejoined TG 53.6. Steamed as a unit, conducting flight operations the rest of the day. *1900* An F6F from the USS *Chenango* was ordered to crash land because of a faulty tail hook. Ensign J. M. Ring, USNR, was retrieved from water unhurt. *1955* Returned to station in TG 53.14 and cruised in area NE of Roi Island during the night.

Earl Hicks: Our job was to screen the Jeep carriers operating off the coast of Kwajalein. The Jeeps were there to provide close air support to the guys on the ground and CAPs for the task force. Our job was to protect them from Jap submarines. Though we were too far off the island to see much action, everybody aboard knew how important our job was because we had all seen what happened to the *Liscombe Bay* when the Japs torpedoed it down in the Gilberts. Other times our job was to be the plane guard for the carriers. During takeoffs and landings we would cruise in a carrier's wake and rescue the pilots that couldn't land. One time we were plane guarding a carrier when the planes came back all shot up. A bunch of us guys up on the bow were making ten-cent bets on which planes would make it and which ones would not.

Author's note: Within a week, one of the most complicated amphibious campaigns in history, involving landings on thirty islets, had been completed, and the whole of Kwajalein Atoll was in American hands. The lessons learned at great expense in the Aleutians and Gilberts paid handsome dividends on Kwajalein, as the number of

Americans killed in action was limited to 1 percent. In fact, Operation Flintlock had been so successful that its unused reserves would become the invasion force for Operation Catchpole, the taking of Eniwetok Atoll on the archipelago's western perimeter.

Before moving up the Pacific highway to Eniwetok, Admiral Nimitz dispatched Admiral Marc Mitscher's Task Force 58 on Operation Hailstone, an offensive sweep of Truk, the Imperial Navy's principal base in the Central Pacific.

Truk consists of several volcanic islands inside a coral ring and is situated at the geographical center of Micronesia, the Milky Way–like archipelago of more than five hundred islands stretching from due south of the Marshalls to just east of the Philippines. Truk is seven hundred miles equidistant from Rabaul in the Bismarcks and Eniwetok in the Marshalls. Since 1942, it had been the headquarters for the Imperial Navy's combined fleet and was much feared in the American press, which referred to it as "Japan's Pearl Harbor" and "The Gibraltor of the Pacific."[1] From its Truk base, the Japanese fleet posed a serious threat to MacArthur's pending operations in the Bismarcks, as well as to those of Nimitz at Eniwetok. Undeterred by the fear emanating from the press, Nimitz sent Task Force 58 to the island with orders to wreak havoc.

For three days, beginning on February 17, aircraft from Mitscher's fast carriers flew 1,250 missions over Truk, raining destruction on facilities, personnel, planes, and ships. At the same time, TF 58's battleships and cruisers, under Admiral Raymond Spruance, circled the island fortress with guns blazing. Combined, these forces destroyed more than 265 aircraft and sank more than two hundred thousand tons of shipping. However, the most significant loss suffered by the Japanese was the invincible position Truk occupied in the imagination of the American press.

Operation Hailstone set a new standard for carrier warfare. Because of the total dominance demonstrated by Task Force 58 at Truk, no longer would fast carrier task groups be used as weapons of hit and run. Now the American carriers would hit at dawn and stay till dusk for days on end.

Eniwetok

Second in size to Kwajalein, Eniwetok consists of forty small islets surrounding a central lagoon of 388 square miles. Its very name, "land between east and west," suggests its strategic significance to both sides in the Pacific theater. For the onrushing Americans, the atoll would provide an airfield and an exceptionally large lagoon to support the invasion of the Mariana Islands, which lay only one thousand miles to the west. Though *Dale* would get little rest between Operations Flintlock and Catchpole, she would get a change of duty, as orders came for her to become a gunslinger in Admiral Jesse Oldendorf's fire-support unit.

During the invasion of Tarawa in the Gilberts, U.S. Marines had suffered severe casualties because of an inadequate pre-invasion bombardment, but as the war progressed across the Pacific, the fire-support unit of Admiral Jesse Oldendorf became increasingly proficient. To avoid Oldendorf's shore bombardments, Japanese defenders began ceding beaches to the invading marines and focusing their defense inland.

USS Dale War Diary, *February 13*: Received CDS 47 secret serial 006 of 12 February 1944, giving "General Instructions" for Eniwetok operation.

John Kelsch: When we arrived at Eniwetok the entire fleet opened up on the forty little islands that ringed the lagoon.

Darel Bright: Our firepower was arranged so everyone could get his licks in. On the outside ring there was a screen of destroyers to protect against air and submarine attack. Then inside, at about thirty miles out, escort carriers launched and recovered planes. Inside the carriers were battleships, firing 16-inch guns, and then cruisers, firing 8-inchers. And finally, right up close to the beach, would be us tin cans. We could always tell when the battleships were firing their 16-inchers because the two-thousand-pound rounds would make a terrific roaring sound as they came in over our heads!

Bela "Shorty" Smith: The *Dale* was positioned off the island and ordered to cover a part of the island with gunfire. It was hard to see exactly what we were shooting at because of all the smoke and dust. So we just shot it up until the Japs shot back. Then we'd zero in on their gunfire and blast away until they quit shooting.

Charles O'Rorke: We got detached for some close-in shore bombardment on one of the little islands. Now, those coral islands do not have any mountains or hills. Most are just slices of sand and coconut trees. When you see them from a distance, they are just thin slivers of white and green separating the blue sea and sky. Somehow, we found ourselves shooting from one side of the island, while everybody else was shooting from the other side. While we were blasting away with our 5-inchers, the big old battleships on the other side were booming away with their giant 16-inchers. We had the Japs coming and going. Trouble was, the battleships were right close to the shore, which meant the trajectory of their rounds was flat. And so a bunch of those 16-inch rounds hit that narrow slip of corral and ricocheted right off in our direction. You could hear them roaring past right over our head, and they didn't sound very friendly at all! Captain Aldrich said, "Let's get the hell out of here!"

John Kelsch: There were only two ways into Eniwetok lagoon, and one of them was through a very narrow passage between two islands. Everyone was really nervous because nobody knew how the Japs would react when we steamed through that narrow passage into the lagoon.

A. D. Payne: When we cruised into Eniwetok lagoon, there were twenty-five or thirty of us lining the deck to catch the action. We were close enough to the island to count the leaves on the trees. We could hear all kinds of things going on, like the big boom of naval guns and the rat-a-tat of airplanes strafing. It was a real show! Ahead of us the battleships and cruisers went through the passage into the lagoon with their big guns depressed and pointed directly at the islands on each side. There was no enemy reaction to them at all. What we didn't know was that the Japs were just playing possum. They had successfully hidden from the cameras of the carrier planes and the binoculars of ships' lookouts and were just lying low. When *Dale* slid into that narrow passage, a Jap somewhere in the jungle couldn't stand it anymore and opened up with his machine gun. Bullets were flying everywhere. You've never seen sailors diving for hatches so fast in your life!

Author's note: On the morning of February 18, 1944, U.S. Marines landed on Engebi Island, Eniwetok Atoll. After ferocious fighting with ill-prepared defenders, Engebi was secured the same day, including its airfield. On February 22, all Japanese resistance ceased and the entire Eniwetok Atoll fell into American hands.

Majuro

Eugene Brewer: Majuro became one of the fleet's main rest areas in the Central Pacific. By "rest" I mean it was one of the few places we could go ashore and have a beer party with our ration of three warm beers. There wasn't much for us to do on those sandy beaches except eat tangerines and loaf about. And did we ever get sick of tangerines! Sometimes we would get up a little game of beach football, using a coconut as the football. We would run up and down the beach for a while and then jump into the lagoon for a swim. One time a big shark swam up real close to us without our knowing about it. We learned of its presence when an army sentry on the beach opened up on it with a machine gun. Don't know what frightened me more— the shark with the teeth or the grunt with the machine gun!

Author's note: The occupation of Kwajalein and Eniwetok, together with the neutralizing of the great Japanese stronghold at Truk, turned the momentum of the Pacific war in favor of the Americans. Lessons learned in the Aleutians and Gilberts led to masterful planning for the Marshalls, and thus the Americans were able to pierce Japan's inner defensive perimeter with less than 1 percent of its fighting men killed in action. Most importantly, the campaign restored the American public's trust in its navy. When compared with the unmitigated disaster of the Kiska invasion only six months previously, and the bloody battle for Tarawa in the Gilberts, it was easy to see lessons learned and put to use would make the road across the Pacific less costly.

For the Japanese there was only discouragement. The U.S. Navy had become so thoroughly dominant there was simply nothing the Imperial Navy could do to support its bypassed island garrisons on Jaluit, Maloelap, Mili, and Wotje. Those marooned on the tropical outposts had little to eat, except that which they could fish or farm—or each other.

March to May: Caroline Islands
and New Guinea

After a few days of rest, *Dale* became a minion of Task Force 58, then assembling in Majuro Lagoon, for operations Desecrate, Reckless, and Persecution. Desecrate was a March 28 to April 3, 1944, Task Force 58 carrier raid on Palau to prevent Japanese air forces from threatening MacArthur's invasion of Hollandia in northern New Guinea; Reckless and Persecution were April 22 Task Force 58 operations in support of MacArthur's invasion of Hollandia.

Consequent to the raid on Truk, the Imperial Navy had repositioned its surface fleet to Palau in the western Carolines. This move, however, once again put the Imperial fleet squarely between MacArthur and Nimitz; only this time the American invasions were to occur on the north coast of New Guinea and at Saipan in the Marianas. Thus, mighty Task Force 58 was again sent on the prowl with instructions to rout the Japanese from Palau and attack their positions throughout the Central and South Pacific.

Three of the Fifth Fleet's four carrier task groups gathered in Majuro Lagoon. Each task group was made up of two or three *Essex-* and *Independence*-class carriers. These fast carrier task groups were combined into Task Force 58 under the command of Admiral Marc Mitscher. On March 22, Task Force 58 sortied from Majuro Lagoon to wreak destruction upon the enemy.

Task Force 58 Raids

From the very beginning of war, the U.S. Navy's Pacific fleet included "fast carrier attack forces." But when the new *Essex-* and *Independence*-class carriers arrived in late 1943, those carrier forces came to be known as "The Fast Carrier Task Force."

The Fast Carrier Task Force was divided into carrier task groups, each of which contained between three and five carriers and escorts, including one or two of the new fast battleships, cruisers, and destroyers. Submarines often accompanied the groups to scout enemy positions and pick up downed pilots.

The Fast Carrier Task Force, designated Task Force 58 when operating under Admiral Nimitz or Task Force 38 when operating under Admiral Halsey, was the Pacific war's equivalent of the great fleets of big-gunned battleships that occupied the stage of earlier wars. When at sea, Task Force 58 was a sight to behold. Said navy historian Samuel Morison, "The age of steam has afforded no marine spectacle comparable to a meeting of Fast Carrier Forces Pacific Fleet. Now that the seaman's eye has become accustomed to the great flattops, and has learned what they can do to win command of the sea, they have become as beautiful to him as to his bell-bottomed forebears. They and the new battleships with their graceful sheer and boiling wake evoke poetic similes."[2]

A. D. Payne: You could see ships for as far as the eye could see—from horizon to horizon. There were ships everywhere! Though no one told us what our strategy was, we all figured it out soon enough. The idea was to run in on a Jap-held island from several directions, pound the hell out of it, and then look for any sign of organized resistance to show up. After our airplanes had flown off over the horizon we would be left with nothing to do but guard against attacks from airplanes or submarines. We would wait anxiously for our planes to return, and when they did, everyone would man the rails to see how we did.

Orville Newman: Those Task Force 58 carriers ran us ragged. They were faster than the *Dale* and so were the new battleship escorts. On top of that, we were always on the outside of the formation. If we were on the starboard side, and the formation turned to port, poor *Dale* would have to rattle, shake, and shiver at full steam as she tried to keep up with the turn. And those carriers were always turning one way, and then the other. I don't know how she held together.

USS Dale War Diary, *March 30*: Cruised in company with TG 58.2 in formation 5V en route Palau Island area. TGs 58.1 and 58.3 also present. *0630* Carriers commenced launching initial striking force. *0847* Proceeded to pick up survivor of fighter plane forced landing. Picked up Lt. W. L. Gibbs, uninjured. *1202* TG 58.2 formed cruising disposition 5VD to prepare for repelling air attacks. *1915* All hands to general quarters—enemy planes reported bearing 285° T, 25 miles, 9 of which were reported shot down by CAP. *2050* Several flares observed on starboard quarter. *2118* Ships ahead commenced firing. *2122* Observed eighteen short bursts from USS *Baltimore* close to our stern. *2125* USS *Dale* opened fire on enemy aircraft. *2305* Secured from general quarters. *2320* Had contact on two groups of unidentified planes, which approached from the east. Enemy planes did not close formation.

Hugh Melrose: One of *Dale*'s jobs was to plane guard for the carriers. This meant we had to get in close behind the carrier for launching and recovery. When carriers launched, the entire formation would turn into the wind and increase speed to thirty knots to give the heavily loaded planes additional lift for takeoff. When carriers recovered everyone would again turn into the wind to make it easier for planes to land on pitching decks. During recovery the planes would fly really low right over us. We could see the battle damage to the planes. Sometimes the damage was so severe the pilot would have to ditch in the water. *Dale's* job was to rush in and pick up survivors. The plane usually floated long enough for the pilot and crew to get out, and they all wore Mae West life vests. Each plane also carried a small inflatable rubber raft and green dye so search planes could spot the pilot and crew if they crashed away from the carriers. When we rescued a pilot and crew, we would take them below for a cup of hot coffee and some medicinal brandy. Then, while they were showering, the crew would clean and press their clothes. When we handed them back to the carrier they would be clean and pressed and good as new. One time an F6F pilot on his first combat flight was ordered to ditch because he couldn't catch the wire. So he landed in the water right next to *Dale*, stepped off onto a wing, and then climbed into *Dale's* whaleboat without so much as getting a foot wet!

Darel Bright: The rookie pilots were taught how to land back in the States. They painted the flight deck of a carrier on a runway someplace, and the rookies would practice on it before they actually landed on a carrier. But, with the excitement of combat and the pitching decks of heavy seas, things were a lot different out in the war zone, and some of those young pilots had a tough time of it. One time several of us were up on the bridge, watching a plane trying to land on the carrier. Each approach he was waved off and had to go around for another attempt. Finally, Gene Brewer, our signalman, yelled at the carrier, "Just shoot the son of a bitch down! We'll pick him up!"

Warren Deppe: Whenever we returned a pilot to the carrier we were always rewarded with five gallons of ice cream. It may not sound like a big deal now, but ice cream was very precious back then, and we didn't have the equipment to make our own. So it became a tradition much appreciated by all. The carriers got their pilots back and we got some ice cream. Fair trade! But one time when we returned a pilot, an officer on the carrier called over on the loud speaker to say they were fresh out of ice cream and couldn't send any over. Callahan, our XO, called back on our loudspeaker, "Then we'll throw the son of a bitch back into the drink!"

John Kelsch: We lost a lot of airplanes. Some were shot down by Japs, but many were lost to accidents. We saw a lot of planes simply pushed over the side of the carriers because they were too damaged to fix. The carriers were always in need of replacement planes. Fortunately, our plants back home were able to turn planes out fast enough to replace those lost. Special aircraft carriers would bring them out from the States. When we retired from the scene of action to refuel, the carriers would get replacement planes and pilots. Though we lost a lot of planes, we managed to save a lot of pilots, and every time we pulled one of them out of the drink it made us all feel real good.

Author's note: The U.S. Navy dedicated itself to the rescue of pilots downed in the Pacific Theater. Owing to the effective work of destroyers, seaplanes, and submarines, the effort saved many pilots. For example, during three days of strikes on Palau in late March 1944, twenty-six out of forty-four men from twenty-five planes lost in combat were rescued. The U.S. Navy's investment paid handsome dividends when experienced U.S. pilots met inexperienced Japanese pilots in the First Battle of the Philippine Sea, which became known as the Great Marianas Turkey Shoot for the number of Japanese planes shot down.[3]

USS Dale *War Diary, April 21:* Steaming as before. *0525* TG 58.2 launched first strike on Hollandia Bay, Dutch New Guinea. *0910*

Torpedo plane from USS *Yorktown* made crash landing and at 0922 USS *Dale* picked up survivors, all uninjured. Note: Crossed equator at 0323.

A. D. Payne: Like sharks, we were always on the move. We would run in on a target, turn into the wind, launch our planes, then hightail it somewhere else to recover them. We would blast a place to smithereens and then move on to the next place. Much of the time we were running at thirty knots, which meant we had to fuel every three or four days from tanker groups waiting between one target and the next. Sometimes we got too close to the enemy to use the TBS, so then we had to use semaphore flags or lights. My job as a signalman was to watch for signals from the task force, and then relay the information up the chain of command. These signals would come in just before sunset. And boy, you better not miss any signals, because after the sun went down it was as black as ink.

John Kelsch: In the radar shack, ten minutes might seem like an hour, or an hour might seem like ten minutes, depending on what was going on. Generally, you think you should be doing a lot all the time, but most of the time you only do a little. In fact, 99 percent of the radar work was navigation and only 1 percent spotting enemy aircraft. You're always watching the relative position of other ships and shorelines, and feeding information to the bridge. Of course, there were those times when hours went by like minutes!

Hugh Melrose: During the strike against Truk we went in with three carrier task groups. *Dale* had a station in the screen of Task Force 58.3, which was built around the *Bunker Hill*, *Monterey*, and *Cowpens*. These carriers launched and recovered their planes in a circle of ocean about four miles in diameter. One of our new fast battleships was also inside the circle to protect against enemy air attacks. A ring of six light and heavy cruisers was built around the carriers, and then an outer ring of thirty-two tin cans. Whenever a carrier launched or recovered aircraft, one of the tin cans was detached to serve as its plane guard.

The approach to Truk was timed for the dark of the moon. Ships were blacked out and radio silence enforced. Cruising speed was usually between twenty-four and twenty-seven knots, which we called our "Get in and get out speed!" The senior watch officers were concerned for our safety in those conditions, as we were zigzagging all night by a plan pre-assigned by blinker signals a half hour before sunset. At lunch earlier that day, Lieutenant Hagmann talked about how easy it would be to have a collision at speed if one of the ships in the formation did not turn exactly on time. It was something to think about!

During the approach that night, I had the mid-watch as JOOD. When I relieved the previous watch, we were on station and cruising at twenty-seven knots. At 0200 the zigzag plan called for a turn of ninety degrees to starboard. The *Dale* was in the eight o'clock position in the screen with respect to base course. Another destroyer had the six o'clock position about a mile away on our starboard quarter. I looked on the chart and saw that if that destroyer failed to turn on schedule we might collide. So, about two minutes before the turn, I called down to CIC to apprise them of the situation. I asked that range and bearing to that ship be called every thirty seconds or so after the turn began. I plotted our position and that of the second destroyer on the chart board. After about three readings I saw we were indeed on a collision course. I notified the OOD of our predicament and asked permission to reverse propellers if required.

Now, you might think only those on the bridge would know what was going on with the ship in the middle of the night, but that was not true. Everyone aboard the *Dale* was always tuned in to the vibration of the engines and propeller shaft coming up through their bodies from the metal deck plates. It was like living inside a musical instrument that played one note. The instant something caused the note to change, everyone knew about it. Well, I was about to change octaves on the crew of the *Dale*!

After the next report from CIC, I signaled "All stop" down to the engine room. Now, imagine steaming along at twenty-seven knots and then, all of a sudden, the engines and propeller shaft stop turning! Everyone felt the change instantly, whether they were sleeping or awake.

I waited through two more range and bearing reports and saw the situation with respect to the sleeping tin can was not changing fast enough, so I ordered, "Both engines astern one-third!" When those big screws reversed direction at over twenty knots, it created a huge vibration that rumbled and shook the *Dale* for a good fifteen seconds. Her stern dug down into the ocean and her bow reached up for the sky. The crew came piling out of every hatch to see what was going on. It was much more effective than any general quarters!

That sleeping destroyer crossed our bow with three hundred feet to spare and disappeared off the Sugar George radar over the horizon. About an hour later it came sneaking back to its position in the task group.

USS Dale War Diary, *April 25*: Steaming as before in area to the south of Truk Island. *0629* USS *Macdonough* on picket duty reported an unidentified surface contact 6 miles from her which disappeared at *0651* at a range of 1,800 yards. Underwater sound contact was made and USS *Stephen Potter* was ordered to assist. *0644* Carriers launched aircraft for strike on Truk and carried out air operations during the rest of the day. *0930* USS *Macdonough* reported destruction of enemy submarine. *1930* USS *Dale* and USS *Aylwin* left screen to take picket station bearing 250 T, 12 miles from TG center.

Hugh Melrose: On the way back from Truk we ran into some heavy weather, which always made for an interesting unrep. Tankers were lined up across the open ocean like tollgates at a bridge. *Dale* was assigned one called "Ready." As JOOD I gave the "Up helm" order and we began our approach to the tanker.

By this stage of the war *Dale* had gone through a lot of changes. Seems like every time we put into port or tied up to a tender they would add some new, must-have equipment to the superstructure. The result of all this new stuff was that *Dale* was becoming very top-heavy, which meant she rolled like crazy in heavy seas, especially when she was low on fuel.

Dale was low on fuel, and we were steaming through heavy seas, so you can imagine how tough it was getting hooked up to that tanker. Sure enough, a big swell came barreling along and *Dale* rolled way over on her beam. Down in the wardroom, where the captain was having lunch, dishes began flying from one end of the table to the other. Some, of course, landed in the captain's lap, which quickly resulted in a call to the bridge: "This is the captain speaking. . . . Who has the helm?"

"Lieutenant J. G. Melrose, sir!"

"I might have known it was you, Melrose!" After that episode I put in my application for flight school, and the captain signed it right away!

Author's note: Task Force 58 raids into the heart of Japanese-held territory in the Central Pacific demonstrated the total dominance of the U.S. Navy's growing sea power. The raids neutralized Japan's vast web of Caroline Islands strongholds, including the mighty Truk, and turned the garrisons guarding those islands from one of Japan's few remaining assets to another of its many liabilities. In early May, the ships of Task Force 58 sailed into Majuro Lagoon for some well-earned rest before taking the next step toward Japan—the Mariana Islands.

Majuro

Mike Callahan: Those Task Force 58 raids had taken it out of us. In a little over a month and a half we had raided Japanese positions at Palau, Yap, Ulithi, Wolesi, Wakde, Hollandia, Sawar, Aitape, Truk, and Ponape. For much of this time we were steaming at twenty-seven knots, which meant we needed to be refueled about every four days. As the *Dale*'s executive officer, my job was to hold the ship and the men together. I'll tell you, after those raids both the ship and the men were ready for a rest, even if it was at Majuro.

Darel Bright: We didn't get much rest when we were running with Task Force 58. The few times we did were when the fleet sailed into the protection of Majuro Lagoon. There wasn't much there, other than some solid land to stand on. During those rest breaks we got to go ashore for beer parties. They gave us each a ration of three warm beers. Well, come to think about it, Majuro must have had something to hold our attention, because one time Wescott and I missed the last boat back to the *Dale*. We had to spend the whole night ashore, which had to be the worst place in the world to go AWOL!

Billy Walker: Unlike the deck crew, those of us who worked in the fire room rarely got any sun and so our bodies were always white as a sheet. We were looking forward to a little sunshine when we got to

Majuro. But that little sunshine turned out to be too much in short order. Once ashore, I drank my beers and got to splashing around in the water and having a lot of fun. Finally, someone came up to me and told me that I had better get out of the sun, as I was turning beet red. When I went back aboard I was assigned to a work party unloading ammunition. But when the bosun saw me he said, "Walker, you'd better go below and lay up for a while." That was great news, because my back was blistered and I was in real bad shape.

Bill Eggenberger: One of the good things about serving on tin cans was nobody got excited about how you looked, especially out there in the middle of the Pacific. Captain Aldrich was that way. As long as you did your job, and did it well, he cut you a lot of slack about how you dressed or polished your shoes. But down in Majuro that attitude got me into trouble. One day I had the coxswain duty and was ordered to go ashore and pick up the commodore. Well, my dress whites were simply too dirty for the job, so I borrowed my leading petty officer's, as he and I were about the same size. On the way back to the ship I could see the commodore was eyeing my uniform. "Son," he finally said, "I know you haven't been in the navy long enough to get all those stripes. You are out of uniform!"

Robert "Pat" Olson: Hadley was the lead petty officer of the section and my boss. One day he said, "Follow me." We were the last in a nest of six tin cans and had to cross all six to get to the tender. Nobody paid us any attention, as people were always coming and going in the nest.

Hadley had found a bunch of ice cream mix and made up his mind to appropriate some of it for the *Dale*. He told me to carry as many containers as I could, and we made it back with six big ones. We hid them under the low-pressure turbines down in the bilges. Problem was, *Dale* didn't have equipment to make ice cream. So we improvised and stirred up the ice cream mix with some powdered milk and water, and then poured it into ice trays and placed them back in the icemaker. The ice cream didn't turn out all that good, but at least it was ours!

Elliot Wintch: There wasn't much entertainment for the crew out there on those coral atolls, so the ship's evening movie was always an event. One time I decided to add a little merriment to the event. Previously, I had talked the mess gang into giving me the juice from some canned cherries. I poured a bunch of it into a five-gallon jerry can and then added water and sugar. After it fermented into a tolerable cherry wine, I poured it into smaller containers, took it to the ship's movie, and passed it around. After a few sips of cherry wine some of the guys stole an officer's hat, put it on the end of one of our 5-inchers, and then hoisted it up into the air, like a big salute.

Harold Zoellner: I joined up with *Dale* in May of forty-four down in the Marshall Islands. They took me out to the *Dale* in a skiff. When we climbed up the ladder, I looked up and there was old Bullneck Green! He went to the same church and schools I did back home. We even ran around together! As a seaman, I would be part of Bullneck's deck crew. After introducing me around, he told me we were going out on a big operation and it was time I learned where my GQ station would be. He led me back to the after deck house, opened a hatch, and descended a ladder. He opened another hatch and descended another ladder. Then he took me down another ladder! Finally, we reached the very bottom of the ship, where he opened another hatch and said, "This is your GQ station!" I looked inside and saw nothing but powder and shells. I picked up one of the 5-inch rounds. It was about two and a half feet long and weighed about thirty pounds. My job would be to load those rounds and the powder cases on a lift. I looked around and tried to figure out how to escape that magazine if something went wrong. There was no other way out, so I gave up thinking about escaping.

JUNE TO JULY: MARIANA ISLANDS

Through experience gained in taking the Japanese-held islands in the Aleutians, Gilberts, and Marshalls, American strategy developed around the belief that Japan would never surrender, that it would hold each position to the very last man. Furthermore, many believed at least one million American lives would be lost in the invasion of the Japanese home islands.

To cope with this eventuality, American planners looked for a location to base their new strategic weapon, the B-29 Superfortress bomber. As the largest bomber to enter service in World War II, the B-29, which had gone into mass production in early 1944, could carry eight thousand pounds of bombs 2,850 miles at 358 miles per hour. The Mariana Islands could provide a base from which the B-29s could reach Japan, but only barely.

The Marianas are an archipelago of fifteen volcanic islands located 3,300 miles west of Hawaii and 1,400 miles east of Japan. In June 1944, American forces would initiate Operation Forager, which had as its objective the capture of Saipan, Guam, and Tinian islands in the southern Marianas. At the same time, American forces were conducting Operation Overlord, the invasion of France. Though resources would be stretched to the maximum by Overlord, Admiral Nimitz would put together an invasion fleet for Forager of 535 ships and more than one hundred and twenty-five thousand troops.

The American move toward the Marianas would catch Japan by surprise, as Japanese planners believed the Americans would invade their weakened base at Truk. But Nimitz left Truk to the special harassing force of Admiral Halsey and remained focused on the Marianas, as they were the main goal of the Central Pacific campaign. The Japanese could not allow the Marianas to be taken, and so would attempt to interdict the invasion with a decisive attack on the U.S. Fifth Fleet.

Saipan

To date, American forces had to contend with three distinct geographies in their invasions of Japanese-held islands in the Pacific Theater. In the South and Southwest Pacific, there were large, mountainous islands covered in dense jungles inhabited by friendly natives; in the North Pacific, mountainous, uninhabited islands with intense cold and excessive precipitation; in the Central Pacific, coral atolls composed of tiny islets ringed by protective reefs. The targeted islands of the Marianas—Saipan, Guam, and Tinian—combined the worst of these geographies with some additional defensive advantages thrown in as well. Saipan and Tinian were both populated by civilians intensely loyal to Japan. Each island was protected by coral reefs and possessed mountainous ridges from which artillery could command invasion beaches and caves in which defenders could conceal themselves. On June 15, American forces would begin their assault on these defensive juggernauts by landing on the beaches of Saipan.

As one ship in a fleet of 535, and a very small one at that, *Dale* would be assigned many jobs during Operation Forager. She would screen Task Group 58.7, the line of seven battleships and four heavy cruisers commanded by Vice Admiral Willis Lee in battleship *Washington*, as they bombarded the beaches and ridges of Saipan. She would be ordered up to Guam to screen Task Unit 53.5.3, a division of cruisers, only to be called back to Saipan to screen the fleet's landing forces while Task Force 58 engaged the Japanese in the First Battle of the Philippine Sea. She would then screen the escort carriers of CTU

16.7.12 as they supported the marines fighting on Saipan, and then steam back up to Guam with the cruisers of TU 53.5.3.

USS Dale War Diary, *June 6*: Moored as before at Majuro Lagoon. *0700* DesRon [Destroyer Squadron] 1 less USS *Dale* underway. USS *Dale* delayed departure in order to pick up officer messenger mail for CDS-1. *1052* USS *Dale* underway. Proceeded to anchor in berth 37 at 1119. *1210* Underway, officer messenger mail having been received. Proceeded from Majuro Lagoon and set course to rendezvous with TG 58.7. *1710* Rendezvoused with TG 58.7 and took anti-submarine screening station. TG 58.7 in cruising disposition proceeding Saipan, Caroline Islands.

June 12: Steaming as before. *0145* Enemy planes reported closing formation. TG formed in cruising disposition 5V, reforming into cruising disposition 5R when enemy attack did not develop. *0457* More enemy planes reported approaching formation. Again TG formed in cruising disposition 5V, reforming at *0625* into 5R, when all radar contacts faded. *0710* Air strikes against Saipan Island commenced.

June 15: *1027* DesRon 1 rendezvoused with TG 50.17 and ships of DesDiv 2 proceeded independently to go alongside respective fueling ships. DesDiv 1 joined A/S screen. *1955* DesDiv 2 rendezvoused with TU 53.5.3 in disposition 5R and proceeded en route to Guam Island. *1948* All hands went to general quarters when enemy plane attacked formation. *2049* Secured from general quarters, enemy planes having retired after inflicting no damage.

Mike Callahan: We were assigned a lot of different jobs during the invasion of the Marianas. When we first arrived we were with the bombardment group working over Guam. But, before the party really got going, the Japanese decided to spoil it by attacking with all their carriers. Our task group was called back to Saipan to screen the invasion force while our carriers went out to meet them. It was amazing! Here we were thousands of miles from our nearest land base and yet we were able to put up over a thousand aircraft to meet them. I was awed. The Japanese attacked with both carrier- and land-based planes. But our planes and pilots were up for it, and shot down over four hundred of them that day. It was such a rout they called it "The Great Marianas Turkey Shoot."

Author's note: Though the U.S. Pacific fleet was clearly ascendant, the Imperial Navy had a plan to give its emperor a decisive, Tsushima-like victory in the Central Pacific. This plan, A-Go, called for luring the Pacific fleet into friendly waters, where land-based airplanes would inflict severe damage on the American ships, and carrier-based planes would finish them off.

To prepare the Imperial fleet for this great battle, Admiral Toyoda Soemu gathered 1,700 airplanes at Japanese bases in Singapore, the Dutch East Indies, the Philippines, and the Marianas, and issued sealed A-Go orders to a combined fleet of nine aircraft carriers and escorts. Then he waited for the U.S. Navy to show up on his doorstep.

Toyoda's doorbell rang on June 15, when American marines hit the beach at Saipan. Toyoda answered by activating A-Go. The five hundred airplanes stationed in the Marianas were ordered to attack the American fleet and sink at least one-third of its ships. The 653 airplanes on his nine carriers were ordered to follow up and sink what was left. Toyoda sent the following message to his fleet: "The fate of the empire rests on this one battle. Every man is expected to do his utmost."

However, when Toyoda's airplanes rose from the airfields of Guam, Saipan, and Tinian to attack American ships, they were shot down by Hellcats of Task Force 58. (Early in the Pacific war it quickly became evident that the Japanese Zero fighter totally outclassed the U.S. Navy's

Wildcat. The Grumman Hellcat entered service in October 1942. With a top speed of 376 mph, six 50-caliber machine guns, and self-sealing fuel tanks, the Hellcat quickly replaced the Zero as the dominant fighter in the Pacific.) Few survived the onslaught, and the airfields from which they had departed were bombed into uselessness.

Unaware of what had happened to the land-based air groups, the Japanese carrier group commander, Vice Admiral Jisburo Ozawa, launched his air attack on June 16, sending wave after wave of airplanes east toward the American carriers.

Before he launched, however, Ozawa had been discovered by an American submarine and one of his carriers, *Taiho*, was torpedoed. The position of Ozawa's force was reported to Task Force 58 commander Raymond Spruance, who readied his command. When attacking Japanese appeared on the radar screens of Task Force 58 CICs, Hellcats were vectored out and met them approximately sixty miles west of the American carriers.

Many of the young Japanese carrier pilots had not completed all of their flight training, and most lacked combat experience. They were simply no match for Yankee pilots in Hellcats. Consequently, the ensuing air battle became known as "The Great Marianas Turkey Shoot."

The Japanese lost 426 airplanes and three aircraft carriers in this, the First Battle of the Philippine Sea. Only twenty-nine American airplanes were lost. Ozawa made it safely back to Okinawa with six carriers, but the carriers had few airplanes or skilled pilots left and were, therefore, useless for all but one last mission. That mission would come in the Second Battle of the Philippine Sea.

Following their great victory, the Americans proceeded with their workmanlike invasion of Saipan, Guam, and Tinian. Though now without hope of help from the outside, the Japanese defenders would fight to nearly the last person.

Harold Zoellner: The Japanese defending Saipan simply would not surrender, nor would the civilians that lived on the island. Instead, they climbed up to the high side of the island and jumped off the cliffs into the ocean. Men, women, and children! I remember clearly watching as the *Dale* plowed through their bodies floating in the water. There was just no way to avoid them, as they were everywhere. I remember one body in particular. He was stretched out on his back with his arms spread out to his sides, his only clothing some white skivvies. I remembered him for years, even after I got home. The image just stuck with me. Even today I remember it as if it were yesterday.

Roy Roseth: We spotted a Jap pilot down in the water and went to pick him up. We threw him a life preserver but he would not take it. He just waved it off, like there was some other opportunity waiting for him. We threw it out again and again, and finally he swam over and grabbed on. They locked him up in the post office, which was the only cage we had aboard the *Dale*.

John Cruce: At first, everyone treated our POW like he was a monkey in a cage. They poked cigarettes at him and tried to tease him into talking. They named him Hirohito.

Robert "Pat" Olson: I looked at him and got to thinking, "There but for the grace of God go I." He could see what I was thinking by the look on my face, and he became happy and very friendly. But then I got to thinking, "Hey, if this guy had the least chance he would probably kill me and throw me to the sharks." He could read that thought in my expression as well, and he became sad and morose, and started shaking and shivering.

Roy Roseth: I had to stand guard over him a couple of times. After a while we got to feeling sorry for him, and even fond of him. Soon guys were coming by to slip him cigarettes and candy. Others gave him clothes. When an officer came by we would signal him to hide his cigarettes.

Harold Zoellner: A boat came over from a four-piper to pick up Hirohito. It had a big marine in it. I mean this guy was big! We brought Hirohito up to the deck, which was not high off the water. Now Hirohito was just a little guy, not very tall at all. Well, that big marine reached up from the boat and grabbed Hirohito by the scruff of his neck and lifted him down into the boat just as pretty as you please. He pointed his submachine gun at Hirohito to let him know who was boss. The last we saw of Hirohito he had a big smile on his face and was waving goodbye from the back of the boat.

Guam

USS Dale War Diary, *June 23*: Steaming as before. *1044* USS *Dale* went alongside USS *Marias* to fuel. *1300* All hands to general quarters as enemy dive-bombers attacked USS *Kitkun Bay* (CTU 16.7.12) and USS *Gambier Bay* about 11,000 yards on our starboard quarter. USS *Dale* ceased fueling and rejoined A/S screen. Enemy planes inflicted no damage and escaped unscratched. *1350* Secured from general quarters. *1438* USS *Dale* went alongside USS *Marias* and resumed fueling. *1525* Completed fueling. Proceeded to deliver coupling received from USS *Marias* to USS *New Mexico*, returning to USS *Marias* to deliver exchange coupling at 1549. Rejoined A/S screen.

July 17: Steaming in company with TU 53.5.2 en route to Guam, Mariana Islands. *1425* USS *Honolulu* and USS *St. Louis* proceeded to bombardment area in vicinity of Agat Bay, Guam Island. DesDiv 2 formed screen to seaward and patrolled between Orote Point and Facpi Point.

July 18: Steaming as before on night retirement. *0700* USS *St. Louis* screened by USS *Dale* and USS *Aylwin* left formation and proceeded to fire support area northwest of Guam Island. USS *Dale* and USS *Aylwin* patrolled to seaward of USS *St. Louis* while she bombarded beach in vicinity of Saupon Point, Guam Island.

Harold Zoellner: One time we went in to fire on an enemy-held beach on Guam. We were with a big task group of cruisers and battleships. First in the line were the minesweepers, then us tin cans, then the cruisers and, finally, the battleships. This big parade of ships moved along parallel to the island at some distance while the battleships opened up with their 16-inch guns. We moved along down to the end of the island and then turned in closer so the cruisers could open up with their 8-inch guns on the way back up. While we were waiting to get close enough for our 5-inch guns, a bunch of us guys were hanging around the after deck house watching the battleships in action. When they let go with a broadside you'd see giant tongues of flame coming out of those 16-inch guns. Then you'd see the big projectiles come out of the gun, and you could follow them as they reached up into the sky. When they reached the top of their trajectory you'd lose them and just have to guess where they were going to land. On Guam about the only thing left standing was a smokestack. You could see the big boys were trying their best to knock it down. Finally, we turned in close enough for us tin cans to go to work, so we went to general quarters.

USS Dale *War Diary*, *July 21*: Steaming as before in company with night bombardment group off Asan Point, Guam Island. *0404* USS *Dale* left A/S screen to close Asan Point to conduct short-range bombardment in support of underwater demolition activities. All hands went to general quarters. *0526* Commenced firing until 0645 at which time proceeded to take A/S patrol station in TG 53.3 screen on eastern side of northern transport area.

Mike Callahan: Early one morning we were ordered in to support the underwater demolition teams clearing the beach before an invasion. The boats carrying the frogmen went in right under our fire and deposited them in the water. They swam in and blew up the coral and coconut log cribs Japs had installed to prevent our landing craft from being able to reach the beach. We kept up a steady fire on the beach until the frogmen were picked up and returned to their ship. When the sun came up we went back to screening some cruisers.

Author's note: Operation Forager included three major land campaigns and the greatest carrier action of the war. Though small groups of Japanese soldiers would continue to resist until September 1945, American forces succeeded in taking effective control of the Marianas by August 12. With this victory, the Americans had cracked the shell of the Japanese inner defensive perimeter; destroyed the air groups of the Imperial Navy; forced the Tojo-led government of Japan to resign from power; and laid the Japanese home islands open to the depredation of B-29s.

AUGUST TO OCTOBER: UNITED STATES

As America consolidated its newly acquired possessions, a conflict developed among its strategic planners: Should the next step toward the Japanese home islands be Formosa and the Bonins, or the Philippines? While this decision was being debated at the highest levels, the USS *Dale* received some long-awaited orders.

With the exception of a few weeks in a San Francisco navy yard, the USS *Dale* had been at sea for thirty-three months. She had fought her way out of Pearl Harbor; raided deep into the Coral Sea; screened battleships during the Battle of Midway; pioneered Espiritu Santo; dodged torpedoes along Torpedo Alley; fought in major naval engagements at Guadalcanal; steamed around the Bering Sea for nine months; fought the Battle of the Komandorski Islands; invaded Amchitka, Attu, and Kiska; steamed down to the Central Pacific; invaded Makin and Tarawa in the Gilberts, then Kwajalein and Eniwetok in the Marshalls; steamed throughout the Central Pacific with Task Force 58; then invaded the Marianas. In August, the USS *Dale* was ordered to the navy's shipyards at Bremerton, Washington, for a complete overhaul.

Bremerton

Orville Newman: Try as they might, the Japs couldn't seem to get a hit on the *Dale*. But one of our own ships got her! We were getting ready to go stateside and had to offload all our "Buck Rodgers," which were the 5-inch rounds with magnetic proximity fuses. No ship was allowed to take them out of the battle zone, so we had to give them to a cruiser anchored nearby. After we transferred the Buck Rodgers we pulled away from the cruiser, but its metal boat scupper got caught in one of our portholes and ripped a hole in our bulkhead. I got the job of welding a metal plate over the hole and had to hang over the side of the ship all night, as we were scheduled to depart early the next morning. I was still welding when the ship weighed anchor and began working her way out of the harbor. I guess the skipper figured I could finish as he worked the *Dale* out to the open sea! I finished, but just barely! I had worked all night without a protective sleeve, and the wind-blown sparks had burned up my arm. You can still see the white scars running up and down my arm today. When finished, I went down to the sickbay to have my burns fixed. The pharmacist mate put medicine on them, and then gave me eight containers of brandy and said, "Here, go drink these and have a good sleep." I did, and slept for two days!

Harold Zoellner: We were not allowed to say much in our letters home. If we did say something of any consequence, the ship's censor would just ink it out. So we had to develop little codes to get by the censor. For example, when we were ordered back to the States from a long stay down in the Marianas, I wrote home that I was going to visit cousin Jimmy. Since everybody back home knew Jimmy was stationed in Hawaii, they would know which direction I was headed.

USS Dale *War Diary,* *August 17:* Steaming as before en route from Pearl Harbor to Navy Yard, Bremerton, Washington. At 0250 sighted Cape Flattery light bearing 055° T, 27 miles. *0455* Screen of TU 12.7.1 formed in column 3,000 yards ahead of guide, steaming down Straights of Juan de Fuca. *0900* Hove to off Port Angeles while USS *New Mexico* and USS *Yorktown* awaited official boarding party. USS *Dale,* USS *Aylwin,* and USS *Farragut* proceeded independently to Navy Yard, Puget Sound. At *1542* anchored eight hundred yards south of pier No. 4, at which time a lighter came alongside and transfer of ammunition commenced. *1745* Completed transfer of ammunition. USS *Dale* got underway and moored alongside pier 5C.

Harold Zoellner: We had been at sea for eight months without having been anyplace where you could spend money. So there were a lot of guys who had a lot of money. Somebody set up a pool to bet on the time our anchor would fall in the States. As time went on this pool grew and grew. When we finally anchored in Puget Sound, everyone was watching the clock. This redheaded boy, forgot his name, won eight hundred dollars cash. That was a lot of money in those days! Everybody warned him not to take the cash ashore, but he was feeling mighty big and nothing we said could stop him. Sure enough! Next morning he came straggling back to the ship all beat up and broke. Somebody rolled him and took all his money.

Bill Eggenberger: Seattle was the best liberty port of the war. They put *Dale* in dry dock and us in barracks. After years of steaming from one end of the Pacific to the other, we finally had a month of shore duty, and were we ever ready for it!

Earl "Jitterbug" Pearson: Bremerton was the best liberty port of the war, and I had a secret weapon for enjoying every second of it. The weapon? Roller skates! No kidding! Now, right outside the gates of the naval base there was a sailor bar, and sure enough, almost every sailor would stop right there. Many of them wouldn't make it out of that bar until they were poured out. But not me! I kept going right past the bar until I got to the roller rink. Oh sure, I'd go out for a drink or two with the boys, but what I really liked was skating. Most of the guys thought I was nuts, but I wasn't! You see, there was no better way to meet girls than to skate around a rink in your dress blues! Back in those days I was limber enough to do tricks, like wrapping one leg around my neck while skating on the other. Yeah, most of the guys thought I was crazy. They'd see me leaving the base with the skates and just shake their heads. But heck, I just laughed all the way to the bank!

Bill Ryan: When we docked in Bremerton I received word that my grandmother was sick and it didn't look good for her. She had raised me down in Gainesville, Florida. I asked for an emergency leave, but since she wasn't my parent, the navy wouldn't grant me leave to go home for a visit. They said it wasn't my turn. But they did give me a seventy-two-hour pass and told me to stay within fifty miles of the base. I decided to go home anyway. The boys said I was crazy and that I'd never make it back in time! Well, I got on a plane and we took off. Seemed like we landed somewhere in Montana, and then in Chicago where I changed planes for Nashville, and then on to Jacksonville. I got out of the airport and hitched a ride to Green Coast Springs, and then another to Interlocken and another to Gainesville. I spent that day at home and then someone gave me a ride back to Jacksonville to catch a plane. I got back to Bremerton an hour late. I'm really glad I did it because my grandma died when I was out there in the Pacific somewhere. I got to say goodbye to her when she was still alive.

Robert "Pat" Olson: Once ashore in Bremerton we discovered girls everywhere, and if you had a uniform on, they all wanted to meet you. It was like being a champion rodeo cowboy! After a couple of weeks I was granted a twenty-day leave and went home to Molt, Montana. The day after I got home dad suffered a ruptured appendix and ended up in the hospital in nearby Billings. Mom, brother Clair, and I took some rooms in a boarding house to be with Dad. One evening at the dinner table Clair nudged me with his elbow and said, "Hey, that cute little gal at the other end of the table has been trying to get your attention, but you won't even look at her!" I looked down the table and saw this country gal with a twinkle in her eye and thought, "She'll never catch me. I'm a tin can sailor!" But there was something in her look that caught my attention, and whatever it was would not let me go.

Mike Callahan: Before we left to join the fleet, which was down in San Pedro, Lieutenant Commander Aldrich turned command of the *Dale* over to Lieutenant Commander Zimny. As *Dale*'s executive officer, I had had a pretty easy time of it because I got along well with Captain Aldrich. That all changed when Zimny took over. I was thirty-two years old at the time and he was only twenty-five. He was a little Caesar and thought that I didn't know a thing about being a destroyer officer, even though I was an ASW expert. One evening at dinner in the wardroom he told a story about how, when he was younger, he had hung his kid brother upside down from a clothesline and poured hot wax into his eyes. When he finished telling the story, he got up and left the wardroom. Everyone just sat there and stared at the bulkhead, wondering what life was going to be like aboard the *Dale*.

San Pedro

Robert "Pat" Olson: We had steamed down the coast to San Pedro in order to join our squadron, which was getting ready to leave for the western Pacific. We all knew it would be a long time before we got back to the States again, so everybody was out to live it up as much as they could in the short amount of time we had left. Sometimes we lived it up too much. One of those times I had the mid-watch down in the fire room. My job was to keep steam up in one of the boilers so the ship would have power. Sometime after midnight, Nixon came stumbling down into the fire room and started bad-mouthing poor Walker. Nixon was very drunk, and yelling and cursing at Walker. Walker was a great big kid, and a second-class fireman. Nixon was a little guy, but a first-class fireman. The argument quickly turned ugly, with little Nixon chasing big Walker around the fire room with a doggin' wrench. It was funny watching Nixon chase Walker around like that, as he was making lots of noise banging the doggin' wrench against all the metal. But it was also scary, because, with all the pipes and gauges and ladders around, someone could get hurt pretty easily. Walker was big enough to take Nixon down with one punch, but couldn't afford to because Nixon outranked him. And I couldn't do much, as both out-ranked me. Finally, Walker got creative and started pretending that Nixon had beaten him up, and begged for mercy. "Please, Nixon, enough! Enough! I can't take it anymore!" Nixon relented, and the two became old friends again.

A. D. Payne: A shipmate and I were taking in the sights down in San Pedro when a couple of good-looking gals pulled up to the curb in a convertible. They chatted us up for a while and next thing you knew we were riding around town with the top down. Well, it wasn't too long before they pulled into a driveway and asked us in to their home. We all went inside, but when the gals went into the kitchen for some beers I became frightened of what could happen and said to my shipmate, "We've got to get out of here! We've never met these girls and we don't know anything about them." He must have been as afraid as I, because he quickly nodded his head and we slipped out the front door and high-tailed it down the street. I guess we just plain chickened out!

USS Dale War Diary, *October 10*: Moored as before. *1545* Underway, assisted by pilot and tug. *1607* Pilot left ship. Proceeded out of San Pedro Harbor. *1613* Passed from inland to international waters. *1619* Passed buoy #1 too close to port side and hit same on port quarter and the propeller guard. No damage to propeller was apparent, but later on increasing speed to 20 knots noticed considerable vibration. Steamed at various speeds to investigate damage but at 1750 a knock was heard in port reduction gear. Stopped all engines and engineering officer was lowered over side to inspect port propeller. USS *Farragut* and USS *Aylwin* screened while standing by. *1825* Engineering officer hoisted aboard and preliminary investigation revealed one small dent in hull and one blade of port screw bent forward three or four inches along tip. *1830* Pursuant to verbal orders proceeded to return to Los Angeles Harbor on starboard engine only. Sent radio dispatch to COMINCH and CinCPac, reporting damage incurred and requesting ComServPac to grant availability at Naval Drydocks, Terminal Island, San Pedro, California.

USS *Dale*

From: The Commanding Officer

To: The Commander in Chief, United States Fleet

Subject: Report of Damage to Port Propeller

USS *Dale* sortied from San Pedro Harbor on 10 October 1944. Passage through the net was made at 1615 and course of 159° T was set to pass to port of the turning buoy.

On clearing the net, the Commanding Officer noted that a destroyer was approaching the turning buoy inbound and that a tug with tow was also approaching. Course was changed to 170° T to pass turning buoy close aboard to starboard in order to afford greater maneuvering room to above mentioned vessels. In order to eliminate any possibility of collision with these vessels, the Commanding Officer made final decision to pass to the starboard of the turning buoy. Course was accordingly changed to 220° T and speed increased to 15 knots.

As soon as ship steadied on 220° T, the Commanding Officer estimated that ship would clear buoy safely. The Commanding Officer was at all times kept properly advised by the navigator. As the buoy passed abeam of this vessel, the Commanding Officer realized that ship would not clear the buoy. The port engine was immediately stopped and the buoy then hit at frame 159 to port, and then bounced off the propeller guard. No shock was felt on the bridge.

Elliot Wintch: We were anchored in San Pedro Harbor waiting to have our propeller repaired, and were just a stone's throw from the beach and all those city big lights. But the captain was so mad at having run into the buoy he wouldn't allow liberty for anyone on the ship. That's right, nobody got to go ashore! There was a lot of discontent among the crew, and it was rumored some guys were going over the side at night and swimming to shore, but I certainly wouldn't have done anything so risky, especially with the new captain!

Commander Destroyer Squadron One, Pacific Fleet, 14 November, 1944

Subject: Report of Damage to Port Propeller

Lieutenant Commander S.M. Zimny became Commanding Officer of the USS *Dale* during her recent Navy Yard overhaul ending about 1 October, 1944. The subject damage occurred while en route to the Forward Areas via San Pedro.

The accident was avoidable and apparently was caused by the lack of experience of the Commanding Officer who gave primary consideration to the convenience of the approaching tug and destroyer instead of to the safety of his own ship. This incident should serve to improve Lieutenant Commander Zimny's judgment in similar matters.

It is recommended that no disciplinary action be taken.

A letter of caution will be addressed to Lieutenant Commander Zimny by the Type Commander.

USS Dale War Diary, *October 20*: Anchored as before. *2255* Underway. Proceeded out of Los Angeles Harbor independently en route to Pearl Harbor.

Pearl Harbor

Dan Ahlberg: All was not love and kisses when I went aboard the *Dale*. I had been waiting at Pearl thirty days for her to arrive. I lived in the barracks at the submarine base and drove trucks around the island for the Seabees. It was good duty! When the *Dale* finally pulled in I went aboard and reported to the chief petty officer in charge of the sonar, whose name I can't remember. He took one look at me and gave me a direct order not to touch any of his equipment and to stay out of his way.

Looking back on it, I guess you can't really blame him. At eighteen, I was the youngest guy on the ship and already a third-class petty officer. That chief had probably been in the navy five or six years before he became a petty officer. I had enlisted in an accelerated training program, which meant I spent only three weeks in boot camp before going into intensive training at the navy's West Coast Sonar School. Most of the students in the school were second-class or better and had been out in the fleet for many years. They thought boys like me, who had only three weeks of boot camp, were a pain in the butt, and that we should have been sent out to the fleet before going to sonar school. The very idea of giving an eighteen-year-old kid a third-class rating was sacrilege to them.

When I reported aboard the *Dale* I got the same kind of reception. Matter of fact, the chief didn't even assign me a bunk, so I hung my sea bag from a hook and slept on a cot over the hatch to the ammunition magazine. Whenever they called general quarters, I stowed my cot and found a place to stay out of the way.

My only saving grace was that I was able to help people type letters. One guy I helped was barely literate, but he was also the strongest man on the ship and we became fast friends. He could pick up a depth charge and put it up on the rack all by himself! He was the bosun mate in charge of the fantail. We were assigned shore patrol duty together and made a good team. If I couldn't talk drunk sailors into behaving, he could beat the hell out of them. He also kept me reasonably sober; and heck, there wasn't enough booze in the world to get him drunk!

Charles O'Rorke: After completing the day's training exercises, *Dale* would anchor with other cans in a nest. Guys that didn't have liberty didn't have much to do, so the ship's movie became the evening's entertainment. My job was to find the movies, and it was a good job, too! I had the ship's car, lots of freedom to run around wherever I wanted, and an extra dollar a day. That was thirty dollars a month! But there was one kicker. If I picked out a bad movie, I had hell to pay with the crew, and there was nowhere to hide from them on the *Dale*. Whenever I picked a movie the crew didn't like, I had to quickly redeem myself with a good one or things would get real dicey for me. And, when it got right down to it, I really didn't know how to tell a good movie from a bad one! I remember going over to pick up a movie the day before we departed for the western Pacific. When I got to the disbursing office there were only two movies left. I was totally stumped about which one to pick, and was thinking about how there would be hell to pay for months if I picked the wrong one. Then, as if by some kind of miracle, Henry Fonda, the movie actor, walked in the door and said, "Hello!" I held up the two movies and explained my predicament. He picked out a movie and said the crew would love it. And they did!

Robert "Pat" Olson: Nobody knew what was going to happen to us out there in the western Pacific. We knew we were in for more invasions, and maybe even the big invasion of Japan itself. As the days got closer to leaving Pearl, the anxiety of not knowing what was going to happen to us kept building. When our last day at Pearl finally arrived, everyone was in the mood to hit the beach. As luck would have it, I had the duty that night and couldn't go ashore. When the guys returned to the ship, it quickly became apparent they had got their hands on some rotgut liquor, because they were all as drunk as skunks. I berthed in a bottom bunk, and that night everybody above got sick and threw up. Right then and there, I decided if we ever got into a situation like that again, I would forego all my notions of temperance and get drunker than everyone. What a mess!

NOVEMBER TO DECEMBER: PHILIPPINES

Which archipelago would the tsunami-like American offense overwhelm next: Formosa and the Bonins, or the Philippines?

Admiral Chester Nimitz argued that his seemingly unstoppable fast carrier and amphibious fleets be employed first at Formosa, and then at the Bonins. When combined with the newly acquired Marianas, the three positions would allow American forces to sever Japan's supply lines with the South Pacific and China, and provide ideal bases from which to launch an invasion of Japan's home islands. General Douglas MacArthur argued that he should be allowed to fulfill his "I shall return!" promise to the people of the Philippines, and that the navy's fleet should support this effort.

Only one person had the power to decide between MacArthur and Nimitz. President Franklin Roosevelt boarded the heavy cruiser *Baltimore* for a trip to Hawaii and a July conference of the three. MacArthur, who had a significant following among voters in the United States, presented several arguments, not the least of which was that the president might well lose the November election if he failed to keep the promise MacArthur had made in his name to the people of the Philippines. Nimitz also presented his arguments, but they were not as persuasive as MacArthur's.

As a consequence of Roosevelt's decision for MacArthur, the

CHINA

Okinawa

JAPAN

Task Force 58
Raid on Hong Kong
January 14, 1945

Hong Kong

Formosa

Task Force 58
Raid Formosa
January 9–15, 1945

Invasion of Luzon
January 1945

Typhoon Cobra
December 18, 1944

Hainan Is.

Task Force 58
Raid on Hainan Is.
January 14, 1945

Thailand

PHILIPPINES

Luzon Is.

French
Indochina

Camranh Bay

Task Force 58
Raid Camranh Bay
January 12, 1945

Leyte Is.

Invasion of Leyte
October 25, 1944

Sulu
Sea

Surigao
Straight

Second Battle of
Philippine Sea
October 23–26, 1944

South China Sea

Mindanao Is.

Malaya

Invasion of Balikpapan
July 1945

Borneo

Celebes

Sumatra

Balikpapan

**PHILIPPINES, SOUTH CHINA SEA, AND BORNEO—
1944 TO 1945**

offensive units of the U.S. Pacific fleet would be given two identities: When supporting General MacArthur in the Philippines, the task forces, groups, and units would operate as the Third Fleet under Admiral Halsey, and be designated "Task Force 38." When following Admiral Nimitz's plan, they would be the Fifth Fleet under Admiral Spruance, and be designated "Task Force 58."

While *Dale* was sitting snug in her Bremerton dry dock, other tin cans were screening the invasion of the Palau Islands in the western Carolines. The objective of this invasion was to take Japanese airfields that controlled the sea-lanes of the Philippine Sea and threatened MacArthur's invasion of the Philippines. Though the brutal fight for Palau was disdained by many as being superfluous, the U.S. Navy did gain access to a protected anchorage at Ulithi Atoll that could house the entire Pacific fleet.

While *Dale* was steaming out of San Pedro for Pearl Harbor, U.S. forces invaded Leyte Island in the central Philippines.

The Imperial Navy had long planned for such an eventuality. Their general plan for a decisive victory in the Central Pacific was called *Sho-Go*, which simply meant "Victory Operation." Because the Imperial headquarters did not know where the United States would invade, several specific Sho plans were drawn up. Sho-1 was the battle plan for a U.S. invasion of the Philippines. Sho-1 called for a task group of carriers—the carriers rendered impotent by the First Battle of the Philippine Sea—to lure the carriers of Admiral Halsey's Task Force 38 to the northeast. Two task groups of battleships, cruisers, and destroyers would then steam into Leyte Gulf from different directions and crush the invasion force of General MacArthur's Seventh Fleet.

The commander of Japan's Combined Fleet, Admiral Toyoda Soemu, was determined to commit his all to Sho-1. When explaining why to an interrogator after the war, he said, "Should we lose in the

Philippines operations, even though the fleet should be left, the shipping lane to the south would be completely cut off so that the fleet, if it should come back to Japanese waters, could not obtain its fuel supply. If it should remain in southern waters, it could not receive supplies of ammunition and arms. There would be no sense in saving the fleet at the expense of the loss of the Philippines."[4]

Sho-1's carrier force did lure Halsey's Task Force 38 away from Leyte Gulf, and one of the battleship task groups did steam into the Philippine Sea and threaten the Seventh Fleet in Leyte Gulf, but it was not enough to win the day. Thin-skinned American escort carriers, destroyers, cruisers, and the old, slow battleships dredged from the bottom of Pearl Harbor turned them back. At the end of the Second Battle of the Philippine Sea, there was very little left of the Imperial Japanese Navy. Also known as the "Battle of Leyte Gulf," the series of naval engagements between October 23 and 26 cost the Japanese four aircraft carriers, three battleships, ten cruisers, and eleven destroyers, while the Americans lost three aircraft carriers, two destroyers, and one destroyer escort. Toyoda had gambled it all, and had lost it all.

As the USS *Dale* steamed west toward the Philippine Sea, she would find herself fighting a different kind of war. The Japanese fleet, for all intents and purposes, was gone. No longer would *Dale* face the prospect of engaging one of the Imperial Navy's massive battlewagons in a gunfight. But the new war would certainly be no less dangerous than the old war. Indeed, *Dale* would now have to brace for ill winds more fearsome than 16-inch rounds fired from Japanese battleships.

Eniwetok

USS Dale War Diary, *November 18:* Steaming as before with CTU 12.5.7 en route Eniwetok. *0415* USS *Farragut* dropped astern of formation, being unable to maintain formation speed of 22 knots because of excessive roll. USS *Monaghan* assumed duties of Screen Commander. At 0530 USS *Farragut* rejoined formation, which had reduced speed, and resumed duties of Screen Commander. At 0936 USS *Farragut* lost two men over the side, [who] were expeditiously recovered by USS *Monaghan*.

Dan Ahlberg: Relations aboard the *Dale* had deteriorated. There were now two camps: the new guys behind Captain Zimny and the old guys behind XO Callahan. I wasn't in either camp. Mostly I just stayed out of everyone's way, as ordered by the chief.

This went on until the day the sonar went down at Eniwetok. A quartermaster found me camped out on my hatch cover and ordered me to report to Captain Zimny's quarters. I did not know where the captain's quarters were located, so the quartermaster had to show me the way. Captain Zimny looked at me for a second or two, and then said, "What's wrong with that damned sonar, Ahlberg?" I told him I did not know. He said, "Well, why don't you know? You're a rated sonarman, aren't you?"

"Yes, sir," I replied. "But with all due respect, sir, I've been ordered to stay away from the sonar equipment and to get lost. I've done that, sir! I have not stood any watches nor met with the sonar officer, sir!"

With that, all hell broke loose! I was sent out to await orders. The chief and the sonar officer were found and ordered to the captain's cabin. I was told later the chief told the captain he wasn't about to let a dumb eighteen-year-old kid touch his sonar equipment. The skipper told the chief that he had raised all sorts of hell to get me, and if the chief didn't like it he could and would be replaced. The chief had been on the ship a long time and apparently thought he could buffalo the new skipper! But he couldn't, and the captain relieved him of his duty!

The captain then ordered me to go fix the sonar. I got the sonar officer to take me to the transmitter, which was located way down in the bowels of the ship. The dammed keying relay was stuck, so I took it out, polished the points, and tuned the transmitter. I then went up to the bridge to check the receiver. The second- and third-class sonarmen on watch made stupid jokes about me. They knew their chief had been sacked because of me—and let me know my name was mud, and it would stay mud until the war was over.

I reported to the captain the keying relay was temporarily repaired, but that the repair wouldn't last very long. If he wanted something that would last longer, I would need to install the spare. Then the fun began, because nobody would tell me where the spare was. I got a storekeeper to help and we searched all the bilges and dry storage areas. When we finally found the spare relay it turned out to have been one already worn out!

I put in a request for a new relay. But when I went to the tender with all the proper paperwork in hand, complete with the captain's signature, they refused to let me have the part because it was the only one they had, and it was promised to another destroyer. I went through all the right motions to no avail, so I just flat stole it. I got caught just as I was leaving the tender. They took the relay away, and then an officer and a SP took me back to the *Dale* with court-martial papers for stealing Title A, which was top secret equipment in very short supply. I was in big trouble!

When they left the captain ordered me to report what had happened. When I told him about the part, he asked if it was what was causing us so much down time. I replied in the affirmative and said the one we were operating on would soon fail completely. I then took him down to the transmitter and showed him how the contact points had been worn down to nothing from repeated cleaning.

The captain said, "Okay, Ahlberg, let's go to work." He then tore up my court-martial papers, put on his hat, and we headed back to the tender in our whaleboat. He said, "Take me where that part is kept." I did so. He pushed past the storekeeper and picked up the box containing the relay switch. He handed it to me and said, "Is this the switch?" When I confirmed he turned to the storekeeper and handed him the paperwork. But still the storekeeper wouldn't let us leave with the switch, so the captain marched both of us right up the chain of command to the captain of the tender. I was ordered to wait outside with the part.

A few minutes later Captain Zimny came out and said, "Okay, Ahlberg, let's go back to the ship. But that dammed relay switch better work." Thank God it did!

Mike Callahan: I wasn't the only officer that didn't get along with Zimny. Robinson was another. Zimny just terrorized him. Much to the amusement of everyone aboard, Robinson had the ship's carpenter build him a little one-man sailboat. Then, whenever we would anchor somewhere to await orders, Robinson would put the little sailboat into the water and sail away!

Ulithi

When the Americans took Palau, the Japanese abandoned Ulithi Atoll, leaving behind a lagoon large enough to hold the entire American fleet. Ulithi quickly became the staging point for fleet activities throughout the western Pacific, and much effort was devoted to developing facilities for rest and recreation. Within a short amount of time, the islands surrounding the lagoon had airstrips, ball fields, swimming beaches, and an officer's club. One of the tiny islands, Mog Mog, just one-half-mile wide and three-quarters-mile long, was the traditional center of Ulithi culture. During the American occupation, its community was resettled to other islands and it became "Beer Island" for tens of thousands of enlisted men, who would drink more than 7.6 million cans of beer and soft drinks on its sandy beaches.[5]

There was one other aspect of Ulithi and the Philippine Sea sailors found interesting—weather. Each year the Philippine Sea hosts an average of twenty typhoons and countless tropical storms. Unlike Atlantic hurricanes, which are confined to a season, Pacific typhoons come and go as they please. Ulithi Lagoon afforded sailors respite from tossing seas while their ships were anchored within its confines, but all guarantees of comfort vanished when they put back to sea.

Elliot Wintch: Though Ulithi Lagoon was big enough to hold the entire Pacific fleet, and often did, it was always easy to spot the *Dale* and her sister *Farragut*s. They would be the ones swaying back and forth like drunk sailors walking line abreast down the sidewalk. *Farragut*s were built before the war started, and each time we went in for repairs, or tied up to a tender, they would add new equipment topside. We had new guns, radar sets, and radio masts. All this new stuff was great, but it also weighed a lot and was located high above our center of gravity. The slightest swell set us to bobbing back and forth. But while we swayed in the sober waters of Ulithi Lagoon, we rocked and rolled in the Philippine Sea!

USS Dale War Diary, *November 25*: Anchored as before in berth 111 while awaiting arrival of mail. *1240* Underway from berth 111. *1410* Proceeded to sea to join TU 30.8.5 having received all mail for Task Groups 38.2, 38.3 and Com 3rd Fleet. *1940* Joined TU 30.8.5, taking station in A/S screen.

Bob Johnson: The fleet had grown into hundreds and hundreds of ships by the time we got to invading the Philippines. Each one of them needed to be fueled hundreds and even thousands of miles from the nearest base. *Dale's* new job was to screen the tankers that would fuel the fleet at sea. These unreps were not easy, especially in heavy seas. One time *Dale* was taking on fuel in heavy weather when the hose broke free and spewed bunker crude all over the decks. It was a terrible mess, and everyone in the crew was ordered to grab a rag. We were on our hands and knees all day, and used every rag on the ship, but we barely made a dent on the mess!

Harold Zoellner: Each day we went to general quarters at dawn and dusk, because that's when we were most vulnerable to aircraft attacking out of the sun. During one dawn GQ, I was coming up on deck through the starboard hatch when the ship rolled heavily to port. The hatch, which had been held open by a hook fastened to the bulkhead, came free and slammed full force into my face. I stood there dazed, somehow holding on to the hatch frame. Then the ship rolled to starboard and the hatch flopped the other way and slammed down on my hand. By then blood was flowing freely down my face and I was incapable of moving. Just before the ship rolled back to smack me in the face again, a corpsman happened by and pulled me out of the hatchway. Blood was streaming down my forehead into my eyes. I couldn't see and thought for sure I was going blind. The corpsman led me down to sickbay where the doc stitched me up.

USS Dale War Diary, *December* 8: Steaming as before. *0700* TU 30.8.5 commenced scheduled firing exercises. *0933* Completed exercise. TU proceeded to enter Ulithi Lagoon, Caroline Islands. *1100* USS *Dale* commenced patrolling off entrance to Ulithi Lagoon while Oiler units of TU 30.8.5 entered Lagoon, finally entering the Lagoon at 1137.

Typhoon Cobra

The American invasion of the Philippines was threatened during October and November by a new Japanese weapon—the suicide bomber. In the air, these martyrs were *kamikazes*, the "breath of god" or "divine wind," who crashed bomb-laden airplanes onto the decks of American ships. At sea they were *kaitens*, or "turning of the heavens"— 24-inch torpedoes containing 3,000-pound charges with midsections elongated to create a space for a suicide pilot, who rammed into the hulls of American ships. In one month, Japanese suicide bombers hit twenty-two ships of Task Force 38, including ten carriers.

On December 11, Task Force 38 would sortie from Ulithi Lagoon with a plan to stop the suicide bombers. The plan, called "Big Blue Blanket," referring to the blankets used by football players on the Naval Academy's Big Blue football team, called for pulling a continuous cover of navy and marine corps fighters over Japanese air bases in the Philippines. Every Japanese plane that tried to rise up through this coverage would be shot down. Because this plan called for continuous air coverage, the fast attack carriers of Task Force 38 would require frequent fueling from tankers at sea. Destroyers from DesRon 1, including the USS *Dale*, would screen these tankers.

Dan Ahlberg: We were supposed to check all systems the day we entered port so we could fix anything that was not working before we left again. We were also supposed to recheck everything the day before we left to make certain nothing had reared its ugly head while we were in port. When we pulled into Ulithi the sonar checked out okay. But the day before we were to leave it did not register correctly.

To confirm my readings, I signaled a friend on another tin can to measure a ping for me. [*Author's note*: Sound emitted from the sonar transmitter—a "ping"—travels through water to a target, and then bounces back from the target to a receiver. Distance and direction can then be measured to the target.] After I pinged him he sent a message back via Morse code, which said our signal strength was low and had the wrong spread.

I had to wait for the captain to come back from the officer's club to deliver the bad news. I knew he would be three-sheets-to-the-wind, and would not be one bit happy about having to tell the squadron commander *Dale* could not screen the convoy.

When the quarterdeck petty officer saw the captain returning I got ready to make my report. I waited until he was at the evening meal in the wardroom so other officers would be around. Needless to say, my name was mud! "Goddamn, Ahlberg! You told me the sonar was okay just a couple of days ago, and now you're telling me it's down. This better be good!"

I presented a record of my readings to him and then gave him the real bad news. "Captain," I said, "our readings were good when we pulled in, but now they're bad! And I can't fix the sonar, sir, without retracting the sonar dome all the way out of the hull. And we can't do that, sir, unless we go into dry dock!"

Cussing a blue streak, he ordered me back to work. Later, a couple of technicians came over from the tender to check my readings. I was literally sweating blood while they ran their checks, and was much relieved when they confirmed my diagnosis.

Harold Zoellner: During this time we were steaming in and out of Ulithi Lagoon, escorting tankers back and forth to the fleet. One time we were getting ready to sortie with a task group of tankers when our sonar went down. Our job was to screen those tankers from Jap submarines. Without sonar we were pretty much useless. So, instead of going out with the tankers, we headed over to the tender for some parts. Our sister, the *Monaghan*, had arrived early in the morning and was turned right around and sent out with our tankers. *Lucky guys!*

USS Dale War Diary, *December 11*: Anchored as before. USS *Dixie*'s visual to Maintenance Officer, ComServRon 10, stated that USS *Dale* was ready for undocking and that USS *Dixie* was unable to effect repairs [to] USS *Dale*'s sonar gear. *0800* TG underway for sea. *0819* Underway. Proceeded to enter floating dry dock ARD 13 in berth 410 for examination of sonar gear. *1027* Rested on keel blocks in floating dry dock. *2230* Lt. Bowen Blair assumed duties as Executive Officer of USS *Dale*, relieving M. D. Callahan of such duties pursuant to BuPers restricted dispatch.

Dan Ahlberg: Apparently, no one had overseen the repair of *Dale*'s sonar while she was being overhauled at the Bremerton Navy Yard. They didn't bring the sound head up because the original hole made for it was too small. So, rather than fixing the problem while the ship was in dry dock, they just ignored it. Someone screwed up!

I was totally miserable the day *Dale* went into dry dock. I was eighteen years old and responsible for *Dale*'s missing her convoy duty! I smoked a carton of cigarettes and drank gallons of coffee while they pulled the sonar head out. To make matters worse, the entire crew had to turn to and paint the ship's hull. It was hot as hades in the dry dock and nobody was my friend!

I was standing there when they finally cut off the dome and took the sonar head out. The technicians took one look at it and discovered burned wires. Turns out our sonar was failing because of an electrical short. I was happy as a kid with a new toy when this was confirmed.

Eugene Brewer: We hung around for quite a while at Ulithi, waiting for our sonar to get fixed. One day our sister, the *Aylwin*, came into the lagoon and we knew right away something very bad had happened. She was missing her entire forward stack and was pumping water out of every compartment. Guys lined the decks to watch her come in. We wondered what could have happened, as the waters in Ulithi Lagoon were so calm.

Dan Ahlberg: The ship that took our place when the sonar went down—the *Monaghan*—did not come back. We were told she was lost in a typhoon and that a search was being conducted for survivors. The ships that did make it back to the lagoon were all beat up.

Harold Zoellner: For years I dreamed about our sister ships that were lost in the typhoon. I knew many of those guys, as we used to tie up in nests together and share movies. In my dreams I would see a big wall of water coming to overwhelm me. I called them *"Monaghan* dreams." They stayed with me for many years.

Author's note: On December 18, ships of Admiral Halsey's Task Force 38 met with Typhoon Cobra in the Philippine Sea. Typhoon Cobra was a powerful, compact storm. So powerful, in fact, that destroyer *Dewey*'s barometer read 27.30 inches of mercury, which is one of the lowest barometric pressure readings ever recorded.

Ships of Task Force 38, critically low on fuel, experienced a hellacious time surviving Typhoon Cobra. No ships experienced more difficulty than *Dale*'s decade-old sisters, *Hull* and *Monaghan*. The top-heavy old tin cans rolled up to seventy degrees while battling the howling winds and towering waves. But after fighting for many hours, both ships succumbed to Cobra's venom, rolled over, and sank. A newer *Fletcher*-class destroyer, *Spence*, also went down.

In one strike, Typhoon Cobra took the lives of 790 tin can sailors.

As *Dale* waited out the few remaining days of 1944 in a Ulithi dry dock, the loss of *Hull*, *Monaghan*, and *Spence* weighed heavily on the spirits of her sailors, who believed Cobra to be a portent of things to come in 1945. They were right.

1945

America's Pacific offensive had become relentless. During the past year, the Yanks had conquered the Marshalls, Marianas, New Guinea, and Leyte Island in the Philippines. The U.S. Navy crushed Japan's Imperial Navy in two major naval engagements, leaving it only two aircraft carriers without airplanes and three battleships with little fuel. America's battle fleet now had more than a thousand ships and was growing in size and strength day by day.

Though left with only a few ships, Japan was determined to extract the maximum price for every square inch of its remaining territory. The Japanese still had airplane factories, hundreds of airfields, and an endless supply of young men willing to fly airplanes into the steel hulls of American ships. Japan also maintained hope that the divine winds (or *kamikaze*, the origin of the suicide bomber term) that had destroyed Kublai Khan's invasion force in the thirteenth century would once again swoop down and drown its enemy. That invasion had been the only severe threat to Japan from outside invaders prior to World War II. In November 1274, an armada led by Kublai Khan landed at Hakata Bay. The Japanese were no match for the Mongol cavalry and were forced to retreat to the hills. The Mongols returned to their ships for the night, where a severe storm caught them, sinking two hundred ships and drowning thirteen thousand soldiers. The remaining Mongol ships retreated back to Korea, ending the invasion attempt. The end game of the Pacific war would present many opportunities for ships of the U.S. Navy to steam full speed into harm's way. In fact, nearly one-half of the navy ships lost in WWII went down in 1945. The USS *Dale* would get her fair share of harm's way. Indeed, wherever the fight went, *Dale* was sure to follow.

JANUARY: PHILIPPINES AND SOUTH CHINA SEA

The Philippine archipelago comprises more than seven thousand islands, most of volcanic origin and quite small, running north to south along the eastern side of the South China Sea. The nation's eleven largest islands make up approximately 90 percent of its land area, which is about equivalent to the land area of Italy. This north-south chain of islands was a barrier guarding Japan's domination of the immensely important sea-lanes of the South China Sea. Were the Philippines to fall to the Americans, Japan would likely lose its access to the natural resources of Southeast Asia.

The Americans planned to punch through the island barrier, swarm into the South China Sea, invade Luzon, and take back Manila, the nation's capital. At Leyte Gulf, the U.S. Navy assembled its invasion fleet and its Task Force 38 carrier force for this purpose.

The ships of Task Force 38, sailing into harm's way thousands of miles from safe harbors, would require ammunition, food, and fuel. The support ships of Rear Admiral Donald B. Beary's Task Group

30.8 would satisfy these needs, as Task Force 38 flew cover for the invasion of Luzon and then steamed into the South China Sea for raids on China, Formosa, Luzon, and Okinawa. *Dale*'s job would be to escort these supply ships as they nourished the fleet.

Ulithi

USS Dale *War Diary*, *January 1–5*: Anchored in berth 9, Ulithi Lagoon, Caroline Islands, awaiting replacement parts for defective sonar gear.

A. D. Payne: Our sonar gear was down, and while we waited for the parts to arrive, we had plenty of rope-yarn Sundays. Often the captain would send us ashore to Mog Mog Island with a ration of three cans of beer. I hadn't learned how to drink yet, so I would sell my three beers to someone else. Oh, there were always plenty of guys willing to pay good money for my beer.

Robert "Pat" Olson: I wasn't a drinker and so always sold my ration of beers to the highest bidder. One time a guy offered me twenty bucks for my three cans! Twenty bucks was a lot of money back then, and though I didn't like beer, and certainly liked money, I got to thinking, "If that guy is offering me twenty bucks for three beers, there must be something in those beers that I've been missing." So I kept the three beers, opened one, and tried to drink it. But try as I might, I couldn't drink the beer. So I sold my remaining cans to the guy, who had by then amassed a collection of about twenty cans. He sat under a coconut tree and drank every one of those beers. And he wasn't a big guy, either! There were all kinds of guys in that shape on Mog Mog Island.

Dan Ahlberg: There was one universal truth aboard the *Dale*: everyone hated Axelrod! He was a sleazy lawyer who had pissed someone off at the JAG office in Washington, D.C., and got sent out to sea. He went by the book like he wrote it with God telling him what to say. He was a total pain in the ass!

Axelrod would sneak around *Dale* with a watch bill to catch sailors showing up late for duty. Boy, if he caught you showing up one minute late you had hell to pay! One night it was raining cats, dogs, and fish. You couldn't see the gun mount twenty feet away. We were all standing on the lee side of the bridge out of the rain. The weather-side watch, who couldn't see a thing in that driving rain, came over and joined us. Suddenly, Axelrod appeared on the bridge and started screaming at the OOD, Lieutenant Bright, that the weather-side watch should be put on report for leaving his post without a relief. Now, Bright was a big old farm boy from Nebraska, and the third man in *Dale*'s chain of command. Bright took one look at Axelrod, ordered him out to the weather side, and told him to keep binoculars glued to his eyes until the watch changed. As Axelrod stood there in the driving rain with binoculars glued to his eyes, Bright asked me what the crew thought of him. I replied, "Well, sir, he should probably stay off the fantail in bad weather."

There was a lot of time to waste while we waited for our sonar parts in Ulithi. On the day in question, everyone who did not have the duty went ashore for a big softball game. These games were usually a lot of fun because officers and men would play and drink together instead of being segregated. Well, one thing led to another and soon the guys were drinking more than they were playing. Bosun Mate McNabb commandeered a landing craft from another ship, which he put to use as a party boat for the crew, who by then were all buck naked and drunk as skunks. You have to remember, with all the enlisted men on all the ships in Ulithi Lagoon, there simply wasn't much room on Mog Mog, and so having your own party boat was quite a luxury, even if it didn't happen to belong to you.

Sure enough! Axelrod appeared on the scene, climbed aboard the boat, and began berating Lieutenants Cook and Fishman for fraternizing with the crew, and McNabb for stealing a boat from another ship. The crew, by then thoroughly drunk, took issue with Axelrod and threw his hat over the side. This made Axelrod real mad, but when he protested, the crew threw him over the side as well.

I was the quarterdeck petty officer and watched all the fun and games through our twenty-power long glass. The sight of that boatload of naked drunk sailors, which was then circling Axelrod in the water, was quite hilarious. But I was happy to see Lieutenant Cook, who at least still wore skivvies, order McNabb to pick up poor Axelrod.

I don't remember who had shore patrol that day, but I remember they were as drunk as everyone else and lucky if they still had on a pair of shoes much less any other clothing. By the time they got back to the *Dale*, everybody but Axelrod was in pretty rough shape. We laid them out on the torpedo deck like a bunch of sun-bleached seals and the corpsman checked them over to make sure no one was badly hurt.

Axelrod then ordered me up to the bridge and began dictating charges against the mutinous crew. He talked and talked and talked, and I wrote and wrote and wrote. He was so wrapped up in detailing all his charges he failed to see I was not using a pen like the rules required, but a number two pencil. I covered several pages with his charges and had just finished writing when Captain Zimny came back from the officer's island. He and the other officers were every bit as drunk as the crew, but at least they still had their clothes on.

After chow that evening, I was ordered to report to the captain's cabin with the quarterdeck log. I also brought along a new pink pearl eraser, just in case. When I arrived, Axelrod was there bitching to the captain about everything. The captain dismissed him, took a look at the log, and noticed right away everything had been written in pencil and I had a big eraser in my hand. "Get to it, Ahlberg!" he ordered. Next morning at captain's mast, McNabb was busted down to Seaman First for two months and the starboard duty section was restricted to the ship for two Mog Mog beer parties.

USS Dale *War Diary*, *January 7*: Resting on keel blocks in ARD 15 undergoing sonar repairs. *1105* Commenced flooding dry dock in order to undock because of storm warnings, but at 1240 commenced to re-dock in accordance with verbal orders of ComServRon 10. *1838* Underway from floating dry dock. Proceeded out into harbor and anchored near USS *Prairie*. *1947* Reported to ComServRon 10 that sonar repairs were completed. *2000* Captain P. V. Mercer, USN, ComDesRon One shifted his flag from USS *Dewey* to the USS *Dale* and arrived on board with staff. *2020* Underway and proceeded to rendezvous with TU 30.8.9. *2144* Passed through entrance gate of Ulithi Lagoon and from inland to international waters.

Philippines

Dale joined the fleet at Leyte Gulf where it was engaged in the invasion of Luzon Island. Lacking warships to defend its positions in the Philippines, the Imperial Navy would be forced to respond with the only weapon it had capable of stopping American ships—suicide bombers. Between January 3 and 13, fifty-three U.S. Navy ships would be struck by kamikazes off the coast of the Philippines.

Lowell Barker: I was OOD one day while we were in Leyte Gulf, waiting for the convoy to form up. Everybody was on edge because of reported kamikaze activity. Suddenly, several ships were struck by kamikazes and blew up. The air filled with AA bursts and everyone on the bridge was looking for kamikazes trying to sneak up on us. One was spotted at some distance and we opened up with our 5-inchers, but he kept boring right in on us. Then the 40mms opened up, and then the 20s. Closer and closer he came. Suddenly, his plane erupted in flame, exploded, and crashed into the water less than a hundred yards away. Boy, we had to get him, and we got him!

USS Dale *War Diary,* *January 14*: Steaming as a unit of TU 30.8.11 in the Mindanao Sea en route to fueling area in South China Sea. *0230* Cleared friendly task unit, which was previously reported by USS *Converse* making eastern transit of Mindanao Sea. *0323* In a TBS transmission addressed to ComScreen the *Bangust* reported having felt two heavy underwater shocks. A minute later the *Kyne* reported seeing six faint torpedo tracks and the *Bangust* conjectured the possibility the shocks experienced by her could have been "dud" torpedoes striking her hull. However, evidence was lacking and the TU proceeded as before.

Dan Ahlberg: We were escorting tankers from Leyte Gulf through the Surigao Straights into the Sulu and South China seas. Our mission was to draw the Japs' attention away from the big push, which was Luzon. We started through the straights about sundown and were called to general quarters. The tankers we were escorting were really slow. It was pucker time!

The water in those straights was really shallow, so my attention was divided between my sonar and GQ stations. The sonar was located in a little room off the bridge. The room also contained our chart table, fathometer, chronometer, and the captain's steaming bunk. There were two sonarmen and the skipper in a room meant for one person. My GQ station was up forward at gun two, a 5-incher.

Every time we got close to a really shallow stretch of water, I would run back to the sonar room and watch the fathometer. Whenever a lookout yelled [he] spotted a torpedo wake, or saw a torpedo boat sneaking out from the shoreline, I would run to beat hell from the sonar room down to my gun position. The shoreline on both sides was mighty close and mountainous, so torpedo boats were hard to spot against that black backdrop. Our radar signals were also confused by the proximity to land, so everyone was really jumpy.

When the danger passed, I would run back up to the sonar room again. Back and forth! Back and forth! As I remember it, we never fired, but some of our sister ships in the screen did.

Later that night I had the bridge watch. We were told to watch out for Japs swimming out with satchel charges from the land. I saw what I believed were swimmers and shot them with my .45 handgun. I was raised in Texas and was a pretty good shot in those days. I could even hit a running rabbit with a pistol shot. Trouble was, my thumb was pinched by the automatic's slide and started bleeding. Everybody came running over to see what the shooting was about and saw me, an eighteen-year-old punk, standing there sucking on my thumb with a smoking .45 in the other hand. They must have thought I had gone crazy, as whatever I was shooting at had long since disappeared in the ship's wake.

One thing for sure, everyone breathed a sigh of relief the next morning when the sun came up and we steamed out of those confined straights into the Sulu Sea!

Author's note: While *Dale* escorted tankers of TU 30.8 out to meet the carriers of Task Force 38 in the South China Sea, the U.S. Navy's invasion fleet landed on Luzon, thus beginning the long and arduous task of retaking the principal island of the Philippines from the Japanese.

South China Sea

After busting through the Philippine Islands, Task Force 38 would steam thousands of miles throughout the South China Sea to lay Halsey's Big Blue Blanket over Japanese airfields and shipping lanes. The shipping lanes of the South China Sea, a portion of the Pacific Ocean stretching roughly from Singapore and the Strait of Malacca to the Strait of Taiwan, were absolutely critical to Japan's survival as a world power. Japan used this body of water, which today hosts the world's second busiest sea-lanes, to ship oil from mineral-rich Borneo and Indonesia north to its home islands, and ammunition, equipment, and food south to its troops in occupied territories. Without free access to the sea-lanes of the South China Sea, Japan would run out of oil in the home islands and lose the ability to fight for the captured resources in the south. Halsey's intrusion would be met by fierce storms of kamikazes and typhoon winds. Through it all, the task force would be nurtured by the support ships of Task Group 30.8, which would be protected by the USS *Dale* and her sister tin cans.

USS Dale *War Diary, January 17:* Steaming as a unit of TU 30.8.11 in fueling area in South China Sea. *0500* In preparation for fueling exercises with TF 38 and on orders from CTG 30.8, TU 30.8.11 divided into four units in accordance with CTG 30.8's TBS transmission. *1830* Fueling exercises for the day completed. A heavy sea and wind of gale proportions had hampered fueling exercises during the day, and later in the evening conditions became even worse, necessitating fleet course to clear storm area. Even though completely ballasted, the *Dale* experienced rolls up to 45°. TG was composed as follows: *Lexington* (CTG 38.2), *Hancock* (CTF 38), *Hornet*, *Independence*, *Enterprise*, *New Jersey* (Com3rd. Flt.), *Wisconsin*, DesRons 52 and 62, *McCord*, *Hazelwood*, *Haggard*, and *Franks*.

January 18: Steaming as a unit of TU 30.8.2 in formation with TG 38.2 and in general company of TF 38. Because of continuing heavy seas, the fueling exercises scheduled for this day were not held.

Bob Johnson: In the South China Sea we had weeks of weather that was either bad, worse, or worst. Sometimes all you could do was tie yourself down and hold on. I remember looking out over the waves and seeing a tin can do something that scared me out of my socks. That destroyer went completely airborne, like a fish jumping out of the water! I clearly remember seeing both of its propellers spinning in the air. Its sonar dome, which extends down from the bottom of the ship, completely cleared the surface of the water. I thought, "If this is what's going on, we don't have a chance!"

John Overholt: The storm just kept getting worse and worse. I was down in the galley baking bread when the ship heeled way over on its side. Everything went flying! The bread flew one way, the pans another, and I a third! I've never had to work in conditions like that before. And I certainly don't want to again!

Earl "Jitterbug" Pearson: If you saw it in the storm, you'd a known why they called it a "mess hall." There was food scattered across the decks everywhere, even out to the torpedo tubes!

Lester Dailey: We were escorting the support ships fueling the aircraft carriers on their raid into the South China Sea when we ran into the storm. It was so violent we figured we were all doomed. Less than a month before we lost three tin cans in a storm and were well aware of what happened to the guys down below. Nobody wanted to go below for fear of being trapped when the ship rolled over. I'm sure glad I wasn't with those poor guys down in the engine room! I stayed right there and held on to the chart table through the entire storm. It was the most frightening experience of the entire war!

George Crandall: I was the OOD during the storm and had to be strapped into the chair because *Dale* was taking rolls of up to seventy degrees. There was no way I could stand on the deck. My big worry was that if we kept taking rolls like that, we would take water into the stacks, which would put the fires out in the fire room. Then what?

John Kelsch: My job was to use the Sugar George radar to keep *Dale* in formation with the rest of the fleet. There was no way you could actually see anything with the naked eye. You couldn't see where the sea ended and the sky began! It was real tough reading the radar because of the interference of the weather and our relationship with other ships. In order to see where another ship was on the Sugar George, both ships had to be on an even keel. But each ship was rolling way over on its beam, and so all I could see on the screen was momentary glimpses of other ships. I had to extrapolate our relative position. We were scared as hell of running into each other in that stuff.

Darel Bright: It was an incredibly helpless feeling and totally frightening. Everyone aboard the *Dale* was seasick. Callahan and I stood the watch together on the bridge. There was no general quarters or anything, just regular duty stations, but nobody could stand watches topside because of the ferocity of the winds. The weather was so heavy we couldn't tell where the sky ended and the sea began. We had to keep heading right into the wind and waves, otherwise we would roll sixty degrees and more. During Typhoon Cobra, *Hull* and *Monaghan* got themselves broadside to the waves, rolled over, and never came back. Luckily, we had fuel aboard, and that fuel acted as ballast and kept our top-heavy old ship from turning turtle. It was terrifying . . . totally terrifying. There was no place to go . . . no foxhole to hide in, and no way to retreat. You were just there until it was done with you.

John Kelsch: I was stationed right below the bridge in the radar shack, which was high above the ship's center of gravity. Being up high like that had a way of really accelerating the ship's rolls. I kept watching the inclinometer peg at sixty degrees! With each roll we'd get whipped because we were so high above the center of gravity. I was really frightened by how close our stacks came to the waves, because if water poured down into them, we'd have lost all power.

Elliot Wintch: We were taking rolls of seventy degrees, which made the open decks of the *Dale* the most frightening place on earth. We had lines rigged fore and aft, and to get from our berthing compartment to our duty station we had to cross the deck in a safety harness.

Eugene Brewer: You must remember the *Dale* had no fore and aft passageways below decks. If you worked aft and wanted to get some chow, you had to cross the open decks, which were constantly awash in giant waves. We rigged lifelines fore and aft, and timed our movements to conform to the rolls of the ship and movement of the waves. You had to perform some fancy trigonometry to figure out how to avoid being washed over the side. It was the only time during the entire war that everybody wore life jackets.

Charles O'Rorke: Giant waves lifted the bow way up into the air, and then rolled along underneath the ship until the bow plunged down into a trough. Then the ship would roll way over to port and way back to starboard, sometimes sixty to seventy degrees and more. Everyone was real seasick. There was just no way to avoid it. We had ropes running fore and aft to help us get from one place to the next, but sometimes they didn't help. One of our bosun mates was washed clean off the deck by a big wave, and then washed right back aboard by the next one. He was one happy guy!

John Kelsch: Those old tin cans were made very top heavy by all the new equipment they added throughout the war. For us to survive that storm, we had to lower the ship's center of gravity as much as possible. They sent the cooks and other ratings down into the magazine to secure all the ready ammunition. It must have been terribly nauseous bobbing around down there in the magazine while handling all that heavy ammunition. Anything above decks that couldn't be taken below was tossed over the side.

Bill Ryan: They took us off the fire control tower and sent us down to the mess hall where they tied off ropes from the starboard bulkhead to the port. When the ship would heel way over on her starboard side, we'd all climb the ropes to port, and vice versa. This went on all night long! It was totally out of control down in the mess room. There was no hope of eating and, besides, we were all seasick as hell!

Ernest Schnabel: They kept us all on duty throughout the storm to be human ballast down below. They had ropes tied off, port to starboard, throughout the ship. Whenever the ship would take a heavy roll, we would all scramble up the rope to the high side and hang on for dear life.

John Overholt: Down below in the berthing compartments we were spread-eagled on the deck, because hardly anyone could stand up. The ship was taking terrifying rolls to port and starboard. When she would get to the extreme of a roll, she would just hang there motionless. Everyone held their breath, wondering if this would be time she would roll all the way over. Then she would free herself and roll back, and we would all let go of our breaths in one big "WOOOoooooooooooo!"

Robert "Pat" Olson: You had to adapt to the conditions. When the ship buckled under you, you had to let your knees buckle with it. But sometimes it was very difficult to adapt, like when we hit that storm in the South China Sea. It was so rough down in the fire room that the big steel-tread deck plates covering the bilges flew loose and crashed all around us. We had to dodge them while shuffling about on the angle iron framing that had held them, and all while the ship was rolling and pitching like a bucking bronco. Made you wonder which one of us was going to have his head smashed in. We all got plenty scared down there!

Darel Bright: The only difference between kamikazes and typhoons was time. Oh, the terror was the same, but when kamikazes attacked, it was all over in a matter of minutes. There was not much you could do to protect yourself. It was just the luck of the draw. Some ships got hit; others did not. But it was all over in a few minutes. Typhoons were different! They would last for hours, and even days. Every second, you just hung on and waited for the wave that would roll you all the way over. You were terrorized the entire time.

Dan Ahlberg: During the storm a big wave caught me from behind and washed me into a gun mount. I broke four ribs and wrenched my back, which still troubles me today. The ship's doctor said my injuries were sufficient to warrant a transfer off the *Dale*. And hell, by then I had already requested transfer four times. But after the storm I knew for a fact the USS *Dale* was one lucky ship. I told Doc and Captain Zimny the only way I would leave her now was feet first or in a body bag.

Bill Ryan: The next morning the sun came out. There were birds everywhere and driftwood and stuff floating on the surface of the ocean.

USS Dale War Diary, *January 21*: Steaming as a unit of TU 30.8.1 in assigned area awaiting orders. CTG received orders from Com3rd Fleet to consolidate cargo and depart for Ulithi, Caroline Islands. *1035* TU commenced fueling exercise to consolidate cargo among oilers as directed by CTG in his TBS transmission of 1005. *1820* Completed fueling exercises and proceeded en route to Ulithi Atoll, Caroline Islands.

Author's note: Between January 10 and 21, Task Force 38 steamed 3,800 miles throughout the South China Sea, raiding French Indochina (Vietnam), China, Formosa, Luzon, Okinawa, Tokyo, and Kobe. Though severely hampered by foul weather, Halsey's carrier pilots sank forty-four Japanese ships totaling about 132,700 tons. Of these ships, fifteen were combatants and, of the twenty-nine merchant marine ships, ten were tankers. Though Task Force 38 lost twenty-three planes, most of the pilots and crew were recovered safely by screening submarines and tin cans. In a message to the fleet, Admiral William "Bull" Halsey said, "We have driven the enemy off the sea and back to his inner defenses. Superlatively well done."[1]

JANUARY TO MARCH: IWO JIMA

With Leyte under control, Luzon invaded, supply lines relatively secure, and General MacArthur's promise to return fulfilled, the U.S.

IWO JIMA, OKINAWA, AND JAPAN—FEBRUARY TO
AUGUST 1945

Navy turned its attention back to the next step in its delayed march across the Central Pacific—Iwo Jima.

Eight square miles of sulfur-belching rock dominated by Mount Suribachi (which would be made famous in the flag-raising photograph captured by Joe Rosenthal), Iwo Jima is part of the Volcano Islands, which constitute one-third of the Bonin Archipelago. Situated some 660 miles south of Tokyo, Iwo Jima was being used by Japanese forces as a staging area for kamikaze attacks on American shipping. Were the Americans to take Iwo Jima, it would deprive the Japanese of this critical staging area, provide bases from which P-51 fighters could escort the giant B-29s to Japan and back, and accommodate emergency landings from damaged B-29s struggling back to their bases in the Marianas.

Operation Detachment, the seizure of Iwo Jima, called for weeks of preliminary bombardment from carrier- and land-based bombers; days of shelling by battleships, cruisers, and destroyers; and then a landing by seventy thousand U.S. Marines. Arrayed against this mighty force were twenty-seven thousand Japanese soldiers, who had spent months tunneling in for a battle that Lieutenant General Holland M. Smith would call the "most savage and costly battle in the history of the Marine Corps."[2]

When Task Force 38 passed from the control of Admiral Hasley to Admiral Nimitz, it became Task Force 58. Similarly, the fleet's support unit, Task Unit 30.8, became Task Unit 50.8. The change in numbers, however, meant little to the USS *Dale*, as she would continue to protect the ships that armed, fed, and fueled the fleet as it steamed into battle.

USS Dale *War Diary*, *March 1*: Steaming as a unit of Task Unit 50.8.28 en route to fueling rendezvous with Task Unit 52.2.5. In accordance with CinCPac directive *Dale*, along with *Aylwin*, *Farragut*, *Macdonough*, and *Dewey* were reassigned to DesDiv 10 of DesRon 5, DesDiv 1 being dissolved by the same directive. At 0130 made radar contact on Minani, Iwo Jima, Volcano Islands, bearing 330° T, distant 45 miles.

March 2–4: Steaming in company of *Saugatuck* en route to Iwo Jima, Volcano Islands. *0700* The *Saugatuck* reported to CTF 51 for duty and *Dale* proceeded with *Saugatuck* in accordance with CTG 51's TBS message to join the *Pamanset* who was just off Iwo Jima. At 0735 *Saugatuck* and *Dale* joined the *Pamanset* and *Dale* patrolled station ahead of the two vessels while a transfer of fuel was taking place from the *Pamanset* to the *Saugatuck*. In accordance with CTG 51.2's message, the *Dale* proceeded to patrol an area off southern tip of Iwo Jima, arriving in area at 1013.

Robert "Pat" Olson: We had dusted the top off Iwo Jima real good. There wasn't a thing left standing after weeks of bombing and shelling, and not a chance for life to exist anywhere on that island. Well, the joke was on us, because the Japs had played a little game of prairie dog on us and tunneled way down deep, where they sat out our softening-up bombardment. Then, when our marines went ashore, they popped up out of their holes and blasted away.

Author's note: Robert Olson was most likely referring to the prairie dogs of his Montana homeland when he described the Japanese tactics on Iwo Jima. However, hide and seek "prairie dog warfare" was earlier defined by Confederate General Simon Bolivar Buckner during America's Civil War.

John Galica: My battle station was pointer on the starboard 40 mm. When the 5-inch guns were working over Iwo Jima we didn't have anything to do but watch. We could see our marines fighting the Japs as plain as day. It was just like being in a giant movie theater. The marines looked just like toy soldiers as they worked their way along the cliffs.

Eugene Brewer: We were right in under Mount Suribachi, firing our 5-inchers in support of the marines. You could see it plain as day from the bridge. We would lay in 5-inch fire a couple hundred yards in front of the marines in a rolling barrage. As they advanced, the marines would call in requests for us to lay rounds in caves and such.

Bill Ryan: Mount Suribachi was full of caves. I was up on the range finder, ranging the fall of shot into the mouths of caves the Japs were hiding in. We thought we were doing a great job, because we were putting our shots dead on the money, but it didn't seem to make much difference to the Japs. Even if we landed a shot into the mouth of a cave, they would just go down their tunnel and pop out of another hole.

George Crandall: I was up in *Dale*'s gun director, talking directly with the marines fighting on Mount Suribachi. We spent about two days helping them out with our 5-inchers. The Japs were encased in deep caves and fortifications. Whenever the marines would come up against one of these strong points they would call for help. We would lay a few rounds in for distance, and the marines would call back, "Down a hundred! Now, right fifty!" Then we would lay a round or two right into the Japs' lap and the marines would move up to the next strong point. I spent all that time on the radio talking with those marines as they worked their way from cave to cave. Boy, was I ever glad to be in the navy!

Dan Ahlberg: I was on the bridge, watching the marines through our twenty-power binoculars scramble up Suribachi. We spotted a Japanese cannon, firing out of a cave high up on a cliff face, but when we called in a request to fire on it, we were turned down because it wasn't our assignment at the time. Captain Zimny was steaming mad. We watched helplessly as a squad of marines scaled the cliff and lowered a satchel charge into the cave. The explosion blew out the cannon but killed the marines as well. With our twenty-power binoculars you could practically count the whiskers on the guys' faces.

Roy Roseth: We got into some real sport at Iwo Jima. They detached us from screening duty to support the ground troops with gunfire. We could see the flag on Mount Suribachi really well. We also got the job of escorting the hospital ship out to sea for burial duty. I don't know how many guys aboard the *Dale* knew what we were doing. But with binoculars you could see them sliding the bodies into the sea from underneath a flag. We heard there were five hundred bodies buried at sea by that ship. I suppose they had a weight of some kind tied in with them, because they sank right away. You could watch them dropping bodies over the side for a while, and then *Dale* would turn in a different direction and you'd lose them. But when we shifted course again, there they'd be, dumping bodies over the side.

USS Dale War Diary, *March 11*: Moored along the destroyer *Melvin* in berth 330 of the southern anchorage, Ulithi Lagoon, Caroline Islands. At 2012 all hands went to General Quarters as condition "Red" was ordered throughout the harbor because of enemy aircraft in the vicinity. Just as the alert was sounded a large fire and what appeared to be an explosion was observed in the northern anchorage area and from the information received over the voice circuits the target was deduced to be the escort carrier *Sangamon*. At 2105 the area was clear of all enemy planes and no fires visible, so condition "White" was set.

Author's note: Iwo Jima did not come cheap. What had been planned as a fight of a few days took a solid month. At a cost of tens of thousands of lives, Japan lost another link in its inner defense and the Americans gained a vital base close to Japan's home islands that would double the effectiveness of its B-29 attacks. The 3rd, 4th, and 5th Divisions of the U.S. Marines suffered 26,000 casualties, with 6,800 deaths. It was indeed, as Lieutenant General Holland M. Smith said, "the most savage and costly battle in the history of the Marine Corps."

Ships of the U.S. Navy did not have it quite so bad. Compared to campaigns in the Philippines, where kamikazes brought a daily dose of death and destruction, it had been an easy fight. Kamikazes had to fly long distances over water to reach Iwo Jima, and thus were easily discovered and quickly managed. The smooth sailing, however, was over for the U.S. Navy.

MARCH TO JUNE: OKINAWA

The next step for American forces was to go for the heart of Japan's defense—the Ryukyu Islands.

The Ryukyu Archipelago is a combination of three island groups immediately south of Japan's home islands. These islands separate the Philippine Sea from the East China Sea. Most of the islands are of volcanic origin with rugged hills and little flat land. The largest and most important island, Okinawa, is situated only 350 miles from Japan's home islands to the northeast, Formosa to the southwest, and China to the northwest. Okinawa was large enough, and flat enough, to support airfields and fleet anchorages.

If American forces could capture Okinawa, it would effectively seal Japan within its borders and provide a base from which to invade its home islands. Thus plans for Operation Iceberg, the capture of Okinawa, were put into effect. Operation Iceberg would employ thirteen hundred ships that would put ashore one hundred and eighty-three thousand troops and seven hundred and fifty thousand tons of supplies. It would dwarf all other amphibious operations of the Pacific war.

There was, however, a logistical challenge to Operation Iceberg that made its outcome doubtful—distance. The nearest American base, Leyte, is 900 miles to the south. Ulithi and Guam are more than 1,200 miles away, and Pearl Harbor is more than 4,000 miles to the east. The Yanks were a long way from friendly shores and in the heart of kamikaze country.

The Japanese would meet this invasion with all the force they could muster. A directive from Imperial General Headquarters designated Okinawa to be the focal point of the decisive battle for the defense of the homeland. The one hundred ten thousand troops that had spent months digging in to enforce this edict were determined to do so, to the very last man. Thousands of kamikaze pilots stationed at airfields in Japan, Formosa, and China waited for their moment. They would attack alone, in pairs, small groups, and in giant Kikusui flights containing hundreds of airplanes. Between June 6 and 22, Japan launched ten massive waves of upward of two hundred planes against the American fleet invading Okinawa. The code name for this operation, *Kikusui*, translates as "floating chrysanthemums," and was the symbol used by Kusunoki Masashige, a fourteenth century Japanese hero.

Fully aware of Japan's suicidal intentions, the U.S. Navy did its best to reduce the number of kamikazes by working over Japanese air-bases with the fast carriers of Task Force 58. These high-speed, hit-and-run carrier raids in the western Pacific became known as "Haul

Ass with Halsey" after the commander of Task Force 38, Admiral William "Bull" Halsey. The "Haul Ass with Halsey" raids began in October 1944 with attacks on Japan, China, Formosa, and the Philippines.

The first American step toward Okinawa was taken when the Americans landed on Kerama Retto, a group of small islands fifteen miles west of Okinawa. The Keramas would provide the Americans with a fleet anchorage, a seaplane base, and a platform for its long-range artillery to support the upcoming landings on Okinawa proper. In addition, the Americans captured 350 suicide boats that had been positioned on the small islands to attack the American invasion fleet.

Finally, after months of softening up by the American fleet, sixty thousand American troops went ashore on Okinawa proper on Easter Sunday morning, April 1. Thus began three months of the most gruesome fighting of the Pacific war.

Dale would continue to escort Rear Admiral Beary's logistical support ships throughout the fight for Okinawa. Beary's Task Unit 50.8 maintained about ten fleet oilers, five ammunition ships, two escort carriers, and one or two provision ships on station with the fleet at all times. Every day this support group would service one of the carrier groups of Task Force 58.

Early in the morning, prior to the arrival of ships of the carrier force, a fueling line of designated oilers, ammunition ships, and provision ships would clear the main body of the logistic group. A line of five oilers would set a fueling course some 1,500 to 2,000 yards apart, while four ammunition ships and provision ships formed a similar line astern the oilers. As these ships fueled, provisioned, and rearmed the fleet, other ships of the support group would consolidate cargo and hurry the ships emptied in this manner back to Ulithi for new cargo.

Dale would make five cruises between Ulithi and Okinawa during the struggle for the Ryukyus. She would escort ships into and out of Kerama Retto anchorage, stand picket duty, and protect against swarms of kamikazes.

USS Dale *War Diary*, *April* 6: Steaming as a unit of TG 50.8 in assigned fueling area. *0015* Made radar contact on TG 58.4, 22 miles to the northwest. At 0020 the *Lackawanna* reported hearing cries for help in the water close aboard her, and the *Dale*, on orders from ComScreen, proceeded to search the area. The search was abandoned with negative results at 0130, and the *Dale* left to rejoin TG 50.8.

April 7: A mine was sighted at 0830, 1,500 yards off starboard beam and *Dale* left station to destroy it. A second mine was sighted 1,000 yards off the port beam at 0834. The *Sederstrom* was directed by ComScreen to destroy the second mine. At 0910 the *Dale* succeeded in destroying her mine after expending 144 rounds of 40mm and 360 rounds of 20mm ammunition, and then proceeded to resume station in screen of formation.

Eugene Brewer: A lookout called out, "Mine! Mine off the starboard bow!" The ship's momentum carried us right up to the darned thing. We were only about a yard or so away before we finally got stopped. The captain worked us slowly and gently away, and then we blew it up with 20mm fire. It blew up so close to us that shrapnel hit all over the bridge. One of the small pieces hit Garlinghouse right on the cheek. Had we run up and hit that thing, *Dale* would have sunk like a stone!

USS Dale *War Diary*, *April* 23: Steaming as a unit of TU 50.18.63 en route to Kerama Retto. Made radar contact on Okinawa at 0138, thirty-five miles to the northwest. Sighted the hospital ship *Comfort* at

0340, twelve miles to the southwest. The Southern entrance was reached at 0720 and *Dale* and *Aylwin* commenced patrolling off the entrance to cover the entry into the anchorage area of the *Mayfield*, *Victory*, and *Suamico*.

Dan Ahlberg: I remember Kerama Retto very well. We spent some really bad nights in that hellhole. The first time we were there, we anchored for a couple of days in line with a slot in the mountains. The Jap pilots would fly through the slot knowing that when they cleared the slot there would be a ship waiting right there for them to crash.

We were ordered to anchor where several ships had already been sunk by the kamikazes. We would be the first in a line of ships. Outside of us there was a light cruiser, then a heavy cruiser, and then Bull Halsey's battleship. When we went into that anchorage I remember being on the fathometer and sonar with a couple of the other guys. We were trying to make sure that we didn't drop the hook on top of one of those sunken ships because we didn't want to get snagged. I believe one was a seaplane tender, but don't recall what the others were. We had just enough speed up to steer while we were creeping into that anchorage. Finally, we made it over the sunken ships and yelled, "Clear!" The anchor dropped safely onto a sandy bottom. By the grace of God, and a lot of luck, the flying weather was bad during the time we were anchored there, and so we survived another day.

George Crandall: Kerama Retto was not a pleasant place to be. It was a bunch of small islands a few miles off the coast of Okinawa that we used as a fleet anchorage for the invasion. The problem was the kamikazes. Every day they would crash ships that were participating in the invasion. Some ships were sunk or scuttled and the rest would be towed into Kerama Retto for temporary repairs. One time I counted over sixty damaged ships anchored there, and most of them were tin cans. During daylight hours, the anchorage was fairly quiet because the Japs were out attacking the fleet near Okinawa. But every night they would carry out small air raids over Kerama Retto. To protect all those defenseless ships, LCVPs with smoke-making gear laid a thick blanket of smoke over the harbor. It was spooky. We could hear kamikazes buzzing over us, but we couldn't see them. Some ships tried firing their 20mm guns up through the smoke, but the kamikazes just followed the tracers down through the smoke and crashed those ships.

The planes were not all we had to worry about. The Japs also had suicide boats that would speed out among the ships and drop a depth charge or two under your fantail. There were also Japs on the island, and rumor had it they were swimming out to the ships at night, climbing up the anchor chains, and stabbing sentries.

Those nights were real spooky. The water would be calm and oily and the air filled with smoke. There was a lot of garbage floating in the water, and you never knew if it was garbage or a suicide swimmer. So you shot at it. There were sentries shooting at floating objects throughout the anchorage, and all the shooting really got on your nerves!

Harold Zoellner: I saw a destroyer escort in the anchorage that had been hit by kamikazes on both ends. The bow and stern were both blown away. I don't know what they planned to do with that tin can's remains, but there were guys working away on it!

USS Dale *War Diary,* *April 23*: At 2109 all hands went to General Quarters when a sound contact was made at a distance of 1,500 yards on a bearing of 015° T. An embarrassing barrage of three charges was dropped at 2113. After dropping, however, contact was not regained, and Operation Observant was commenced. Operation Observant was completed at 2306 and a retiring search was initiated immediately thereafter.

Lowell Barker: We made a sonar contact with what we believed to be a submarine off Okinawa. Captain Zimny decided that he would direct the attack himself. He ordered up "full speed ahead, right full rudder" and "drop depth charges" all at about the same time. Well, what happened next is not to be forgotten! The depth charges blew up right underneath *Dale* and severely damaged her stern. We were dead in the water for hours and we knew there was a Jap sub out there somewhere!

Dan Ahlberg: We picked up a sub and made a run on it. The officer making the run botched it big time, because the exploding depth charge lifted us up some ten or fifteen feet and nearly blew the stern off. It split three of the *Dale*'s bottom plates and I couldn't hear out of my right ear for days. Since I had done arc welding in my dad's auto business, I helped Healy, the first-class ship repairman, weld up the cracks. We were both small men and so could [fit] down below where there wasn't much room. We closed the door to the compartment, pressured-up the room with air, and then opened the hatch to the bilges. We stuffed strips of bed sheets into the cracks and then welded a plate over them. *Dale* still had those bed sheets in her hull when she was decommissioned in Brooklyn.

USS **Dale** *War Diary, April 25:* At 1832 *Dale* proceeded to take night picket station fifteen miles to the northwest of formation center. A sound contact was reported by the *H. F. Clark*, which was in the formation screen to the south at 1914, just four minutes after *Dale* arrived at picket station. TG 50.8 executed emergency evasive maneuvers. At 1930 *Dale* had surface radar contact four miles to the northwest. All hands went to General Quarters and closed contact at flank speed. Two minutes after radar contact had been made, however, it was lost, and, on the assumption that contact might have been a submarine, a sound search was commenced. Radar contact with unidentified object was regained at 2002 bearing 010° T, 3,600 yards. Commenced closing contact at flank speed, but contact opened, giving erratic plot. Made visual search since visibility was good (moonlight—visibility four miles) but with no success. By 2012 had made five more similar contacts with ranges varying from 1,500 to 5,000 yards. In light of all the evidence, the contact was evaluated as false, probably due to freak atmospheric conditions, and further investigation was halted.

John Kelsch: One of our most dangerous jobs was standing picket duty off Okinawa. We would go out beyond the fleet fifty miles or so and make figure eights in the water while we searched for incoming kamikazes with our radar. There would be about eight of us tin cans stretched along a line about twelve miles apart. We'd all be sweeping for the same thing.

A destroyer's best defense is speed and maneuverability. Standing picket duty took that defense away because we were always going in circles in one place. The kamikazes and their fighter escorts figured out pretty quick we were sitting ducks! It seemed like the first wave of kamikazes always went for the picket ships, and that made us all nervous as hell. We'd be listening to the TBS, which is how rumors got passed from one picket ship to the next, and hear things like, "Just heard the 560 got hit!" Then we'd get to thinking, "Hey, maybe we're next!"

Ernest "Dutch" Smith: Back then, radar could only see to the horizon. So they sent us out to where the top of our mast could be seen poking up above the horizon and made us stand picket duty to protect the fleet. Each DD or DE was stationed about twenty miles from the next, so each ship's radar would overlap with the next one in line. This way we could pick up any kamikazes coming for the fleet. Trouble was, once the kamikazes saw us pickets, they thought we were the fleet! Once we were caught out there by a huge flight of kamikazes. They knocked the stuffings out of the other tin cans in the line, but somehow, just missed us.

George Crandall: We were on picket duty one day when a lone kamikaze attacked us. Everyone aboard the ship knew it was going to be either him or us. If we didn't shoot him out of the sky, he was going to crash us and blow us out of the water.

Roy Roseth: He attacked from astern. They all liked to attack from astern because then only our aft-mounted guns could be brought into action. But every gun that could shoot did shoot. First the aft-mounted 5-inchers opened up, then the 40mms, and then the 20s. Our tracers were reaching up to him, and his tracers were reaching down for us. Finally, one of our rounds hit the damned thing and it exploded and crashed right into our wake. It was sure good to see him go down!

USS **Dale** *War Diary, May 5*: Steaming in company with the *Sebec* en route to Okinawa. Made radar contact on Okinawa thirty-four miles to northwest at 0059. At 0320 all hands went to general quarters for possible air attack, numerous unidentified aircraft in vicinity.

Elliot Wintch: We were alongside a tanker refueling. *Dale* was on one side and *New Mexico* was on the other. Suddenly, the GQ klaxon sounded its "bong, bong, bong!" and the forward fuel controller ordered all hoses secured. I looked up and saw two kamikazes barreling in on us. They had us dead to rights and it looked like curtains, for sure. But then the heavy cruiser *Baltimore* pulled up to starboard and opened up with its broadside. It was truly awesome the way she filled the sky with steel. The kamikazes didn't like what they saw and went for a couple of Jeep carriers instead. Didn't do them any good, though, because the *Baltimore* blew them both right out of the sky. That was a real scary one, because if those kamikazes had hit the tanker we were tied up to, we would have all bought the farm!

USS Dale *War Diary*, *May* 6: Anchored in berth K100, Kerama Retto, Ryukyu Islands, awaiting daylight before departing. At 0204 all hands went to general quarters when enemy aircraft were reported in the vicinity. Smoke boats began laying a smoke screen over the anchorage; AA fire was observed over Okinawa. By 0456 the enemy aircraft had left the area, having inflicted no damage on our forces. At 0750 sortied through the northern entrance to Kerama Retto Bay. Formed TU 51.15.30 with the *Saranac*, CTU being Commanding Officer of the *Dale*. Course was set to rendezvous with CTG 50.8. At 0831 all hands went to general quarters for possible air attack. There were many enemy aircraft in the vicinity. Sixteen minutes later, at 0847, sighted a Japanese plane, a "Val," diving through heavy AA fire over Kerama Retto Bay. Later the seaplane tender *St. George* reported that she had been hit by a suicide plane of the "Val" type. Also the *Hamlin* reported that she had shot down one enemy plane of the "Tony" type.

Elliot Wintch: We ran a lot of errands for the fleet. One of them was running personnel and mail back and forth from ship to ship. One evening we took a captain over to his new ship, which was a tin can tied up in a nest with two others down the harbor a ways from where we were anchored. The guy was really friendly. While we motored over to his ship in the whaleboat, he asked questions about the living conditions aboard old tin cans like the *Dale*. He seemed to be genuinely interested in how we were all holding up. At dawn the next morning, a lone kamikaze came flying down the chute. Everyone in the anchorage was shooting at him, but he made it through and crashed into that captain's new ship, hitting it right below the bridge. The ship went down with one-third of its crew. The only thing left was the bow sticking straight up out of the water. I never did hear what happened to the captain.

Harold Zoellner: We were escorting a tanker down a narrow channel into an anchorage near some small islands off Okinawa. After we dropped the tanker off, we turned around and proceeded back out the channel. But just after we turned around, five kamikazes came roaring down the chute headed for the anchorage. The skipper ordered, "Full speed ahead!" Down in the fire room we had to run around and light off all sixteen burners in order to get him his two hundred pounds of pressure. While the skipper was making evasive turns in that little channel, one of the kamikazes crashed into a seaplane tender and exploded. My uncle was aboard that tender and I worried about him until they signaled over the next morning. He was okay.

Warren Deppe: We were fueling from a tanker near Okinawa. When we finished we cut loose and backed away. Another tin can pulled in and took our place. Just then a single kamikaze snuck in and crashed the tanker, causing a huge explosion that engulfed the tin can. It happened right there in front of our eyes, plain as day!

Eliot Wintch: One of the Jap planes was coming right for us, but we shot it down right in front of the ship. We steamed right through its flaming wreckage in the water. Another flew right over us, heading for the *Bunker Hill*. It was flying so low it had to climb in order to get over us. We were shooting and so were the guys on the *Bunker Hill*, but nobody got him and he crashed onto her flight deck.

Robert "Pat" Olson: The leading petty officer, Navalinski, ordered me to take the sound-powered phone detail up on the bridge. The job was simply to relay messages from the officers on the bridge to repair parties, the after steering station, generator station, two fire rooms, and the engine room. But I had spent the entire war down in the fire room. Very few officers ever showed up down there, and those that did were engineers, just like the rest of us. I didn't like the idea of going up on the bridge at all! But Navalinski was insistent. "Olson. You're the only one around here that can stay awake, so get your butt up there and man those phones!"

I'm here to tell you, it was plenty easy to stay awake, because what greeted me up there on the bridge was the greatest show on earth! Right at dawn, the anchorage was attacked by a massive flight of kamikazes, and every ship there opened up with every gun they had. The sky literally exploded with tracers stitching back and forth among the black puffs of the antiaircraft rounds. There were dogfights between our planes and the kamikazes, and the air was filled with flying metal. You could see some of the kamikazes explode into pieces and watch as the pieces fell crazily down to earth. But some of them got through and hit our ships, and the resulting explosions blasted wreckage way up into the sky. It was spectacular, like watching every fireworks display you've ever seen in your life rolled into one big blast.

I became concerned about being so fascinated with the battle and got to thinking I would screw up if I didn't pay attention elsewhere. So

I turned my back to the battle and watched the reactions of the people around me on the bridge. They were extremely busy! The captain was listening intently to radio reports from other ships while, at the same time, doing a series of energetic calisthenics. It was very early in the day, so I figured he was either trying to wake himself up or control his nerves. Orders and reports came in rapid succession from other ships and were passed along to the captain by the other officers on the bridge. They were all as cool as cucumbers. The captain would ask questions, listen to answers, process the information, figure out what to do, and then issue orders. Whenever they made a change, it went through me, so I had to be on my toes and totally alert. After what seemed like hours, but was really only minutes, it was all over. But in those few moments, I had had all the fireworks I needed for the rest of my life!

Author's Note: On June 4 to 5, while Task Force 58 was dodging kamikaze attacks, it ran into Typhoon Viper southeast of Okinawa. Though small in size, Viper was incredibly powerful. As was the case with Typhoon Cobra, Admiral Halsey maneuvered his task force around trying to avoid the storm's fury, but instead ran it smack into the eye of the storm. As a consequence, thirty-six of his forty-eight ships suffered damage, including four battleships, eight carriers, seven cruisers, and eleven destroyers. Seventy-six aircraft were destroyed and six men lost their lives. *Dale*'s luck held and placed her at anchor in Kerama Retto while Viper ran amok at sea.

USS Dale War Diary, *June 5*: Underway at 1104 in accordance with CTG 31.15's visual dispatch to proceed out of Kerama Retto anchorage and form TU 31.15.17 with the *Enoree* and thence proceed to rendezvous with TG 30.8. By 1143 sortie with the *Enoree* was effected and set course for rendezvous. Commanding Officer of the *Dale* was CTU 31.15.17.

After three months of intense fighting, Okinawa fell to the Americans on June 22. It was the largest land-sea-air battle in history, with some two hundred and fifty thousand perishing, including approximately one-third of the island's civilian population. There were many civilian suicides and, at battle's end, nearly one-half of all surviving civilians were wounded. Japanese combatants, determined to fight to the last man, nearly did. Of the one hundred thousand who fought, only seven thousand survived. The Japanese also lost 7,830 airplanes in the three months of fighting.

American forces suffered 12,281 dead, including nearly five thousand sailors who fell to the kamikaze. More than twice as many Americans were killed and wounded at Okinawa than at Guadalcanal and Iwo Jima combined. Thirty-six U.S. Navy ships were sunk and 368 suffered various degrees of damage.

The fight for Okinawa gave American forces much to consider for the coming invasion of the Japanese home islands. The experience guaranteed Japan would turn all of its home islands into vast fields of death. Few ships of the U.S. Navy would survive the coming invasion of Japan unscathed, and every sailor aboard every ship was acutely aware of what was to come.

JUNE TO JULY: BALIKPAPAN

Dale's task group was dissolved on June 11 and she departed for Leyte, where she joined the screen of aircraft carriers sailing on the 26th to support the seizure and occupation of Balikpapan, Borneo, the petroleum center of Netherlands East India. This would be the last amphibious operation before the invasion of Japan, and there was a considerable amount of controversy as to the strategic need to capture and invade the area, as the few ships left in the Imperial fleet simply could not gain access to its oil. But strategy was not the business of the USS *Dale*, and so off she went to Balikpapan.

USS Dale *War Diary, June 26*: Anchored in berth 33, San Pedro Bay, Leyte Gulf, Philippine Islands. SOPA was ComThirdFleet in the *Missouri*. In accordance with *Dale's* mailgram, underway and proceeded out of San Pedro Bay to await sortie of TG 78.4 composed of *Suwanee, Block Island, Gilbert Islands, Donaldson, Mitchell, Cloues, Lamons, Kyne,* and *Dale* (Commanding Officer was ComScreen). Course was set for Balikpapan, Borneo.

Lowell Barker: Captain Zimny was appointed commander of our destroyer division for the foray down to Borneo, which meant he would be responsible for the two other destroyers in the escort force. Before we left on this mission he called the engineering officer, Floyd Elliot, to his quarters at 0200. Zimny made Elliot stand at attention and said, "I want to make sure that nothing goes wrong with the *Dale* when we go down to Borneo, so promise me nothing will go wrong."

Elliot said, "Sir, I'll do by best to make certain nothing goes wrong."

But Zimny said, "That's not good enough, damn, it! I want you to promise nothing will go wrong!"

"I can't promise that, sir!" replied Elliot. "This ship has been at sea almost continually for three years. She's old and worn out! All I can promise is that I will do my best to make certain nothing will go wrong!"

"That's still not good enough," said the captain. "I want your promise here. I want your promise that absolutely nothing will go wrong with this ship!"

"I can't do that, sir," replied Elliot.

Zimny and Elliot went back and forth like this till 0400, but Elliot never did back down. I'll tell you one thing, though. Nothing went wrong with the *Dale* on our way down to Borneo and back.

USS Dale *War Diary, July 2*: Commanding Officer of the *Dale* was designated ComScreen for TG 78.4. Flight operations in support of the landings in Balikpapan, Borneo, continued throughout the day.

Lester Dailey: We operated with three escort carriers as they bombed the oil fields of Borneo. *Dale*'s job was to keep all the ships in their proper order, which was really difficult because of all of the maneuvering we had to do. It took the entire signal crew to keep things squared away. They even enlisted me, a quartermaster! We must have done a pretty good job, because they gave the entire signal crew a medal for their efforts.

USS Dale *War Diary, July 3*: CTG 78.4 in *Suwannee* took tactical command at 0732. Scheduled flight operations in support of the landings were completed at 1914, after which course was set for San Pedro Bay, Leyte Gulf, Philippine Islands.

July 4: At 0200 TG passed Manimbaya Point, Celebes Islands abeam to starboard, distance 29 miles.

July 5: King Neptune and his royal party came aboard to greet his subjects and initiate all pollywogs.

Harold Zoellner: When we took the escort carriers down to Balikpapan we crossed the equator. There were a bunch of us aboard the *Dale* that had not crossed yet, and everybody wanted to have a ceremony. The captain wouldn't allow it because we were going into action in enemy-held territory. But on the way back up he gave the go-ahead. Even he had to go through the ceremony, as he had never been across the equator before. They took all us pollywogs up to the deck in the middle of the night and said, "First one to see equator line in the water does not have to go through the ceremony!" We stood there all night in our skivvies looking for that damned line and nearly froze to death! When daylight finally came they started the ceremony on the fantail. They lined us up and made us crawl through the line of shellbacks one at a time, and each one of them swatted us on the butt with paddle or hose. Then they made us kiss the baby's belly, which had been smeared with something that looked suspiciously like crap. Then there was the barber, who cut just about anything he wanted to, and the dentist, who brushed our teeth with an old foxtail brush dipped in a bucket of dirty slop water he got from dishwashers in the galley. This went on and on. It was the day of the shellbacks!

Lowell Barker: It wasn't safe to be disliked when *Dale* crossed the equator, and two of my fellow officers were simply hated by the men. One was a CIC officer whose name I've forgotten. He was a shellback. The other guy was named Axelrod. He was a pollywog.

Long before we crossed the equator, the shellbacks aboard the ship got to work making their paddles. One of the bosun mates, a great big burly guy, made a paddle out of a two-by-four three feet long. He drilled holes in it so the air would not cushion its impact, and he did all this dirty work out in the open where everyone could see what he was doing. When finished, he showed it around the ship to inspire his fellow shellbacks and frighten all of us pollywogs.

That CIC officer was a real obnoxious son of a bitch. Nobody liked him and he had no business being an officer. He was mean to the men and none of his fellow officers liked him. When he learned we were going to have an equator ceremony, he told anyone who would listen he had already been across the equator on another ship. "I've got my shellback card to prove it!" he said, and showed it around as proof.

When the CIC officer went to take his shower the day before we crossed the equator, a fellow officer snuck into his locker and stole the shellback card out of his wallet. Later that day, when the guy was bragging around the ship about having crossed the equator, someone said, "I've never seen that card of yours. Mind if I take a look?" Well, when he opened his wallet, that precious shellback card wasn't there! He searched high and low, but couldn't find it anywhere. When he became convinced the card really was gone, he went stark raving mad and ran howling up to the captain's cabin. The captain was asleep in his bunk, but that didn't make any difference to the CIC officer, who shook him awake by the shoulders and shouted into his face, "Somebody's got my card! Somebody's stole my card!"

The captain called Doc up to his stateroom and ordered him to knock the poor guy out with something, which he did. But the poor guy never did recover his marbles. After we got back to port we took him ashore, released him from the ship, and never saw him again.

The morning we crossed the equator we got our orders to report to the deck with nothing on but our skivvies. They lined us up and the first to go through the line was Axelrod. Now, Axelrod had been telling everyone who would listen that he had been sent out to the *Dale* by mistake. "I've got connections in Washington," he would say, "and they're going to get me released from this rust bucket any day now!" This, of course, did not endear him to the crew.

Anyway, Axelrod was first in line. We all got down on our hands and knees and started crawling through the line.

That bosun mate with the big paddle was the first person Axelrod had to crawl past. I was about twelve officers back in the line, but could see everything that was going on. When Axelrod crawled past, the bosun took his big old two-by-four paddle, swung from his heels, and sent Axelrod flying a good six feet across the deck. In one swift whack, Axelrod the haughty asshole became Axelrod the wounded animal. We had to crawl all the way around the ship like that, and everybody had paddles. It really wasn't safe to be disliked when the *Dale* crossed the equator.

Elliot Wintch: When we got back to the Philippines from Borneo they held a war bond drive aboard the ship. The watch that bought the most war bonds would get to have a big beach party. We had been at sea for a long time by then, so just about everybody on the ship was buying war bonds. Luckily, I was on the winning side and went to the beach for the party. The sand was made up of tiny pieces of coral and shells polished smooth and bleached white. We played football and tackled each other in the soft sand. Then we swam out and explored the coral reefs and some sunken LSTs. It was paradise!

Robert "Pat" Olson: I grew up in the dry lands of Montana and so never did learn how to swim. And even though we were always surrounded by thousands of miles of water, there just wasn't anyplace to learn how to swim on the ship. I should have remembered that fact when we went over to the beach for our war bond party. But the white beach and warm water were so inviting I simply got seduced into the water. Well, sure enough, an undertow picked me up and carried me out to where the water was over my head. I survived by bouncing off the bottom to the surface for a gulp of air. I tried paddling back but the current was too strong. I was doing too much paddling and getting too little air, and I kept drifting further and further out. Finally, this guy swam out, wrapped his arms around me, pulled me back to the beach, and laid me out on the sand where I fought for my breath. When I finally caught my wind, I jumped up and ran down the beach without so much as a thank-you to the guy that had saved my life. Next day someone in the chow line remarked, "Say. Wasn't that you rescued yesterday on the beach?"

"Who? Me?!!" I replied.

JULY TO AUGUST: ULITHI, GUAM, AND JAPAN

It was now time for the end game, and the question in the minds of all was, "How can the Pacific war be ended?"

On the American side, many argued that a naval blockade, combined with strategic bombing, would force Japan to surrender without a significant loss of American lives. However, those who fought the Japanese at Guadalcanal, New Guinea, Attu, Tarawa, Kwajalein, Saipan, Guam, Iwo Jima, Okinawa, and hundreds of places in between argued that blockading would choke Japan's will to fight, but not kill it; and bombing would destroy Japan's cities, but leave its armies intact. Japan would then be left to fight at the negotiating table. What would the politicians give the Japanese? Would they be allowed to hold their positions in China? Maintain a military?

Most likely, it was the willingness of the Japanese to fight that led to an American decision. As James Jones, author of *From Here to Eternity*, wrote: "Japan was finished as a war-making nation, in spite of its four million men still under arms. But . . . Japan was not going to quit. Despite the fact that she was militarily finished, Japan's leaders were going to fight right on. To not lose "face" was more important than hundreds and hundreds of thousands of lives. And the people concurred, in silence, without protest. To continue was no longer a question of Japanese military thinking, it was an aspect of Japanese culture and psychology."[3]

America would invade Japan with the goal of obtaining its unconditional surrender. In July, the U.S. Navy began assembling its ships for the much anticipated, and thoroughly dreaded, Operation Downfall. The first assault, Operation Olympic, would land on the southernmost island of Kyushu during the early morning hours of November 1. The second, Operation Coronet, would be nearly twice the size of Olympic and would land on the main island of Honshu during March 1946.

As Operation Olympic drew near, the U.S. Navy's Third and Fifth fleets would approach Japan. The sixty-six aircraft carriers of the Third Fleet, together with battleship, cruiser, and destroyer escorts, would first lay Admiral "Bull" Halsey's Big Blue Blanket over Honshu to suppress Japanese air forces. Halsey would then move the Third Fleet south to support the three-thousand-ship invasion fleet of Admiral Spruance's Fifth Fleet, as it approached the beaches of Kyushu. Days before the landings, Halsey's battleships, cruisers, and destroyers would pour thousands of tons of high explosives into the landing areas. Waves of carrier-based aircraft would bomb, rocket, and strafe enemy defenses, gun emplacements, and troop concentrations along the beaches. Each one of the thousands of ships involved in Operation Olympic would require ammunition, food, and fuel. Admiral Donald Beary would satisfy this need with his Logistical Support Group. The USS *Dale* would screen Beary's ships as they fed the fleets.

Japan would meet the American forces landing on Kyushu with Operation Ketsu-Go ("Decisive Victory").[4] An Imperial Army staff officer voiced the goal of Ketsu-Go in 1945: "We will prepare ten thousand planes to meet the landing of the enemy. We will mobilize every aircraft possible, both training and "special attack" planes. We will smash one third of the enemy's war potential with this air force at sea. Another third will also be smashed at sea by our warships, human torpedoes and other special weapons. Furthermore, when the enemy actually lands, if we are ready to sacrifice a million men we will be able to inflict an equal number of casualties upon them. If the enemy loses a million men, then the public opinion in America will become inclined towards peace, and Japan will be able to gain peace with comparatively advantageous conditions."[5]

Lacking a competitive surface fleet, the Japanese would use "special attack" airplanes—the kamikaze—to attack the American fleet.

Throughout the summer, American airplanes had been flying unmo-
lested over Japan, leading American planners to believe Japan had spent
its air force during the invasion of Okinawa. Such was not the case. Japan
had been holding its aircraft, fuel, and pilots in reserve and had been
feverishly building new ones in factories secreted in railway tunnels,
mines, and businesses. By October, there would be nearly thirteen thousand airplanes ready to fly from more than one hundred airstrips—some
with underground hangers. In addition, there would be squadrons of
new, more effective *ohka* ("cherry blossom") rocket bombs. These
rocket-propelled, pilot-directed aircraft with high-explosive warheads
were launched from twin-engine Mitsubishi "Betty" bombers and
crashed into enemy ships. The kamikaze would attack American ships in
wave after wave, day and night, for ten solid days.

When entering the waters of Japan's home islands, American
ships would be attacked by forty fleet submarines, which would
launch Long Lance torpedoes and spawn thousands of suicide sub-
mersibles, including *kaiten*, two-man *koryu* ("rain dragon"), and five-
man *kairyu* ("sea dragon"). When the ships anchored off the invasion
beaches, 3,300 high-speed *shinyo* ("seaquake") suicide boats, small
and agile plywood boats carrying 136-pound torpedoes in their bows,
would attack. When the American landing craft turned in to the
beaches, four thousand *fukuryu* ("crouching dragon") suicide frogmen
would rise up from reinforced concrete dens on the ocean floor and
attack them with contact mines.

Throughout the islands of the Pacific Theater, American invaders
had always outnumbered Japanese defenders by two-to-one, and often
three-to-one. It would be a different story on the beaches of Kyushu,
where the five hundred and fifty thousand invaders would meet seven
hundred and ninety thousand defenders, the elite hard core of Japan's
home army. They were well-fed, well-equipped, and had stockpiles of

arms and ammunition that could be moved around on a transportation system made nearly invisible from the air. Like their brothers throughout the Pacific, they would fight to the last man.

The military effort was only the front line of Ketsu-Go, as Japan had also mobilized twenty-eight million civilians into a National Volunteer Combat Force armed with contact mines, satchel charges, and Molotov cocktails. These *nikaku* ("suicide") warriors, with high-explosive charges strapped to their bodies, would be used in nighttime attacks, hit-and-run maneuvers, delaying actions, and massive suicide charges.

More than 40 percent of all people wearing the uniform of the U.S. military in 1945 would participate in Operation Downfall. General Douglas MacArthur's staff estimated American casualties from the two assaults would be at least one million. Millions of Japanese would participate in Operation Ketsu-Go, and millions of them would likely perish. Indeed, Japan's national slogan for the upcoming invasion was, "The sooner the Americans come, the better. . . . One hundred million will die proudly!"[6]

USS **Dale** *War Diary, July 20*: Anchored at berth 10, Ulithi Lagoon, Caroline Islands. Underway at 0753 on orders from CTU 94.6.2 to patrol station #4, passing from inland to international waters at 0830 and relieving *Wainright* on station at 0900. At 1145 sighted a floating mine 2 miles off the entrance to the lagoon and sank it at 1235 using 30 caliber rifles. The mine was believed to be a Japanese type.

Ernest Schnabel: The Japs had mined the waters around Ulithi and so we always had to be on the lookout. Our job was to destroy them whenever we found them, and we found a lot of them. One day a mine bobbed up out of the water real close to the ship. We blew it up with small arms fire and it showered the ship with salt water and shrapnel. It was truly amazing we didn't get blown up by one of those mines!

USS Dale *War Diary, July 29*: Underway from Ulithi Lagoon, Caroline Islands on orders from CTU 94.6.2 in company of *Dewey, Farragut, Macdonough, Mayo,* and *Cavallero* to cover sortie of convoy UOK 42. Escorts patrolled waters off the channel entrance and in front of heavy ships until taking screening station for convoy, which was fully formed by 1015, at which time course was set for Okinawa.

August 4: Several false sonar contacts reported. Convoy proceeded on course.

Dan Ahlberg: You will see no record of this, but *Dale* did get a submarine off Okinawa! We were screening the fleet and I was standing the mid-watch on the sonar. After about every fourth sweep, I would search ninety degrees to starboard and ninety degrees to port. Suddenly, I came up with the biggest darn sonar contact I had ever heard, about fifteen degrees off the bow. The skipper's cabin was right next to the sonar shack, so I punched his intercom and said, "Sir, I've got a big one!"

The captain came into the sonar shack, gave a listen, and then ordered, "Sonar bearing fifteen degrees off the starboard bow, come right fifteen degrees. Steady . . . On my mark, a shallow pattern. Mark!" We launched a pattern of depth charges, but when the water settled down, the sub was still down there. We figured it was a big mine layer, and chased it around for quite a while before finally losing it.

After the war I was working for an oil company and we were having dinner with a Japanese businessman. The subject got around to the war and he mentioned he had served on a mine-laying submarine damaged by an American destroyer off Okinawa. Turned out to be the same time and place we had our encounter. He said his sub limped back to Japan but had suffered so much damage it never served again.

George Crandall: Captain Zimny was a real son of a bitch. He alienated a lot of the crew by not being fair. If he didn't like you for some reason, he'd pick on some piddling stuff and make a really big deal about it. Oh, he never picked on me because I always did a good job. He never told me I did a good job, he just never picked on me. He picked on other officers, though, and would have them confined to their quarters for days at a time. One day he even sparked a mutiny aboard the *Dale!*

Lowell Barker: Captain Zimny was not the most popular of *Dale's* captains. In fact, he was a pompous little Caesar. Sometimes his dictatorial behavior got us into some sticky situations, like the mutiny.

We had been out at sea for a long time—and were getting real hungry for some sweets—when an AK we were screening called over on its loudspeaker, "Ahoy *Dale* . . . Would you like some ice cream?" The *Dale* didn't have equipment to make her own ice cream, so it was really a treat whenever we could lay our hands on some.

"Hell, yes!" replied Zimny over our PA system. Ropes went back and forth, and soon a five-gallon bucket of frozen ice cream came across. By then, everyone aboard the *Dale* knew fresh ice cream was on the way and the deck was soon lined with hungry sailors, holding spoons. But Zimny said, "Put that ice cream in the officers' reefer." Tempers flared when the sailors realized they would get no ice cream.

Then the officer in charge of the *Dale's* commissary, a good-looking ensign about twenty-one years old, replied, "Cannot do that, sir!"

"What? What do you mean, 'You can't do that?' " shrieked Zimny. "You'll do exactly as I tell you!"

The young ensign insisted, "I'm sorry, sir. I just cannot take that ice cream away from the men."

Red in the face, Zimny shot back, "Okay, then you're going to the brig!"

The ensign stood at attention and said, "Sir, I'll be happy to go to the brig, but first you must sign for all my accounts and for all the ship's money in my safe."

So the captain got out his book of navy regulations and fussed over it for a half hour or so, while the ice cream container just sat there on the deck. By then the entire crew was watching to see what was going to happen. After fussing and fuming over what to do with all those accounts, Zimny slammed the book down and said, "Okay! Give the damned ice cream to the men!" A great cheer went up around the ship, everybody got some ice cream, and that young ensign became a hero.

Earl "Jitterbug" Pearson: There was this young ensign, one of those ninety-day wonders, who got himself into trouble with the captain. Next day he found himself chipping paint next to us ordinary sailors. Boy, did he ever look funny. He was just a young kid and you could tell the *Dale* was the last place on earth he wanted to be.

George Crandall: One night the captain was walking along the main deck just below the wing of the bridge when a signal searchlight fell off the bridge and crashed onto the deck right in front of him. If that thing had hit him, it would have killed him, sure enough. There was no way it could have fallen accidentally; someone had to drop it intentionally. We conducted an investigation but never did find the guilty party. It scared the hell out of the captain, and all the rest of us, too! A captain has to be a bit autocratic to run a ship. But Zimny was not just an autocrat, he was a genuine son of a bitch.

Author's note: At 0815 on the morning of August 6, American forces dropped an atom bomb on the city of Hiroshima. Then, at 1102 on August 9, another was dropped on the city of Nagasaki. Many tens of thousands were killed. While returning to Ulithi to pick up another convoy for Operation Olympic, *Dale* received special orders to report to Guam.

USS Dale War Diary, *August 15:* Anchored at berth 305, Apra Harbor, Guam, Mariana Islands. At 0900, the president of the United States announced that Japan had accepted the terms of the Potsdam Conference and surrendered unconditionally.

Robert "Pat" Olson: When word came through that the war had ended, everyone went wild. We made noise with whatever we could get our hands on. Sirens shrieked, bells rang, and horns bellowed. Sailors whooped and hollered. I was the wildest of all, because when I first went into the navy, I read somewhere you had to do everything you could to keep your head and nerves together so you could survive to the end and be a part of the big celebration that was to come. I believed it, and did everything I could to hold myself together. Well, I held myself together for almost four years on that tin can and made it through to the end. Yes! I celebrated. I whooped and hollered and banged on metal. You bet I did! And I celebrated a bunch for all those guys that couldn't, too!

USS Dale War Diary, *August 16:* On the morning of the 16th, in accordance with CFT 17's operation order of 15 August, proceeded out of Apra Harbor passing from inland to international waters at 0627, to sortie with TG 17.11. Sortie was effected at 0745 and course was set to rendezvous with TG 30.8 near Japan. TG 17.11 was composed of *Proteus, Greenlet,* and *Dale.*

August 19: At 1655 contact was made with TG 30.8. At 1830 TG 17.11 was dissolved and the *Proteus* and *Greenlet* proceeded independently to join TU 30.8.1 while the *Dale* proceeded independently back to Saipan, Marianas Islands.

August 22: At 0355, radar contact was made on Saipan Island, Marianas. At 0634, passed from international to inland waters and proceeded to go alongside *Raccoon* to fuel. On completion of fueling, reported to Port Director for routing to Pearl Harbor. After receiving on board passengers, the *Dale* raised anchor and proceeded out of the harbor alone, bound for Pearl Harbor.

August 30: At 0935 radar contact was made on Oahu Island, 59 miles to the north. Passed from international to inland waters at 1317 and reported to ComCru-DesPac for onward routing to the Panama Canal.

September 1: At 1655 passed into nternational waters with *Dewey* en route San Diego.

September 7: At 1320 passed from international to inland waters of San Diego Harbor with *Dewey* following close behind. Present in the harbor on the *Dale* and *Dewey*'s arrival was the balance of the DesDiv, the *Aylwin*, *Macdonough*, and *Farragut*.

September 11: Entire DesDiv, with *Dale* as flagship, passed into International waters at 1012 en route Balboa, Panama Canal Zone.

September 19: Passed into inland waters of Balboa, Panama Canal Zone at 0911 at the head of DesDiv. By 1017 the *Dale* was moored alongside pier #2, U.S. Naval Repair Base. A few minutes later the *Farragut* followed by the *Macdonough* moored to port.

Earl "Jitterbug" Pearson: We were running light on crew when we reached Panama because many of *Dale*'s crew had been transferred off in San Diego for newer construction. About a third of the crew was given liberty in Balboa. I wasn't one of them, but wanted to get off the ship so badly I volunteered for Shore Patrol duty. They assigned me the red light district, which was a solid block of prostitutes working their little rooms. There were also a lot of bars along the street. Well, given all the booze and broads, and sailors that had seen neither for a long time, you can well imagine what went down. Later, when we had the first *Dale* reunion down in Amarillo, I told everybody not to call me "Jitterbug" anymore, because if they did, I would release the list of names I had collected down in that red light district!

USS Dale *War Diary, September 20*: Underway at 0923 en route New York City in accordance with radio dispatch orders from CinCLant. At 2051 effected passage through the Panama Canal.

SEPTEMBER TO OCTOBER: NEW YORK CITY

Commissioned before the war, *Dale* was now a relic of another era. Her replacements were newer, bigger, broader, faster, and more powerful. America would now tear the *Dale* apart, decommission her, and sell her for scrap, while honoring the sailors who had served aboard her. New York City would host the party.

USS Dale *War Diary, September 25*: DesDiv arrived off the coast of New Jersey very early in the morning, but a very heavy fog had set in necessitating a decrease in speed. Finally, though, at 1000 passage was made into the inland waters of New York Harbor, and some twenty minutes later a Coast Guard pilot was received aboard. In accordance with radioed instructions from Commandant Third Naval District the entire DesDiv first proceeded to Leonardo Pier, Berth 10, Sandy Hook, New Jersey to unload ammunition. By 1323 all ammunition had been unloaded by the *Dale* and she was the first to get underway for the 33rd Street Pier in Brooklyn, New York. At 1647 the *Dale* was moored to the Middle berth. Shortly afterward the *Macdonough* and the *Dewey* moored alongside to form a nest with the *Dale*, and then the *Farragut* and *Aylwin* arrived at the pier to moor to the outside berth, just astern. DesDiv remained at the same berths on the 33rd Street Pier through the balance of the month, making preparations for going out of commission.

A. D. Payne: Right after we tied up in New York City we began dumping stuff over the side. Cartons of cigarettes, sewing machines— you name it, we dumped it. We had to get rid of things, and dumping it over the side was the easiest way to do it.

Robert "Pat" Olson: At the end of the war we had five weeks of liberty in New York City and not a thing to do aboard the ship. After breakfast I would take the subway to Times Square and head over to the USO. They gave us free tickets for anything and everything. After four years at sea, I was ready for some fun, and there was a lot of it to be had in New York City. There was baseball in Yankee Stadium, music in Madison Square, and pretty girls everywhere you looked. A few of my friends were still on the *Dale*, but we didn't see much of each other, as we were all out on the town.

Earl "Jitterbug" Pearson: Boy, did I ever have a great time! Everybody was celebrating and if you were a sailor in uniform, you paid for nothing. If you went to a bar, someone bought you drinks. If you went to a movie, someone gave you tickets.

Each day after breakfast, I would grab my roller skates and head down to Times Square where they had this giant, three-decker roller rink. The beginners skated on the bottom and the experts on top. But it didn't really matter which deck you skated on, because there were plenty of pretty girls on each deck.

We slept aboard the *Dale* and sometimes ate aboard her as well. She was quickly becoming a grand, depressing mess. Sailors were bringing dates aboard and nobody cared. There were no watches to stand and we came and went as we pleased. There was no discipline left at all!

George Crandall: *Dale* was commissioned in 1934. By the end of the war she was an old ship, and there were several generations of newer tin cans to take her place. It was obvious she was going to be decommissioned and sold for scrap, but it was still really depressing. As soon as we tied up, the yard started tearing us apart. I'd come back from liberty and there would be large holes cut into the deck where they had ripped out the engines. I'd go down to my stateroom and it would be filthy and dark, and there would be all manner of things strewn about the deck. It was depressing! *Dale* was always one of the most clean and orderly ships in the navy. We took good care of her, and it was what made her good. When you live on a ship, and get to know her, she becomes a living thing. To see her dirty, ripped apart,and dying was really depressing!

A. D. Payne: I got married as soon as we arrived in New York City. A friend of mine on the ship stood up as my best man. We went on our honeymoon down to Spartanburg, South Carolina, and that was the last I ever saw of the *Dale*.

Elliot Wintch: We decommissioned the *Dale* in New York City on my twenty-first birthday. When the war started I was just a poor kid from Salt Lake City. I was so poor I didn't get my first shoes until I joined the navy. And here I was, twenty-one and on my own in the Big Apple, with money in my pocket!

Robert "Pat" Olson: I don't remember much about *Dale's* decommissioning ceremony. There wasn't much left of her by then, anyway. We stood at attention in our dress blues while some officers gave speeches. They lowered her flag, folded it up, and then it was over.

Oh! There was one other thing that happened. A navy chaplain took us aside and gave us a going-home lecture. "Boys," he said. "You've been out there in the Pacific fighting your way through cruel hard times. You had to become cruel and hard to survive it. Now you're going home to a much different world, and you have to prepare yourselves for it. Soon, you'll be sitting down to dinner with an attractive young gal. Without thinking, you'll want to say, 'Hey! Shove the fuckin' butter over here!' You had to be like that to survive the war, but the war is over. If you want to succeed with a pretty gal, and build a new life for yourself, you have to change your ways when you walk out that gate."

The next day they shipped me off to Bremerton, Washington, to be discharged, and then on to Billings, Montana, where I was to start my new life. Before the navy, I worked for my dad, and so never held a real job before. But that didn't seem to matter! I had confidence. If I could survive the war, I could find a job and build a life.

Though I had always been very shy around girls, I was soon dating Irene, a pretty little country gal I met while home on leave. One day she said, "I'm going to take you home and cook you dinner!" She took me home to her family's farm near the little town of Belfry, where I met her mother, father, younger brother, and sister. Each was bright-eyed and rosy-cheeked. It was spring, and they had been working hard to bring their farm back to life from the long winter.

When evening came, we all sat down to Irene's magnificent dinner. Everybody was happy, expectant, and very hungry. After grace was offered, I turned to Irene and said, "Will you please pass the butter?"

EPILOGUE

Warren Deppe: There were lucky ships, and unlucky ones. Take the *Saratoga*, for example. Whenever the *Sara* stuck her nose out she'd get torpedoed. It was just the luck of the draw, and she didn't draw so well. The *Dale* was a lucky ship, and we were very proud of her. Everybody took special care to keep her clean and in fighting trim, and that's probably what made it possible for us to have good luck.

Ernest Schnabel: It was just amazing. It was like the *Dale* sailed under an umbrella of protection. We went through the entire war and suffered only one casualty, and that was just an accident!

Dellmar Smith: We were young and full of piss and vinegar. We got thirty-six dollars a month, training, three hots, and a cot. That was good living!

Bill Ryan: The *Dale* was the luckiest ship in the navy. I was on her for a little better than three years, so I oughta know. I had me a bunk right next to the bulkhead and could hear the water splashing against the hull. Boy, could I ever sleep! And we had good food. Oh, there were a lot of complaints about the powdered eggs and such. Mostly the guys didn't like the green color. But hell, for a farm boy from the back woods of Florida, those green eggs were good eating!

Herman Gaddis: *Dale* had a good crew, and they were well trained. She always had enough experienced leaders who knew how to transfer their talents to the new guys in ways that allowed us to survive. The navy was constantly transferring men off the *Dale* to crew new construction and replacing them with raw recruits. But she always had enough skilled people aboard to be able to get through. She wasn't the only ship that made it through okay. Others just like her did as well. But then others didn't. She was lucky.

Ernest "Dutch" Smith: Our size made a difference. Compared to the capital ships of the fleet, *Dale* was small potatoes. The Japs always wanted to get the big boys. She was also fast and maneuverable, which made her harder to get. But none of that held true when we had to stand picket duty at Okinawa. We were just sitting ducks.

Charles O'Rorke: We had a good crew, and they trained us really well, too. Toward the end of the war we were pushed back from being on the front all the time by the new 2100s, which were bigger, faster, and more powerful. Still, we were always in there, especially in the Philippines, Iwo Jima, and Okinawa. I think what really made the difference was that *Dale* was a clean ship. You take a ship that's dirty and unkempt and you'll find trouble. Its equipment will fall apart and its crew won't know what to do when trouble comes. That ship will have a hard time surviving.

Bob Johnson: *Dale* was the luckiest ship on the Pacific. Whenever things turned bad on one side of an island, she would be on the other side. Like the time our sound gear went down and we had to stay in port. Our sister tin cans went out and got caught in a typhoon that sank three of them. If it weren't for blind luck, we would be at the bottom of the Pacific, too. The *Dale* was also a clean ship. There was never any debris laying about the decks and the crew always cleaned their quarters and washed their clothes. If you've ever been around a dirty ship, you would know cleanliness makes a big difference. I have to confess that I fell in love with her. Toward the end of the war I used to go up to the bridge and just hang around. They didn't seem to mind having an engineering officer up there, as long as I didn't get in the way. I just loved the peacefulness of cruising into the sunset on those big seas. There were always dolphins, flying fish, and whales keeping us company. It was truly incredible. I'm in my eighties now. Oh, I'm still vertical and making noise, but I don't have all that many opportunities left. But if I did have a chance—if the opportunity did come again—I'd sign up with the U.S. Navy and ask to be assigned to a tin can just like the *Dale*.

Lowell Barker: Chalk it up to luck! What else could it be? That kamikaze off Leyte could just as easily have ploughed into us and sent us to the bottom. But we were lucky. You know, I hated being in that war, but I loved being on that ship, especially when we were cruising through those warm tropical seas at night. We usually stood four and four, which meant we'd work four hours, then sleep four hours. It was very, very satisfying and peaceful, cruising through the great big expanse of tropical sea at night. There I was, a teacher from Texas, in charge of a big navy ship cruising through the night. All I had to do was keep the ship going in the right direction.

Dan Ahlberg: The *Dale* was one lucky ship. When I first shipped aboard as an eighteen year old, I got caught in the fight between the old crew and the new captain. I put in four requests to be transferred, but Captain Zimny turned down each and every one of them. Then, during the typhoon off Okinawa, I got washed off the deck by one wave and then back on by the next wave. I broke four ribs and the doc said it was enough to get transferred back to the States. But by then, I was convinced *Dale* was the luckiest ship in the navy and there was no way they were going to transfer me off her.

George Crandall: We were lucky for one thing, and skilled for another. We were tested and retested by the navy and always came through with flying colors. But when it came right down to it, luck was what brought us through.

Robert "Pat" Olson: It's hard to believe how lucky we were. There were so many times we should have taken a hit. And there were so many times others close to us took the hit. Take the *Liscombe Bay!* I was manning the phones down in the fire room when the guy up on the bridge phone yelled, "Oh, my God! There was a carrier right there a second ago, but it blew up and now there's nothing there at all!" And take our sister tin cans swallowed in one big gulp by the typhoon! Time after time, we just sailed right on through—or right on by. I don't know why. I can't explain it. I'm glad it happened. For some reason, it seems to bother me a lot more now than it did back then.

Don Schneider: I loved the bull sessions we used to have while hanging around the electrician's shop listening to the radio. KOA from Denver would sometimes come in clear out there in the Pacific, and a Minneapolis station, too! The radio reminded us of home, and it would get us to talking. We had good people aboard. There were always enough of the old-timers to teach the newcomers what to do. We lived right, and we were lucky!

Earl Hicks: It was pure luck. The *Dale* never shied away from danger and always seemed to be in a position to get hit. She just never got hit! The Japs had a lot of chances to hit her. Up there in the Komandorski Islands, they had us outgunned two to one and shot at us for three and a half hours. They just couldn't hit us.

Orville Newman: We were one big family aboard the *Dale*. That doesn't mean we all got along all the time. But we were family. It was different on other ships. I spent some time on a DE toward the end of the war and it was different. They got along okay, but they weren't family. There was something about the *Dale* that made us all feel like family. And you know what? We are still family sixty years later!

Appendices

Contributing Crew Members of the USS *Dale*

Dan Ahlberg, Electrician
Lowell Barker, Officer
Eugene Brewer, Signalman
Darel Bright, Officer
Mike Callahan, Officer (Executive Officer)
George Crandall, Officer
John Cruce, Firecontrolman
Lester Dailey, Signalman
Warren Deppe, Torpedoman
Bill Eggenberger, Fireman
Herman Gaddis, Signalman
John Galica, Boatswain Mate
Jean Gould, Officer
Alvis Harris, Radioman

Earl Hicks, Electrician

Cliff Huntley, Electrician Mate

Bob Johnson, Officer

John Kelsch, Radarman

Richard Martinez, Fireman

J. E. McIntyre, Electrician

Hugh Melrose, Officer

John Miller, Radioman

Orville Newman, Fireman

Robert Olson, Machinist Mate

Charles O'Rorke, Electrician Mate

John Overholt, Cook

Ted Palumbo, Radioman

A. D. Payne, Signalman

Earl Pearson, Machinist Mate

Harold Reichert, Store Keeper

K. G. Robinson, Officer (Executive Officer)

A. L. Rorschach, Officer (Captain)

Roy Roseth, Firecontrolman

Bill Ryan, Firecontrolman

Ernest Schnabel, Fireman

Don Schneider, Fireman

Bela Smith, Boatswain Mate

Dellmar Smith, Fireman

Ernest Smith, Coxswain

Jim Sturgill, Machinist Mate

D. J. Vellis, Officer

Billy Walker, Fireman

Elliot Wintch, Electrician Mate

Harold Zoellner, Fireman

USS *DALE* WORLD WAR II BATTLE STARS

World War II battle stars were given for actual operations in a specific area and time that involved clashes with the enemy of sufficient intensity and significance to justify recognition. The USS *Dale* won twelve of the twenty-two battle stars awarded in the Pacific Theater.

1.) **Pearl Harbor**

December 7, 1941

2.) **South Pacific Carrier Raids**

Bougainville	February 20, 1942
Lae–Salamaua	March 10, 1942

3.) **Occupation of the Aleutian Islands**

Komandorski Islands	March 26, 1943
Attu Island	May 11 to June 2, 1943

4.) **Occupation of the Gilbert Islands**

November 13 to December 8, 1943

5.) **Occupation of the Marshall Islands**

Kwajalein	January 31 to February 8, 1944
Eniwetok	February 17 to 25, 1944

6.) **Central Pacific Carrier Raids**

Palau, Yap, Ulithi, Woleai	March 30 to April 1, 1944
Truk, Satawan, Ponape	April 29 to May 1, 1944

7.) **Occupation of Hollandia**

April 21 to 24, 1944

8.) Occupation of the Marianas

Saipan	June 11 to 24, 1944
Philippine Sea	June 19 to 20, 1944
Guam	July 17 to 30, 1944

9.) Occupation of the Philippines

Formosa	January 21, 1945
China	January 22, 1945

10.) Occupation of Iwo Jima

February 15 to March 2, 1945

11.) Occupation of Okinawa

Carrier raids	March 6 to June 13, 1945
Okinawa	March 24 to June 30, 1945

12.) Occupation of Balikpapan

July 15 to 20, 1945

CHRONOLOGY:

NOVEMBER 1941 TO OCTOBER 1945

1941

Nov

As a unit of Destroyer Squadron 1, Destroyer Division 2, supported
Task Force 1, the Pacific covering force of Vice Admiral William Pye,
based at Pearl Harbor, Hawaii.

Dec

Moored at Pearl Harbor when attacked by Japanese carrier force.

As a unit of Task Force 11 under Rear Admiral J. H. Newton, participated in the aborted attempt to relieve Wake Island.

1942

Jan–Mar

As a unit of Task Force 11 under Vice Admiral Wilson Brown, participated in carrier raids on Rabaul, New Britain, and Lae—Salamaua,
New Guinea.

Apr

Trained personnel and escorted convoys from Pearl Harbor, Hawaii.

May

Equipped, overhauled, and trained at Mare Island Naval Shipyard,
San Francisco.

June

As a unit of Task Force 1 under Rear Admiral William Pye, escorted battleships in support of carrier forces engaged at Midway Island.

Jul–Aug

Escorted various convoys between Fiji and the New Hebrides (Vanuatu) in preparation for the assault on Guadalcanal.

Aug–Nov

As a unit of Task Forces 2, 11, 17, and 61, participated in Operation Watchtower, the invasion and occupation of Guadalcanal Island.

Dec

Equipped, overhauled, and trained at Hunter's Point Naval Shipyard, San Francisco.

1943

Jan

As a unit of Task Force 8 under Rear Admiral Charles McMorris, participated in the invasion and occupation of Amchitka Island in the Aleutian Islands.

Feb–Mar

As a unit of Task Group 8 under Rear Admiral Charles McMorris, participated in the blockade of Attu and Kiska Islands.

Mar

As a unit of Task Group 16.6 under Rear Admiral Charles McMorris, participated in the Battle of the Komandorski Islands.

April

As a unit of Task Group 16.6 under Rear Admiral Charles McMorris, participated in the blockade of Attu and Kiska Islands.

May–July

As a unit of Task Groups 16.12, 16.6, 31.1, 31.6, 51.2, and BatDiv 2, participated in Operation Landcrab, the invasion and occupation of Attu Island.

Aug

As a unit of Task Group 16.7 under Rear Admiral Howard Kongman, participated in Operation Cottage, the invasion and occupation of Kiska Island.

Sept

As a unit of Task Group 16.15.7, steamed from the Aleutian Islands to Pearl Harbor, Hawaii. As a unit of Task Group 14.6, participated in a two-day raid on Wake Island.

Oct

Equipped, overhauled, and trained at Pearl Harbor, Hawaii.

Nov

As a unit of Task Group 54.4 under Rear Admiral R. Kelly Turner, participated in Operation Galvanic, the invasion and occupation of the Gilbert Islands.

Dec

Equipped, overhauled, and trained at San Francisco and San Diego.

1944

Jan

Escorted convoys and trained at Pearl Harbor.

Feb

As a unit of Task Group 53.6 under Rear Admiral Van Ragsdale, participated in the invasion Kwajalein Atoll in the Marshall Islands. As a unit of Task Group 31.1, participated in the invasion and occupation of Eniwetok Atoll in the Marshall Islands.

Mar

Escorted various ships and convoys throughout the Marshall Islands.

Mar–May

As a unit of Task Force 58 under Rear Admiral Marc Mitscher, participated in Operations Desecrate I, Reckless, and Persecution, the carrier attacks on Palau, Yap, Ulithi, Woleai, Hollandia, Truk, Satawan, and Ponape.

June–July

As a unit of Task Group 53 under Rear Admiral Jesse Oldendorf, participated in the Battle of the Philippine Sea and the invasion and occupation of Saipan and Guam in the Mariana Islands.

Aug–Oct

Equipped, overhauled, and trained at Bremerton, Washington.

Nov–Dec

As a unit of Task Force 30, participated in Operation Love III, the invasion of the Philippine Islands.

1945

Jan

As a unit of Task Force 30, participated in carrier raids on Formosa, Luzon, Okinawa, Tokyo, and Kobe.

Feb–Mar

As a unit of Task Force 50 under Captain G. C. Montgomery, participated in Operation Detachment, the invasion and occupation of Iwo Jima.

Apr–June

As a unit of Task Force 30 under Admiral William Halsey, participated in Operation Iceberg, the invasion and occupation of Okinawa.

July

As a unit of Task Force 78 under Rear Admiral William Sample, participated in Operation Oboe VI, the invasion and occupation of Balikpapan, Borneo.

Aug 15

Anchored at Guam at war's end.

Oct 16

Decommissioned at New York City.

TASK FORCE ASSIGNMENTS
Destroyer Squadron 1

Destroyer Squadron 1:
Phelps (DD-360)

Destroyer Division 1
Dewey (DD-349), *Hull* (DD-350), *Macdonough* (DD-351), *Worden* (DD-352)

Destroyer Division 2
Aylwin (DD-355), *Dale* (DD-353), *Farragut* (DD-348), *Monaghan* (DD-354)

<u>DATE</u> (d/m/y)	<u>UNIT</u>	<u>COMMANDER</u>	<u>TASK</u>
1941	TF 1	VADM William Pye	Pacific Covering Force/Pearl Harbor
14/12/41	TF 11	RADM J.H. Newton	Jaluit Raid/Wake Reinforcement
09/07/42	TF 11	VADM Frank Fletcher	Operation Watchtower/ Guadalcanal
07/08/42	TF 51 TG 61.1	VADM Frank Fletcher	Operation Watchtower/ Guadalcanal

16/08/42	TF 11	VADM Frank Fletcher	Eastern Solomons
13/01/43	TG 8 TG 8.6	RADM Charles McMorris	Amchitka Landing/ Aleutians
26/03/43	TF 16 TG 16.6	RADM Charles McMorris	Battle of the Komandorski Islands
11/05/43	TF 51 TG 51.2	RADM Francis Rockwell	Operation Landcrab/ Attu
02/08/43	TF 16 TG 16.7	RADM Howard Kongman	Kiska Bombardment
15/08/43	TF 16 TG 16.17	RADM Howard Kongman	Operation Cottage/Kiska
18/11/43	TF 54 TG 54.4	RADM Kelly Turner	Operation Galvanic/ Gilberts
01/02/44	TF 53 TG 53.6	RADM Van Ragsdale	Operation Flintlock/ Marshalls
30/03/44	TF 58	RADM Marc Mitscher	Operation Desecrate I/ Palau

13/04/44	TF 58	RADM Marc Mitscher	Operations Reckless and Persecution/ Hollandia
17/07/44	TF 53 TG 53.5	RADM Jesse Oldendorf	Operation Forager/ Marianas
25/11/44	TF 30 TG 30.8	Captain Jasper Accuf	Operation Love III/ Philippines
30/12/44	TF 30 TG 30.8	Captain Jasper Accuf	Operation Mike I/ Philippines
16/02/45	TF 50 TG 50.8	Captain G.C. Montgomery	Operation Detachment/ Iwo Jima
28/05/45	TF 30 TG 30.8	ADM William Halsey	Operation Iceberg/ Okinawa
01/07/45	TF 78 TU 78.4.1	RADM William Sample	Operation Oboe VI/ Balikpapan

NOTES

1941

1. *www.wtj.com/articles/pacific_war/articles/pearl_harbor.htm*
2. *www.toratoratora.com/we_are/articles/to———ra/default.htm*
3. *War at Sea*, by Nathan Miller, p. 203.
4. *Advance Force—Pearl Harbor*, by Burl Burlingame. Naval Institute Press, 1982.
5. "Massacre on Wake Island" by Major Mark E. Hubbs, U.S. Army Reserve (Retired).
   www.ussyorktown.com/yorktown/massacre.html

1942

1. *http://navy.memorieshop.com*
2. *Blood on the Sea*, Robert Sinclair Parkin. Sarpedon Press, 1995, p. 33.
3. *History of United States Naval Operations in World War II, Volume IV*, by Samuel Eliot Morison, p. 106.
4. *www.ams.ubc.ca/clubs/taekwondo/Choong-Moo.htm*
5. *The Pacific War Encyclopedia*, Dunnigan and Nofi.
6. *History, Volume V, The Struggle for Guadalcanal*, pp. 198–204.
7. *History, Volume V, The Struggle for Guadalcanal*, pp. 277–282.

1943

1. *History, Volume VII, Aleutians, Gilberts and Marshalls*, p. 35. Morison's account of Admiral McMorris's leadership during the Battle of the Komandorski Islands stands in sharp contrast to the accounts given by all of the USS *Dale* sailors interviewed for this oral history.

2. *History, Volume VII.* See page 35 for a complete accounting of shots fired by each ship.
3. From a Radio Tokyo broadcast, as quoted from "Attu Alibi," an Associated Press article of the time posted at *www.coretek.org/gsmith/attu.html*
4. *History, Volume VII,* pp. 61–62.
5. "Massacre on Wake Island" By Major Mark E. Hubbs, U.S. Army Reserve (Retired), *www.ussyorktown.com/yorktown/massacre.html*

1944

1. *History, Volume VII, Aleutians, Gilberts and Marshalls,* pp. 316–317.
2. *History, Volume XII, Leyte,* pp. 86–87.
3. *History, Volume VIII, New Guinea and the Marianas,* p. 33.
4. *www.microworks.net/pacific/battles/leyte_gulf.htm*
5. For an amusing account of activities on Mog Mog, read "What did you do in the war, Daddy?" at *www.kypost.com/news/1998/hicks100998.html*

1945

1. *History, Volume XIII,* p. 183.
2. *History, Volume XIV,* p. 93.
3. James Jones from *www.fas.org/irp/eprint/arens/chap4.htm*
4. "An Invasion Not Found in the History Books," by James Martin Davis. The Omaha World Herald, November 1987.
5. *www.fas.org/irp/eprint/arens/N_11_*
6. *www.fas.org/irp/eprint/arens/chap4.htm*

GLOSSARY OF U.S. NAVY ABBREVIATIONS, ACRONYMS, AND SLANG

90-Day Wonder	Reserve officer trained in ninety-day programs at public colleges.
AA	Antiaircraft Fire
Adm	Admiral
AE	Ammunition Ship
AF	Stores Ship
AirSols	Air Solomons Air Corps
AK	Attack Cargo Ship
AO	Oil Tanker
AP	Transport Ship
Asiatic	WWII expression for crazy, wild, or eccentric behavior.
ASW	Anti-submarine Warfare
AWOL	Absent Without Leave
Bait	Candy or Sweets
BatDiv	Battleship Division
BB	Battleship
Buck Rodgers	Any new or exotic weapon. Named after a science-fiction character in 1930s' vintage comic books.
BuPers	Bureau of Personnel
CA	Heavy Cruiser
Cactus	Code name of Guadalcanal
CAG	Carrier Air Group
CAP	Combat Air Patrol
Capstan	A mechanical device used for moving or lifting heavy weights by winding a cable around a ver-

tical spindle-mounted drum, which is rotated manually by bars fitted into sockets or mechanically by steam or electricity.

Captain's Mast	Nonjudicial punishment hearings in which limited punishments may be awarded by a commanding officer.
Cardiv	Carrier Division
CB	Heavy Cruiser
CIC	Combat Information Center
CinCLant	Commander in Chief, Atlantic
CinCPac	Commander in Chief, Pacific (Nimitz)
CL	Light Cruiser
CO	Commanding Officer
Com3rdFlt	Commander Third Fleet
ComCru-DesPac	Commander, Cruisers—Destroyers, Pacific
ComDesRon	Commander Destroyer Squadron
ComScreen	Commander Screen
ComServRon	Commander Service Squadron
Condition Red	Enemy in Vicinity
Condition White	Enemy not in Vicinity
Crudiv	Cruiser Division
CTF	Carrier Task Force/Commander Task Force
CTG	Carrier Task Group (subunit of a Carrier Task Force)
CTU	Carrier Task Unit (subunit of a Carrier Task Group)
CV	Aircraft Carrier
CVE	Escort Carrier
CVL	Light Carrier
DD	Destroyer

DE	Destroyer Escort
DesDiv	Destroyer Division
Ens	Ensign
Flank speed	Top Speed
Four-Piper	World War I destroyer design, featuring four exhaust stacks.
Gedunk	Specifically ice cream sundaes, but generally all sweet treats, or "bait," not obtainable through a ship's common mess.
General Quarters	An emergency alarm that sends all hands to their assigned battle stations.
GQ	General Quarters
Gun Director	A mechanical computer that automatically controls the laying of the guns without manual intervention by the gun crew.
Handy Billy	A loose block and tackle with a hook or tail on each end, which can be used wherever it is needed. Usually made up of one single and one double block.
Head	Marine toilet. In its original form, toilet facilities were found right forward in the bows, so that the smell would be blown downwind and away from the ship (because sailing ships could not lie directly into the wind when under way). The extreme fore part of a ship was known as the "beakhead," which may have been shortened to "head" over time. *www.hazegray.org/faq/slang1.htm*
HQ	Headquarters
IJN	Imperial Japanese Navy

JAG	Judge Advocate General Corps
Jeep Carriers	Slang for CVE, or "Aircraft Carrier, Escort." Built by the Henry J. Kaiser Company, manufacturer of Jeep vehicles, on cruiser and tanker hulls.
JOOD	Junior Officer of the Deck
Kiyi Brush	A stiff-bristled brush used by deckhands for scrubbing decks.
LCVP	Landing Craft, Vehicle and Personnel
Lee Side	Side of the ship away from wind and sea.
Liberty Ships	A class of 2,751 cargo ships built under an emergency construction program during World War II by the U.S. Maritime Commission.
Long Lance	In the 1920s and thirties, Japan labored to overcome the shortcomings imposed on its battle fleet by the Washington Naval Treaty. One solution was the Long Lance, an extremely powerful, oxygen-powered torpedo with a range of approximately twenty miles.
LST	Landing Ship, Tank
Mess Hall	Area where enlisted personnel are fed. The word *mess* is derived from the Middle English *mes*, which means "food set on a table at one time" and "a group of persons who regularly take their meals together."
OOD	Officer of the Deck
Operation Observant	A period of quiet listening during anti-submarine operations.
Pollywogs	Sailors who have not participated in an equator-crossing ceremony on a U.S. Navy ship.
POW	Prisoner of War

Quartermaster	Naval rating charged with navigation-related duties.
RAdm	Rear Admiral
Raisin Jack	An alcoholic beverage made from fermented raisins and other fruit.
Rope-Yarn Sunday	During the days of wooden ships, an occasional Sunday was set aside for sailors to mend their personal items. Sailors were allowed to take small fiber twists, or yarns, from the ropes used as ship's rigging to make the repairs on clothing. The term *Rope-Yarn Sunday* came to mean time-off for casual work and leisure.
Scuttlebutt	A cask of fresh drinking water. The crew gathers around the scuttlebutt to swap stories, and thus *scuttlebutt* became the word used for gossip, true or false.
Shellbacks	Sailors who have participated in an equator-crossing ceremony on a U.S. Navy ship.
Snipes	Also known as "the black gang." Refers to engineering staff aboard navy ships. Although the origin of "snipe" is uncertain, it may have come from the early days of steamships, when an engineering officer named John Snipes rebelled against the ill-treatment deck crews afforded engineers by having his crew turn off the steam. Thereafter, those who worked on the ships' propulsion systems became known as John Snipe's men, or snipes. (*http://oldsnipe.com/SnipeBegin.html*) *Black gang* came from the days when steamships were pro-

	pelled by coal, because those working on or near the engines would always be covered with coal dust.
SOPA	Senior Officer Present, Afloat
Sound-powered Phones	Phone system powered by voice of user.
SS	Submarine
Sugar George	A microwave surface search radar allowing viewers to "see" the position of targets in any weather condition.
T	Compass bearing in "True" degrees.
TAD	Temporary Assigned Duty
TBS	Talk Between Ships is a short-range, very high frequency radio used to communicate between ships in a group.
TF	Task Force
TG	Task Group (subunit of a Task Force)
Tony	Japanese Number 244 fighter codenamed "Tony."
TU	Task Unit, (subunit of a Task Group)
Unrep	Slang for "underway replenishment."
Val	Japanese Aichi D3A bomber codenamed "Val."
VAdm	Vice Admiral
Watch Bill	Work schedule detailing when a sailor has the watch.
Watchtower	Code name for Guadalcanal Operation.
Weather side	The side of a ship taking wind and seas.
XO	Executive Officer

BIBLIOGRAPHY

Adamson, Hans Christian and George Francis Kosco. *Halsey's Typhoons*. New York: Crown Publishers, 1967.

Burlingame, Paul. *Advance Force—Pearl Harbor*. Annapolis, Md.: Naval Institute Press, 1992.

Calhoun, C. Raymond. *Tin Can Sailor: Life Aboard the USS* Sterett, *1939–1945*. Annapolis, Md.: Naval Institute Press, 2000.

Crenshaw, Russell Sydnor. *South Pacific Destroyer: The Battle for the Solomons from Savo Island to Vella Gulf*. Annapolis, Md.: Naval Institute Press, 1998.

Dunnigan, James F. and Albert A. Nofi. *Victory at Sea: World War II in the Pacific*. New York: William Morrow and Company, Inc., 1995.

———. *The Pacific War Encyclopedia, Volume 1 and 2*. New York: Facts on File, Inc., 1998.

Dupuy, Trevor Nevitt. *The Military History of World War II, Volume 9: Asiatic Land Battles: Japanese Ambitions in the Pacific*. New York: Franklin Watts, Inc., 1963.

———. *The Military History of World War II, Volume 11: The Naval War in the Pacific: Rising Sun of Japan*. New York: Franklin Watts, Inc., 1963.

————. *The Military History of World War II, Volume 12: The Naval War in the Pacific: On to Tokyo.* New York: Franklin Watts, Inc., 1963.

————. *The Military History of World War II, Volume 13: The Air War in the Pacific: Air Power Leads the Way.* New York: Franklin Watts, Inc., 1964.

————. *The Military History of World War II, Volume 14: The Air War in the Pacific: Victory in the Air.* New York: Franklin Watts, Inc., 1964.

Ewing, Steve. *Fateful Rendezvous: The Life of Butch O'Hare.* Annapolis, Md.: Naval Institute Press, 1997.

Gailey, Harry A. *The War in the Pacific: From Pearl Harbor to Tokyo Bay.* Novato, Calif.: Presidio Press, 1995.

Hornfischer, James D. *The Last Stand of the Tin Can Sailors.* New York: Bantam Dell, 2004.

Hoyt, Edwin P. *How They Won the War in the Pacific: Nimitz and His Admirals.* The Lyons Press, 2000.

————. *Storm over the Gilberts: War in the Pacific—1943.* New York: Mason/Charter, 1978.

Ienaga, Saaburo. *The Pacific War: 1931 to 1945,* English translation. New York: Random House, 1978.

Manchester, William. *American Caesar: Douglas MacArthur, 1880–1964*. New York: Little Brown, 1978.

McGee, William L. *The Solomons Campaigns: 1942 to 1943*. Santa Barbara, Calif.: BMC Publications, 2002.

Miller, Nathan. *War at Sea: A Naval History of World War II*. New York: Scribner, 1995.

Morison, Samuel Eliot. *History of United States Naval Operations in World War II, Volume III: The Rising Sun in the Pacific, 1931–April 1942*. New York: Little Brown, 1948.

———. *History of United States Naval Operations in World War II, Volume IV: Coral Sea, Midway and Submarine Actions, May 1942–August 1942*. New York: Little Brown, 1949.

———. *History of United States Naval Operations in World War II, Volume V: The Struggle for Guadalcanal, August 1942–February 1943*. New York: Little Brown, 1949.

———. *History of United States Naval Operations in World War II, Volume VII: Aleutians, Gilberts and Marshalls, June 1942–April 1944*. New York: Little Brown, 1951.

———. *History of United States Naval Operations in World War II, Volume VIII: New Guinea and the Marianas, March 1944–August 1944*. New York: Little Brown, 1953.

————. *History of United States Naval Operations in World War II, Volume XII: Leyte, June 1944–January 1945*. New York: Little Brown, 1958.

————. *History of United States Naval Operations in World War II, Volume XIII: The Liberation of the Philippines, 1944–1945*. New York: Little Brown, 1959.

————. *History of United States Naval Operations in World War II, Volume XIV: Victory in the Pacific, 1945*. New York: Little Brown, 1960.

Parker, Robert Sinclair. *Blood on the Sea: American Destroyers Lost in World War II*. New York: Sarpedon, 1996.

Reynolds, Clark G. *The Carrier War*. Alexandria, Va.: Time-Life Books, 1982.

Roscoe, Theodore. *Tin Cans: The True Story of the Fighting Destroyers of World War II*. Bantam Books, 1960.

Schofield, William G. *Destroyers—60 Years*. Boston: Burdette & Company, 1962.

Sumrall, Robert F. *Tin Can Sailors: USS Laffey (DD-724)*. Somerset, Md.: Tin Can Sailors, Inc., 2001.

Warner, Oliver. *Command at Sea: Great Fighting Admirals From Hawke to Nimitz*. New York: St. Martin's Press, 1976.